ACHIEVING SOCIAL EQUITY

From Problems to Solutions

SECOND EDITION

ACHIEVING SOCIAL EQUITY

From Problems to Solutions

SECOND EDITION

EDITORS

MARY E. GUY

SEAN A. McCANDLESS

Melvin & Leigh, Publishers

IRVINE, CALIFORNIA

This book is dedicated to the tireless advocates, community activists, and public servants who work to achieve social equity for all.

Achieving Social Equity: From Problems to Solutions, Second Edition

Melvin & Leigh, Publishers

Published by Melvin & Leigh, Publishers
6 Curie Court
Irvine, CA 92617

orders.melvinleigh@cox.net
www.melvinleigh.com

Cover design by Jesse Sanchez
Production by Stacey Victor

ISBN: 978-1-7360402-8-7

Printed in the United States of America on mixed recycled paper

Visit our home page at www.melvinleigh.com

Table of Contents

PREFACE

Social equity is about public services being fair for everyone in regard to access, processes, quality, and outcomes. Whether in classrooms or on the frontlines of public service, we often ask "What does fairness mean in X circumstance?" or "Who decides what is fair?" or "Beyond understanding the problems, what are the solutions?" This book's purpose is to teach public service professionals how to address these questions.

Simply put, social equity's effects reveal themselves in every policy domain and in the daily work of all public service professionals. Sentiments regarding different populations have resulted in public investment or disinvestment in ways that have far-ranging effects. Social equity is not a new idea; what is new is the interest in classrooms and communities to pay attention to it and to look anew at the way things are. In response to this, *Achieving Social Equity* is designed for use in courses in public administration, public policy, program evaluation, and capstone courses, as well as courses that focus on diversity, inclusion, accessibility, and social justice.

This second edition provides updated content and acknowledges the resistance and "diversity fatigue" that social equity initiatives are meeting in many places. Chapters provide coverage of these topics: a global point of view, intersectionality, gender equity, LGBTQ+ and race, Indigenous Americans, immigration, race and policing, maternal health among Black women, housing, transit, environmental justice, and what the work of a DEIA officer is like. Prepared for instructors who want to integrate coverage of social equity in their courses, it is written for students who want to learn how to apply a social equity lens to their work.

We embarked on this book after hearing from instructors that they want a text that teaches about social equity across a panorama of issues, from matters of race and gender identity to issues of ethnicity, sexual orientation, socioeconomic status, citizenship status, physical ability, and the intersections that arise from these and more categories. The chapters are written by policy experts and sensitize readers to how social equity considerations should enter into every decision, every program, and every outcomes assessment.

There are five areas of competency that NASPAA—the accrediting body for graduate programs in public administration, public policy, and public affairs—requires curricula to cover. They include leading and managing public service organizations; participating in and contributing to the policy process; thinking critically about problems and decisions; articulating and applying a public service perspective; and, communicating effectively with a diverse workforce and citizenry. This book equips students with the awareness, skills, and strategies they will need to apply a social equity lens as they pursue these competencies.

Whether their careers take them into housing, labor, public works, transportation, health care, social services, DEIA, environmental protection, planning and zoning, parks and recreation, or international affairs, students will encounter questions about equity. Whether they live in a red state or a blue state, whether they work for nonprofits or government, they will find themselves debating plans, programs, and outcomes that impact fairness, rights, and justice. Whether working for federal, state, or local government, for nongovernmental organizations that partner with government, or for international organizations, public service professionals from the executive office to the street level will confront issues of intent, implementation, and impact.

The pursuit of equity is imperative if governance is to be successful, embracing the entire population, rather than the favored few. Whether working as a budget analyst or a parks supervisor, public service professionals must be equipped with the sensitivity, knowledge, and resilience to tackle situations where complex problems intersect in baffling ways. Coverage in this text prepares readers to answer these questions: Does this program further advantage a privileged group? Does it add to the burdens of an already disadvantaged group? Does it narrow the difference between the privileged and the disadvantaged? These chapters provide examples of how a social equity lens can be applied so that public service professionals can "see" equity issues and be responsive to them.

Organization of the Book

The book begins with an explanation of social equity and how accountability for it takes shape. Each subsequent chapter focuses on a subject area, explains how inequities appear, how they are framed, and what solutions are possible. The legal, political, and management dimensions are explored for each. Chapter 13, contributed by the Chief Race and Equity Officer for the City of San Diego, explains DEIA work. The closing chapter explains equity audits and encourages their use as a means for identifying inequities in a way that invites correction. Each chapter closes with a summary of key points and questions that provide a way to spur thoughtful discussion.

The uniqueness of the book is that it takes a forward lens on equity issues. Readers learn how to apply a social equity lens to public service actions. Chapters provide insight into how programs and initiatives function in actuality, and the kind of political, administrative, and community focus that must be present for equity to be achieved. Rather than stopping short by merely "admiring the problem," chapters conclude by presenting remedies.

By the end of the course, students will understand why social equity is an imperative in their work, how to "see" it, how to think about restorative processes, how to weave it into the fabric of their programs, and how to integrate the social equity imperative into public service as a whole.

Pedagogical Features

- Summary of key points, discussion items, and additional resources at the end of each chapter.
- The Instructor's Manual contains a sample syllabus, presentation slides, discussion items, exercises, additional resources, and test questions. You can request it from the publisher at mgmt@melvinleigh.com.

Acknowledgments

The editors gratefully acknowledge the roles that the National Academy of Public Administration (NAPA), the American Society for Public Administration (ASPA), the National Association of Counties, and the International City/County Management Association have played in bringing social equity to the forefront of scholarship and practice. The Standing Panel on Social Equity in Governance is now woven into NAPA's fabric, the Social Equity Leadership Conference is now an annual event, and ASPA's Section on Democracy and Social Justice is committed to furthering scholarship and practice that advances social equity. Additionally, ASPA's LGBT Advocacy Alliance, the Section for Women in Public Administration (SWPA), and the Conference of Minority Public Administrators (COMPA) have been, and continue to be, welcoming spaces for the "other."

1 THE SOCIAL EQUITY IMPERATIVE

Sean A. McCandless and Mary E. Guy

From the Editors

Social equity focuses on questions of who is disadvantaged and who is advantaged and how biases interfere with fairness and justice. It is everyone's responsibility to be mindful of social equity and to be accountable for it. This chapter explains the concept, provides its philosophical and constitutional rationale, explains why it is imperative in the pursuit of public purposes, and urges resilience as public service professionals navigate its roiling waters.

What Is Social Equity?

Public administration has four normative goals called "pillars." Historically, the field has been most concerned with efficiency, or determining how to achieve a goal with the best use of resources possible. In a closely related way, public services should be economical, or cost the "right" amount. And they should achieve their goals, which is what effectiveness means. In this formulation, where does fairness belong? Herein lies the importance of the field's fourth pillar, social equity.

As defined by the National Academy of Public Administration (NAPA), social equity is the fair, just, and equitable management of all institutions serving the public directly or by contract, and the fair and equitable distribution of public services, and implementation of public policy, and the commitment to promote fairness, justice, and equity in the formation of public policy.[1] Laws are to be administered fairly and equitably, and service delivery—whether by government or contractors—is to be delivered with a commitment to fairness, justice, and equity. As stated by Norman Johnson and James Svara, "Public administrators, including all persons involved in public governance should seek to prevent and reduce inequality and injustice based on significant social characteristics and to promote greater equality in access to services, procedural fairness, quality of services and social outcomes."[2] These are complex concepts that we explain, starting with the difference between equity and equality.

Equity vis-à-vis Equality

Equity and equality are not identical. Equality refers to sameness, such as receiving the same opportunities or resources. It is simpler to define and measure equality than equity. Equality requires only that each person gets the same amount of X. In contrast, equity requires that each person gets a sufficient amount of X to create equivalent conditions. The goal of equity is to correct the imbalance between the advantaged and the disadvantaged, whether the focus is on opportunities, access, process, or outcomes.

Here is an example of the difference between equality and equity: Equality dictates that a loaf of bread can be sliced into six equal pieces and six diners will share equally. Everyone gets the same size piece. But does equality take into account what a person has *already* experienced, such as hunger? Equity is more complicated. One slice of bread for a starving person has greater worth than one slice for the person who is well-fed. To give the starving person an extra slice takes it away from someone who would otherwise eat it. In this case, equity is zero-sum in the short run but not in the long run. The starving person gets nutrition, and someone who is not hungry forgoes a slice they did not want, anyway. In the long run, the starving person is benefited by being helped to be more like the others. Conversely, equality is not zero-sum in the short run because everyone gets a slice; there are no winners and losers at the outset. However, the shortcoming of equality is that it results in significant disadvantages in the long run when malnutrition continues for the starving person.

As the extra slice of bread for the hungry person demonstrates, equality is not always fair, and what is fair is not always equal. In equality, no one gets less of what they have enjoyed, and power relations remain the same. Like the starving person, however, different people and different groups have different needs. To be equitable, services may need to be distributed differently. This is how leveling the playing field by boosting marginalized groups advances equity.

The distinction between equality and equity is not without controversy. Simple equality is more readily accepted than actions designed to compensate for complex causes of inequality. This is because the goal of the latter is to minimize imbalance. To create balance out of imbalance requires perturbing the status quo. When there is a finite amount of X and one group gets more of it, the other group gets less. For example, affirmative action initiatives were implemented in the 1970s to overcome discriminatory hiring practices that overlooked otherwise qualified job candidates who were not of the preferred gender or race. The affirmative action protocol directed that when two candidates of equivalent knowledge, skills, and abilities were in the pool, the candidate from the traditionally disadvantaged group should be hired. While opening doors to candidates who would otherwise be excluded, it reduced the number of jobs available to those who had benefited from past hiring practices. Resistance and backlash to overturning traditional patterns of advantage have now reached the point that affirmative action is rarely mentioned and even more rarely practiced.

As resistance to affirmative action demonstrates, power and advantage do not steal quietly into the night. They fight back, seeking to regain what they had enjoyed and to which they feel entitled. Affirmative action is an example of how and why initiatives that advance social equity require constant attention, advocacy, and sensitivity to all the stakeholders who are affected. Social equity is not something that is achieved and can then be forgotten. To achieve it and to maintain it requires constant vigilance.

Equity, Justice, Social Equity, Social Justice, and Liberation

Equity and *social equity* carry related but distinct meanings. When paired with equity and justice, the word *social* elevates the topic from the individual level to a focus on communities of people. And when attention expands from one-of-a-kind, it broadens to consider dynamics that give rise to identifiable groups or communities. "Equity" refers to fairness, but it is often individualized. Social equity, on the other hand, refers to fairness for all groups and emphasizes the need to design public goods—policies, interventions, and programs—to combat historic inequities.

Similarly, *justice* and *social justice* are distinct. "Justice" can be defined as getting one's due, whereas "social justice" acknowledges that to be truly just, societies must focus on designing systems to remedy historic inequities and to benefit the least advantaged. Social justice is instrumental in achieving the broad goals of an equitable society.

Finally, *social justice* and *social equity* are related but distinct. Both focus on the community rather than the individual. Social equity is the pragmatic condition that describes access to, distribution of, and outcomes related to, public goods. Public administration is the vehicle for ensuring both social justice and social equity because its scope of influence is community-wide, reflects procedural decisions regarding access, distribution, and quality, and its end result is measurable by the outcomes that result. Social justice is the broad resolution of inequitable societal conditions. Extending this notion and as documented by Kim Desmond in Chapter 13 of this book, *liberation* is related to social equity and is the result of being free from inequities and injustices.

Another way to think about social equity is that, while equality is about inputs being equivalent, equity is about outcomes being equivalent. Whether in planning or implementing programs, this question must be raised: Who will be advantaged and who will be disadvantaged? With these distinctions in mind, discussion turns now to the role that public service professionals play in working toward social equity.

Social Equity as a Professional Expectation

Social equity is far more complicated than questions about slices of bread. Considerations span all of public service, from homeland security to emergency preparedness to urban and regional planning to law enforcement and corrections, to health care, housing, and education. Budgeting must be equitable if it is to enable public programs that serve all. The social infrastructure of communities must be equitable to enable success for all populations. Equity considerations must be infused in the benchmarks used to evaluate programs. The pursuit of equity is foundational to successful governance and is captured in four large dimensions: procedural fairness, access, quality, and outcomes.[3]

Procedural fairness refers to the steps that decision-makers take, rather than the outcome reached. It involves due process, transparency, equal rights, and representativeness. Procedural inequities occur when administrators *target* groups, making the processes of public services unfair, such as when administrative racism results in disparate hiring practices that result in overrepresentation of majority group members and underrepresentation of minority group members.

Access refers to opportunity and ability to participate in processes and programs. Access inequities are apparent when members of a group have difficulty, for instance, accessing clean water, interacting with public officials, obtaining needed information, or participating in decision-making that will affect them.

Quality refers to the degree to which attributes surpass minimally acceptable levels. Quality inequities occur when, for example, schools are less well-funded and resourced in neighborhoods whose residents are members of marginalized groups.

Outcomes are the effects that policies and programs produce. Questions that guide outcomes assessments are: "Do all groups benefit similarly from the program?" "Are any groups disadvantaged by the program? Outcome inequities occur when, for instance, persons of particular groups inconsistently and insufficiently receive public services. This, then, results in future issues, such as finding it more difficult to get a good job, earn decent wages, have convenient transportation, or live in a safe neighborhood.

The work of public service professionals is to tackle complex, multidimensional problems that intersect with one another in baffling ways. Some combination of, or even all of, the criteria mentioned—access, process, quality, and outcomes—can reveal inequities in any one administrative action or policy. Unlike bottom-line thinking, where minimizing cost is the only consideration, public service professionals are expected to conduct their work with a consciousness not only of cost but also of equity.

There are two approaches for holding the social equity prism to the light to see what is revealed. One is procedural and the other is substantive. The procedural perspective emphasizes citizen engagement in the process of problem definition, program design and planning, evaluation, and feedback. The substantive perspective emphasizes differences in outcomes, asking and answering the question: Who benefits from this program? Who is disadvantaged by it?

Because social equity is an imperative of public service, the work of public administration differs from business management. For there to be a responsive system of governance, social equity must be woven throughout policies, programs, and processes. Cultural norms elevate social equity to its position of prominence as an imperative in American public administration and attention turns now to this subject.

Philosophical and Constitutional Underpinnings

For centuries, philosophers have debated what fairness means, whether it could be achieved, who "deserves" fairness, and what government's role is in achieving it. Broadly speaking, the trajectory of the debate can be summarized as a gradual recognition that fairness and justice should apply to everyone, not just a few.

Notions of fairness have evolved over the centuries. Early philosophers, such as Aristotle, argued that everyone is due fairness and justice, yet what is fair and just differs based upon individual circumstances and people's station in life. Philosophers opined that some people—women, slaves, children—were incapable of self-government and should be ruled by others. Aristotle even went so far as to note that such master–subordinate relationships were natural and beneficial to the one being ruled, whether a wife, a child, or an enslaved person. Over the centuries, the notion has prevailed that some societal inequality is both natural and intended, such that "legitimate" governments should assume social stratification and status differentials among the governed.

By the European Enlightenment of the mid-1700s, thinkers were questioning what governments could legitimately do and not do. Social contract theorists—such as John Locke, Thomas Hobbes, and Jean Jacques Rousseau—all variously argued that there is a "natural law" and that governments form in order to balance the total freedom of nature with the need for order. To these philosophers, governments must act in accordance with natural law and derive their legitimacy through the people's consent. Government's task was to protect so-called natural rights, the most important of which are life, liberty, and property. To them, not everyone is or should be equal.

These philosophers, principally Locke, inspired the men who crafted the U.S. Constitution. The founders wove limitations to government power into the Constitution and later the first 10 amendments to it, the Bill of Rights. Examples include, for instance, the First Amendment's protections regarding religion, speech, the press, assembly, and petitioning the government for redress of grievances. Other examples concern protections like the Fourth Amendment's enshrining of "The right of the people to be secure in their persons, houses, papers, and effects, against unreasonable searches and seizures," or the Eighth Amendment's protections against "cruel and unusual punishments," or the Tenth Amendment's reservation that "powers not delegated to the United States by the Constitution, nor prohibited by it to the States, are reserved to the States respectively, or to the people." These limitations are not absolute, however. Government *can* deprive someone of life, liberty, and property, but it must follow specified procedures to do so. The meaning of these amendments in both theory and practice is the focus of extensive case law, but they establish the idea that everyone is accorded a minimum level of rights.

The Constitution reflects conceptions of freedom, equality before the law, and popular sovereignty, among others. At a minimum, these underpinnings include constitutional values embodied in the phrase "We the people," which is a reflection of the social contract between Americans and their government. The irony is that when the U.S. Constitution was drafted in 1787, adopted in 1789, and amended with the Bill of Rights in 1791, the language of the preamble—"We the People"—excluded many. It did not include women, Native Americans, slaves, and white men who were not property owners. More simply, the Constitution established the basis for popular sovereignty, an essential social contract, for white male landowners. While protections—especially freedom from government interference—gave *de jure* equality before the law for all, the Constitution was the guiding document that benefitted the privileged and saw social and economic stratification as "natural." In sum, although the Constitution situates social equity as an imperative, it also enshrines notions of inequality.

Beliefs about who is included in the "we" of "We the People" have changed since 1787. The Thirteenth, Fourteenth, and Fifteenth Amendments to the Constitution expanded the scope of "We" on the heels of the Civil War. The Thirteenth Amendment abolished slavery, the Fourteenth Amendment bound states to the provisions of the Bill of Rights and mandated incorporation of due process and equal protection of the law, and the Fifteenth Amendment expanded enfranchisement to African American men. Further, in 1920, the Nineteenth Amendment was adopted, which expanded enfranchisement to women. Later, the Twenty-Fourth Amendment prohibited poll taxes, which had prevented many poor persons, especially non-Whites, from voting, and the Twenty-Sixth Amendment lowered the voting age to 18.

Creeping egalitarianism continues. Numerous examples of both statutory law and case law have provided greater protections. For instance, the Civil Rights Act of 1964 (among other laws) outlawed discrimination based on race, color, religion, sex, and national origin. The U.S. Supreme Court has also made rulings that expanded recognition of rights, such as *Brown v. Board of Education* (1954), which ruled that racial segregation in schools was unconstitutional, or *Obergefell v. Hodges* (2015), which provided a fundamental right to marry for same-sex couples.

Still, as documented throughout this book, these legal advancements have yet to overturn the persistent lack of fairness in American society. Laws, customs, and ingrained biases perpetuate disadvantage through voter suppression, biased law enforcement, environmental pollution, economic disparities, and the insouciance for privileges that accompany masculinity and whiteness. Further, some state legislatures have taken steps to limit or ban diversity, equity, and inclusion initiatives, arguing that principles of social equity are tantamount to "prejudice" and "division."

Fairness continues to remain a distant goal. It has taken this long for government to begin to protect marginalized groups, such as Native Americans, women, lesbian, gay, bisexual, and transgender (LGBT) persons, immigrants, and more. The constant push and pull over rights continues. Every three steps forward in fostering fairness for all are met with two—and sometimes more—steps backward.

Social Equity as an Imperative for Public Administration

Public administration encompasses the policies, programs, rules, and procedures used to breathe life into laws passed by city councils, county commissions, state legislatures, and Congress. It involves the work of governmental agencies, as well as collaborative arrangements with nonprofits and businesses. In the broader context, public administration is the conflation of politics, management, and law, pretzeled together to pursue goals.

In the late 1800s when political science—the parent discipline of public administration—was organized, scholars focused on studying how and why governments formed and how legislatures behaved. Public administration began to emerge as a true discipline when political scientists who cared about the administration of public affairs complained that political science devoted too little attention to how governments were actually run. These early views saw public administration as the "action" and "executing" part of government versus the "will" represented by legislatures. While this executive-focused definition of the field is still accurate, more complete definitions acknowledge how the executive, legislative, and judicial branches interact, how intergovernmental levels (federal, state, county, and local) relate, and how intersectoral (public, nonprofit, and private) relations work.

The breadth and scope of public administration matters for social equity because, regardless of decade or issue, it is a part, if not a driver, in discussions of fairness. More problematically, public administration has served both as a vehicle to advance fairness and to hinder it. While some policies adopted at the federal, state, and local levels are in place to ameliorate problems, others are responsible for creating or exacerbating them.

Prior to the latter 1960s, public administration as a discipline had only a smattering of interest in topics of fairness as it related to marginalized populations. There are exceptions, however. It was often women, such as Harriet W. R. Strong, Jane Addams, Mary Parker Follett, and Frances Perkins, who argued most strongly on the need for government to advance social equity. Their views were drowned out by voices that likened government to business, focusing attention on efficiency and economy at the expense of equity. Had women's voices been given the same hearing as that of Leonard D. White and Woodrow Wilson, the field would be less obsessed with designing *efficient* public services, and more intent on designing equitable services.[4] Another example is Frances Harriet Williams, a Black female public administrator, who in 1947 authored an article in *Public Administration Review* on the need for better racial accountability in government agencies like the former Office of Price Administration.[5]

Despite these women's efforts, on the whole, it cannot be said that the field devoted much attention to the "social" in social equity. For instance, early textbooks were silent on issues of inequities based on race and gender. When issues of fairness were discussed, they most often occurred in the context of discussing personnel decisions related to the hiring, promotion, and firing of male employees.

The classical focus on efficiency has overlooked and disregarded too many aspects of fairness. A public service can function efficiently yet still be unfair. The ideal of equal rights and privileges is not achieved when police use their resources to improve traffic safety but fail to ask who is stopped and whether the stop is legitimate in the first place. A board focused on water might provide clean water for their own neighborhoods but overlook contaminated water for those on the poor side of town. The list goes on and on, and the central lesson is that what is efficient is not always equitable.

What Is Efficient Is Not Always Fair, and What Is Fair Is Not Always Efficient

In the late 1960s, George Frederickson[6] and other scholars sought to insert social equity into the public administration canon. After the tumult of the 1960s, with race riots and discord in the cities, it became obvious that what is efficient is not always fair, and what is fair is not always efficient. With the nation's social fabric in tatters, Frederickson suggested that public administration could be better served by emphasizing fairness not only *in tandem* with efficiency but, possibly, *over* efficiency. He suggested that administrators ask not only about policy and programs, but also question who is advantaged and who is disadvantaged by those policies and programs.

Social equity discussions were given further theoretical fuel with the publication of John Rawls' *A Theory of Justice*.[7] Philosopher Rawls asserted that a just society is one that designs and implements policies to benefit the *least* advantaged, not the most advantaged. His work popularized the notion of distributive justice, which refers to the socially just distribution of goods in a society, such that there is perceived fairness in how rewards and costs are distributed across a group's members. An example of distributive injustice is when workers who perform the same job are paid different salaries.

Out of this era came a transition from the word "equity" (meaning fairness) to "social equity" (meaning fairness for all). The latter 20th century led to more focus on issues of social equity, with primary attention to race and gender. Questions arose about the extent of inequity and the factors that contribute to its persistence. This attention has brought about a transition from "admiring" the problem to designing and implementing procedures and structures to correct it. Thought of in terms of remedies, there has been a proliferation of laws passed and programs implemented that are intended to make overt discrimination illegal, and there are programs designed to address targeted areas of inequity. President Johnson's War on Poverty, the Equal Employment Opportunity Commission, the Pregnancy Discrimination Act, the Civil Rights Act and its amendments, Title IX of the Education Act, the Lilly Ledbetter Fair Pay Act, the Affirmatively Furthering Fair Housing Act, all were designed to address inequities. Each of these speaks to a unique problem, and each removes a hurdle. It is evident, however, that laws and targeted programs will not, in and of themselves, create social equity. Why? Because problems are interconnected and grounded in notions about deservingness. Like a game of Whac-A-Mole, social inequities keep emerging.

The focus of social equity has primarily targeted demographic groups based on gender, race, religion, physical disability, or sexual orientation. In terms of race, persons of color are stopped more by police, receive harsher prison sentences, attend poorer schools, live in poorer neighborhoods, have more difficulties accessing higher education, are overlooked for hirings and promotions, and are paid less than their white counterparts. Women experience numerous inequities as well, especially in that they tend to be paid less than men, are frequently stratified in nonleadership positions, are segregated into sex-typed occupations, experience sexual objectification, harassment, assault, and more. The issues become even more complicated when accounting for intersectionalities. A person can face inequities based on skin color, gender, and/or sexual orientation and gender identity. Engaging in "Oppression Olympics" is not helpful, but understanding how inequities are experienced based on different identities aids in naming and claiming the problem.

Inequities persist when administrative and policy environments foster outright or implicit bias. Furthermore, many inequities evident today are traceable to long-standing and formerly "legal" forms of discrimination, often directly encouraged by public policies. For instance, lack of opportunities in education for persons of color is the consequence of prior policies of housing segregation. Hostile work environments for women are manifestations of decades of policies and attitudes toward women that enforced their subordination. Poverty levels of elderly women are disproportionately attributable to the depressed wages they earned during their working years, and so forth.

Finding the Right Language and Levers

There is a complex array of terminology surrounding social equity, how to identify it, and how to ameliorate it. Conscientious administrators want to know which levers to pull to reduce inequities but finding the right language for entering the discussion is challenging. Social equity's close linkage with justice and equality creates definitional complexity. Representative bureaucracy, a tenet of public service that dictates that the public workforce should be demographically representative of the population served, also enters the picture. Social equity is also linked with cultural competency, which directs that administrators should be sensitive and responsive to different populations' cultural needs, attitudes, and styles. Moreover, social equity is linked with diversity, inclusion, and accessibility initiatives because these are ways to overcome subtle biases.

Susan Gooden offers a way out of the terminology quandary by capturing social equity accountability in three steps.[8] First, administrators must *name* inequity and admit where inequities exist. It is not an easy process because public service agencies are reluctant to admit that they have played a role in fostering a lack of fairness. Nevertheless, accountability begins with owning the problem.

The second step is to *blame* inequity on its causes, whether it is due to policies or program rules. Such a process exposes long-standing practices of explicit and implicit patterns of bias.

The third step is to *claim* inequity. By admitting that inequities exist and understanding how they came about, administrators are positioned to move toward remedies. Without being honest about the extent and causes of inequity, levers of change will not turn. Awareness and ownership of the problem can lead to making fairness a priority, reaching out to stakeholders, measuring progress, and giving everyone a place at the table in the problem identification, planning, and decision-making phases.

A Social Equity Lens

Discussions of what it looks like to be more equitable are becoming more common. Many cities and agencies have adopted diversity, equity, inclusion, and accessibility plans. Seattle and King County, Washington, for example, have adopted a pro-equity stance in policymaking, decision-making, planning, operations, services, and workplace practices.[9] The goal is to advance equity and social justice within county government. To do this, King County has an ambitious plan to expand access to opportunity in child and youth development; jobs and economic development; environment and climate; health and human services; housing; information and technology; transportation and mobility; and the justice system.

Other examples come from the nonprofit sector. The Working Poor Families Project is an example of a national collaboration of nonprofits working to identify and implement initiatives that prepare America's working families for a more secure economic future.[10] Another initiative is Equality Indicators, which is a tool that helps cities understand and measure their levels of equality and equity.[11] It measures disparities in multiple policy domains, such as education, housing, and justice, because these are spaces where those most vulnerable to inequality are affected most frequently. Social equity toolkits or scorecards such as these projects are helpful templates to assess program proposals and performance.

These examples demonstrate that an equity mindset is a different way of thinking about public management, one not characterized simply by customer service and efficiency protocols, but rather one characterized by a desire to embody constitutional values for everyone in the community. Social equity is a challenge that touches upon every policy domain and the work of every public service professional. Everyone in the field, especially students of today and public executives of tomorrow, needs to understand what social equity is, what inequities look like, how they occur, and what the levers are at their disposal to address them. In an era of pushback against social equity, as explored in these chapters, the goal of this book is to sensitize readers to the challenges and opportunities that are ahead and to the social equity implications of decisions, processes, and outcomes. The current pushback against social equity makes this all the more urgent. The time for reasonable, actionable solutions is *still* now.

Summary of Key Points

The most important takeaway of this chapter is that social equity is an imperative of public administration and responsibility for it rests on the shoulders of every public service professional. As much as administrative neutrality is taught as a goal, in fact, few actions are neutral in their impact. Biases and blinders result in advantages to some and disadvantages to others. Looking at public actions through a social equity lens helps to identify disparate impacts of seemingly neutral programs.

No policy domain is exempt from equity concerns. Whether housing policy or health care, transportation or immigration, business subsidies or childcare, education or food inspections, the outcomes of programs are likely to produce disparate outcomes for segments of the population. Problems come to government when no one else wants to—or has the capacity to—address them. This is why social equity is a matter that requires attention from the entire public service community.

Equity is more complicated than equality. If they were the same, problems of equity would be easier to resolve. In fact, it is the results of many "equal" programs that have perpetuated social inequity and cemented it into the economy.

Discussion Questions

1. Public services vary in their impact on recipients, depending on the recipient's social, economic, and political status. Are public administrators morally obligated to counter this variability?
2. Identify an issue of social equity in your community. Name it, blame it, and claim it. In other words, identify it, explain the reason for it, and develop a plan for remedying it. Examples might include displacement due to gentrification, disparate levels of resources for public schools, housing insufficiency, shortcomings in public transportation routes, police brutality, and uneven streetlight and road maintenance, among many others.
3. The Constitution's original notion of equality restricted it to landowning white men. Now the Constitution's provisions apply to equality for men and for women, whether or not they are property owners and regardless of their race. Do you think the meaning of equality will expand during your lifetime? Who would the beneficiaries be?

Additional Readings

Guy, Mary E., and Sean A. McCandless. 2012. "Social Equity: Its Legacy, Its Promise." *Public Administration Review* 72 (51): S5–S13.

Frederickson, H. George. 2015. *Social Equity and Public Administration: Origins, Developments, and Applications.* New York, NY: Routledge.

Gooden, Susan T. 2015. *Race and Social Equity: A Nervous Area of Government.* New York, NY: Routledge.

Norman J. Johnson and James H. Svara, eds. 2011. *Justice for All: Promoting Social Equity in Public Administration.* Armonk, NY: M.E. Sharpe.

Notes

1. Norman J. Johnson and James H. Svara, "Social Equity and Public Administration," in *Justice for All: Promoting Social Equity in Public Administration*, eds. Norman J. Johnson and James H. Svara, (Armonk, NY: M.E. Sharpe, 2011), 16.
2. Norman J. Johnson and James H. Svara, "Toward a More Perfect Union: Moving Forward with Social Equity," in *Justice for All: Promoting Social Equity in Public Administration*, eds. Norman J. Johnson and James H. Svara, (Armonk, NY: M.E. Sharpe, 2011), 282.
3. Norman J. Johnson and James H. Svara, eds., *Justice for All: Promoting Social Equity in Public Administration* (Armonk, NY: M.E. Sharpe, 2011).
4. Camilla Stivers, *Bureau Men, Settlement Women* (Lawrence, KS: University of Kansas Press, 2000).
5. Frances Harriet Williams, "Minority Groups and the OPA," *Public Administration Review 7*, no. 2 (1947), 123–128, https://doi.org/10.2307/972754. Susan T. Gooden, "Frances Harriet Williams: Unsung Social Equity Pioneer," *Public Administration Review, 77*, no. 5 (2015), 777–783. https://doi.org/10.1111/puar.12788
6. H. George Frederickson, "Toward a New Public Administration," in *Toward a New Public Administration: The Minnowbrook Perspective*, ed. Frank Marini (Scranton, PA: Chandler Publishing Company, 1971), 309–331.
7. John Rawls, *A Theory of Justice* (Boston, MA: Harvard University Press, 1971).
8. Susan T. Gooden, *Race and Social Equity: A Nervous Area of Government* (New York, NY: Routledge, 2015).
9. See https://www.kingcounty.gov/elected/executive/constantine/priorities/building-equity.aspx
10. See https://www.prb.org/projects/working-poor-families-project/
11. See http://equalityindicators.org/

2 A GLOBAL AMERICA: EQUITY-RELATED OBSERVATIONS FOR PUBLIC ADMINISTRATORS

Kim Moloney

From the Editors

What do American administrators need to understand about their place in the world? Moloney tackles this question by reviewing her own journey. She presents tools to explore our own positionalities and assumptions and encourages travel as well as listening, observing, and reading. Showing how global connections matter for social equity, she argues that we can learn from other countries. Impacts of international public administration, global civil society actors, and transnational public administration are explained.

In U.S.-focused public administration, several claims can be made. The first is that the discipline is largely focused on itself.[1] Second, scholars and practitioners often assume, implicitly or explicitly, that their findings are universal.[2] The implications lead to a third claim. That is, U.S.-focused perspectives are neocolonial,[3] which assumes that the production and dissemination of knowledge begins in the West and then trickles down to the rest. These claims drive the knowledge that is imparted and set priorities for what "matters."

Further, public administration is a discipline that is often White, methodologically American, and often certain that the state (a nation or subunit) is its only analytical unit.[4] It is a discipline where history is underemphasized.[5] But we can do better and must. Our understanding of global equity initiatives is driven by how we understand non-American locations, the effects of non-American actors on global policy, and the multiplicity of non-state actors.

This argument is articulated in seven parts. The first shares stories of positionality and internationalization. The second defines positionality and the hegemonic intellectualism of American public administration. Both sections lead to a third recommending travel and a fourth section on the importance of actively listening, observing, and reading. The fifth asks, given the chapter's internationalization discussion, "so what?" The answer is that every administrative or policy role in America interacts with global communities. The global community is the sixth section, along with proof that the "so what" answer matters. The seventh section concludes by summarizing key points and offering additional readings.

Starting with Story Time

This section starts with storytelling, which is an undersold art within the public sector.[6] The stories were selected to serve as the foundation for what comes next: positionality, social equity, and public service. In my case, they are personal.[7] I am the daughter of high school-educated parents. I had Pell Grants, work-study grants, and worked two jobs per week in college and three during football season.

My résumé omits such stories: waitressing, bartending, fast food worker, swim instructor, lifeguard, sky box work at Wisconsin football games, watering potato plants in labs, secretarial temping, and warehouse work. My "favorites?" Third shift at a 24/7 grocery store. My sole job from midnight to 8 am was to trash cardboard boxes as staff restocked. The other "favorite" was painting hunting ducks on a fast-moving assembly line. Well . . . let's be honest, both were awful jobs.

Yet, since the age of 19, I've had the good fortune to work in 10 countries (two months to four+ years each) and to visit 48. My home was "uneducated," but we had books. Many were about places outside of America. As a young adult, I took public transport since a car would steal money from hard-earned travel savings. By my third university year, I learned to ask professors how I can go here, go there, and do this or that? It was a huge step as I started university unaware of the basics, that is, how to take notes in class.

My first trip abroad was at 12 years old. The goal was to drive around Lake Superior. This required entering Canada. My child's mind knew little about "foreigners." The small things surprised me, like Canadian road signs in English and French given Canada's two national languages. My second trip was after my freshman year in college. I was 19. Studying abroad was unaffordable, but I could use my savings to work abroad (visa still available to college students) in London. I had one skill: lifeguarding. So, I got a job at Hyde Park's Lido (an open-air, public swimming pool). My boss was British, but workmates were from everywhere else. I learned for the first time, in person, that many non-Americans see us as arrogant, overweight, talk too loudly, and have double standards. The latter meant our country's leadership (regardless of party) might want democracy and human rights abroad until our national interest suggested otherwise. Foreign countries were no longer an abstraction to me. It was someone's home.

This was radical for me. Like many Americans, I was raised in a bubble in which we were taught that America is nearly always good. In London, I heard multiple perspectives. An Australian explained why Hollywood limited their cinematic possibilities. An Englishman said that rugby was for men and American football (NFL) was for boys. A Russian had fought in the Soviet wars in Afghanistan. Much to my then-narrow understanding of South Africa, a white South African encouraged anti-apartheid movements. It was not whether each person was right or wrong. Such discussions are for another chapter. It was also not about being stimulated by too many views and thus, retreating with belligerence. I did subsequent work abroad in New Zealand where I learned about its horticulture exports to Japan while pruning calla lilies, and Perú where a think-tank job taught about its class- and race-fueled conflicts. Each opened new doors for me.

My work as an academic in Jamaica, South Korea, Australia, and Qatar has led to new comparative thinking, each deepening my understanding of systemic inequities in America's educational and health care systems. I know, as an American, how hard one has to fight for barely decent health insurance, educational access, and the chance to keep one's financial head above water. As such, I was thrilled to learn in Australia that a minor surgery with a two-day stay had no cost. Not even deductibles. It was covered by national health care. It is the same in my current home of Qatar. My daughter's emergency room visit via ambulance had no expense. Not one dollar was spent. Meanwhile, generic prescriptions in Qatar cost pennies and lifesaving epi-pens are 1/5 of U.S. costs. I was also amazed when my Australian students explained their university loans (tiny when compared to U.S. student loans) are neither due nor garner interest until graduates earn over a salary minimum. Once someone's salary hits that minimum (~US$32,000), there is a compulsory repayment percentage that increases as they earn more.

I visited South Korean museums, which retold the Korean War by stressing how a multinational force authorized by the United Nations had defended Korea. In my high school history books, only American contributions were emphasized. As an academic at the University of West Indies in Kingston

Jamaica, I learned how drug transnationalization negatively altered Jamaican possibilities. Or how one of my Vietnamese graduate students in Australia told me that what Americans call the Vietnam War, the Vietnamese call the "American War." It was shocking to learn that I, as a woman, can safely walk home at night in South Korea and Qatar. Or that in three of the four (Australia, Korea, Qatar), residents do not fear death by firearms because they are banned or highly regulated. Readers have their own stories, of travel, of encounters that surprise, and where lessons challenge biases. Each story showcases your positionality and for nearly all, hegemonic intellectualism. Each concept is the focus of the next section.

Positionality and Hegemonic Intellectuals

Too few academics ask, "am I a hegemonic intellectual?"[8] Or, for you as you read this, too few ask, "am I a hegemonic policymaker, administrator, or student?" Here is the short answer: If you are American—regardless of race, gender, orientation, creed, religion, disability, age—you are a *de facto* hegemonic intellectual. I explain this by defining positionality.

Positionality is understanding the "self as research instrument" and the changes that your own subjectivity will bring to bear on policies and administration.[9] However, positionality extends beyond an understanding of self and whether your traits alter what you understand. Given the dialectic between "objectivism and subjectivism," the search for "pure objectivism is a naïve quest; we can never truly divorce ourselves from subjectivity. We can strive to remain objective but must be mindful of our subjectivities. Such is positionality. We have to acknowledge how we are as individuals, and as members of groups, and as resting in and moving within social positions."[10] We must be cautious about claiming to understand another, how we speak about an "other," and which "conclusions" are discussed.[11] This includes understanding how your questions as administrators and policymakers may also "contribute to the further marginalization of the participants."[12] We can go further. Positionality without active listening, observing, and reading may be little more than unwelcome pontifications.

Given positionality, what is a hegemonic intellectual? The first step is to understand the "intellectual" word. One does not need a PhD to be an intellectual. One can be educated by credentials but not be truly educated. Similarly, one can be without credentials but be educated. Take this example: I am constantly amazed when journalists, academics, and policymakers discuss the "poor," or other marginalized group while dismissing their viewpoint. Too often one has to explain that the poor do not desire to remain poor; they face structural constraints that inhibit dream fulfillment. What appears irrational for an economic elite may be *appropriately rational* for the poor. It is not because the poor are irrational—they are no more or less irrational than economic elites. Instead, rationalities of being poor are different. The poor often know more about what survival requires than do those who judge them.

This example finds parallels in discussions of other marginalized groups. For example, it may be rational for single mothers to take low-paying part-time jobs if childcare is unaffordable. It may be rational to stay in rural areas dominated by low-skill work if one's family is the *de facto* babysitter. It is rational to fill a child's stomach with inexpensive low-quality food if costly high-quality food leads to one meal per day. It is face-obvious that single mothers should want higher-paying jobs that match their qualifications or that families should desire high-quality food, but it may also be irrational in the short- and medium-term. If one would be further impoverished, jeopardized, or harmed, it is rational for the poor to avoid the irrational. Equity-minded administrators work to remove barriers so "rational irrationalities" are overcome.

The other part of "hegemonic intellectual" is hegemony. Hegemony is the dominance of one group over another. Earlier I wrote that "[i]f you are American—regardless of race, gender, orientation, creed, religion, disability, age—you are a *de facto* hegemonic intellectual." By this I mean, if you are American, your country has among the world's highest income. The United States is one of 193 countries.[13] In

2023, *one-quarter* of the world's gross domestic product (GDP is also known as national income) was American. The estimated *world* GDP is $105 trillion with a *U.S.-specific* GDP of $26.8 trillion.[14] U.S. median household income in 2020 was $67,521.[15] On a *per capita* basis, Americans are 7th wealthiest after Ireland, Luxembourg, Singapore, Qatar, United Arab Emirates, and Switzerland. (The first four have per capita incomes greater than $100,000.)

For four-person households with two children under 18, the 2021 U.S. poverty line was $27,479.[16] Ironically, this poverty line is 147.7% of the *world's* per capita income of $18,604.[17] This means that the poverty line for American households *is higher than the per capita incomes of 117 of 193 countries*. In 2021, the world's countries spent $2.1 trillion on military spending. One country, the United States, spent $801 billion or 38% of the total.[18] About 44% of Americans have post-secondary education, the eighth highest in the world.[19] On income, military expenditure, and education, Americans and the American state are hegemonic. If the country is hegemonic and, as noted in the chapter introduction, if public administration is hegemonic, then readers likely are, too. Thus, readers may confuse size or wealth with normative "bests." Normative and empirical "bests" may be best understood by travel and by comparison.

Travel and Its Options

This section notes the importance of travel, both actual and metaphorical, and of repeatedly listening, observing, and reading. I suggest that by traveling, we learn the most about America. Leaving the country to understand the country sounds counterintuitive, but upon explanation, perhaps you will agree. There are three ways to travel. Before discussing each, let's not forget the easiest route: to not travel. In this option, you do not go, you tell yourself that "they" or "it" are "over there" and/or "foreign" and/or "not as good as America" and thus, you close the door to learning. The educated do not sit behind closed doors.

Of the three ways to travel, one option is to "travel lite," like taking a cruise or going to an all-inclusive resort. This is "lite" since such trips envelop travelers in "America-friendly" bubbles in which the people, amenities, and conversations are familiar. The local context may be seen via taxis to/from the airport, half-day excursions, and/or conversations with locals working at resorts. This type of travel is a way to "go abroad" and not leave one's comfort zone.

The second option is to travel or work abroad outside of cruises or resorts. This takes you to locations different from your upbringing, that are not mini-Americas, and where your creative, intellectual, and sociocultural boundaries are challenged. The religious majority, languages, ethnicities, cultures, and/or governmental systems are different from America's.

But must we physically travel to learn about the world? No. A third way is to find non-Hollywood movies, documentaries, books, plays, dance lessons, art showings, bloggers, social media, and/or online newspapers of one's desired locale. If your daily news paints negative views of a country, ask yourself if it is the full story. In nearly all cases, it is not.

For each way of travel, caution is needed. The caution is that it is *your* job to educate yourself. Just as it is not the job of Black Americans to educate White Americans about ongoing legacies of White privilege, and it is not a woman's job to educate men about misogyny, it is also not the job of non-Americans to educate you about their world. No one is required to relive their journey for your education. It is an education that you, as a student or administrator, begin via curiosity. It is an understanding that Americans are only 4% of the world's population, that we share one planet, and that we desire to learn about the 96% who are not American.

Listen, Observe, Read, and Repeat

Regardless of which travel option is chosen, several habits enhance learning. The first is to actively listen. As Americans, we tend to underemphasize listening and overemphasize talking, interrupting, and pontificating. It is about more than listening without interruption; instead, it is *active* listening. This means being intentional, engaged, fully focused, noting nonverbal cues, and placing oneself in the shoes of another. Another habit is to observe in order to see what is outside our windows, to be self-aware enough to recognize our generalizations, to critically reflect, and to push against internal monologues that attach pejorative labels to entire groups. Listening and observation are not one-time events. They are a perpetual exercise.

Such exercises may lead to one of two responses. The first is that, when presented with narratives contrary to one's experiences, the easiest route is to close the door, turn inward to America, and, in effect, dismiss the rest of the world. The second option is to let experiences instill a desire to learn more. What had been a sliver of a door opening as a child in the backseat looking at Canada as we drove around Lake Superior soon became a lifelong endeavor. I had become enamored with repeatedly and actively listening, observing, and reading. It is brave to open a door, to see alternative views, to observe different habits, and to read different literatures. And it is necessary. America is not the world. It is just one of 193 countries.

So What?

For a chapter about social equity, it may seem odd that I have not defined the concept. In fact, while not explicit, the term is implied. I hope the reason is clear: What is understood as equity in one country is not the same in another. Inequities within America are not the same as in South Africa, China, Panama, or Egypt. America's race, gender, and sexual orientation debates need not be the debates, or even provide the framing for such debates, in other countries. Although there is no list of "most discussed categories of inequity around the world," we know from countries in Asia and the Pacific that there is variance on what rises to a national-level inequity discussion.[20]

This leads to the "so what" question. Do the observations mentioned in this chapter relate to public administrators? The answer is unequivocal. Yes. Before expanding on this answer, I encourage readers to reflect and to consider Question 1 at the end of this chapter. If the question appears irrelevant, is it because "the non-American world does not matter to me" because "I wish to be City Manager in Town X," or "I wish to work for a charity focused on children in County Y" or "I wish to work for the Department of Health and Human Services" in Washington DC and thus, "what matters most is Town/County/Department"? If so, read on.

I challenge readers to find any job that is fully disconnected from the world outside of America. Economic inequality, job loss, migration, domestic violence, food deserts, book bans, and gender debates are interconnected with the world beyond America's borders. One of many lessons from the Great Depression is that when we close our borders (politically, economically, intellectually, culturally), our ability to grow as a nation is diminished. For example, think of your current or future job and its focus (health, education, transportation, etc.) and then ask, "which elements of the job interconnect with the world outside of America?" If your answer is "none" or "just one thing," think again. To date, no one has been able to convince me that their job is not influenced by three or more ideas, events, and/or interactions outside of the United States.

Three examples illustrate this point. In health, multiple parts of a hospital (from needles to beds to nurses to medical devices) are reliant on trade, immigration, and complex interactions. We also know that 8.3% of Americans are uninsured, and 43%are inadequately insured.[21] Comparative studies teach us that "the U.S. spends nearly 18% of GDP on health care, yet Americans die younger and are less healthy than residents of other high-income countries."[22] The United States also "has the lowest life expectancy at birth, the highest death rates for avoidable or treatable conditions, the highest maternal and infant mortality, and among the highest suicide rates" when compared to high-income countries. This, despite spending 17.8% of U.S. GDP in 2021 on health care, which is much more than the 9.8% average among high-income OECD countries without such challenges.[23] Among such countries, the United States is the only high-income country without national health care. In other words, health-related jobs interact in substance, trade, comparability, and in outcomes with countries outside of America.

Transport is a second example. It is a cross-border act marked by efforts to ensure that imports of food do not have banned chemicals and that imports do not contain illegal wildlife items like ivory. Moreover, the world's top three cement multinationals are French, Chinese, and German, and each interacts with local roadworks.[24] Similarly, given the integration and growth of the United States, Canadian, and Mexican economies since the North American Free Trade Agreement (NAFTA) in 1993, how should semi-trucks be regulated as they cross borders?

Poverty is a third example. Although not unique to America, the *scale* of American poverty is unique when compared to other high-income countries. Among the 38 wealthy and democratic members of the OECD, the U.S. poverty rate is the eighth highest. When compared to the OECD average, the bottom 10% and 20% of Americans hold less of our national income (2.1% and 6.1%, respectively) than the OECD average. In contrast, the top 10%- and 20%-income brackets of Americans have larger shares of America's national income (28.2% and 43.9%, respectively) than the OECD average.[25] This is striking: the top 20% income bracket in America holds nearly 44% of America's wealth. We can learn from both Slovenia and the Slovak Republic. The lowest 10%-income bracket of Slovenians holds more of its national wealth on a percentage basis than the lowest 10% in other OECD countries. This means that in Slovenia, its poorest are less poor than their fellow Slovenians when compared to other OECD countries. In the Slovak Republic, its bottom 10%-income bracket holds *more* of its national income than any other OECD country. Its top 10%-income bracket holds *less* of its national income than its fellow Slovaks when compared to OECD members.

Inequity and Its Analytical Units

This section has five parts. The first part discusses public administration's favorite analytical unit: the administrative state, meaning its organizational bureaucracy. This is followed by a defense of the art of comparison and its importance for administrative practice. The final three parts discuss the rise of international administration via international organizations, non-governmental organizations via global civil society, and a claim that transnational administration is our present and, increasingly, our future. As you read this, imagine how "being global" interacts with your career goals in public administration.

1. The Administrative State

The administrative state relies on bureaucracy to establish and implement public policies.

In the United States, agencies, bureaus, and departments are located in rural areas, towns, cities, counties, states, and the federal government. While most focus on domestic goals, there are many that also have an international focus. At the federal level, these include the Defense Department, multiple intelligence agencies, two trade agencies, the Treasury Department, the State Department, and the National Security Council. The truth is that there is a false dichotomy between domestic- and foreign-focused agencies, a fact that comes with three implications.

The first is that our understanding of the American administrative state is incomplete. We cannot understand domestic and global interactions that contribute to equity if our economic, trade, and other foreign-focused agencies are overlooked.

The second implication is that a state's administration and policies are influenced by other states and/or non-state actors.[26] Regardless of whether our reference is the empires and kingdoms of old or our current Westphalian order,[27] humans trade goods and services. Whether it was the silk and gunpowder trades from ancient China to the Levant, the Balkans, and further West, trade via 50,000 miles of Roman Empire roads, trade among Incan *ayllu* (groups of families), or the use of monsoon winds to trade among Zanzibar, the Arabian Peninsula, and western India, the exchange of goods, people, and ideas is not new. Nations are interconnected. However, one difference with today is speed. A cross-national deal can be made in seconds, become one of thousands of containers in a 15,000-container ship next week, and arrive in Los Angeles from Korea in four weeks. There is pressure among and between countries to grow, to outcompete for foreign investment, to incentivize domestic innovation, to create reliable legal-regulatory environments, and to provide sufficient social safety nets. Each of these has equity, diversity, and inclusion implications.

A third implication is the scale of interaction. The world's GDP rose from $3.25 trillion in 1900 to $28.85 trillion in 1975 to $108.12 trillion in 2015. In 1900, the world had 2 billion people. In 2022, it was just over 8 billion. There are other shifts, too. Between 1900 and 2019, nearly 500 species have become extinct.[28] Global regulators, such as the Gulf Stream and deep ocean currents, are changing.[29] The consequences are well-known: circulating air, water, and weather do not care about borders. Inequity is not separable from environmental degradation, air and water pollution, land use, poor regulation and planning, and species extinction.

The COVID-19 pandemic cut the income of 99% of the world's population while wealth of the 10 richest men doubled.[30] The pandemic only worsened already-widening inequalities. Oxfam noted that "since 1995, the top 1% [of individuals] have captured nearly 20 times more of global wealth than the bottom 50% of humanity" and "twenty of the richest billionaires are estimated, on average to be emitting as much as 8,000 times more carbon than the billion poorest people."[31] Those billion poorest, as noted earlier, are not Americans. From 1850 to 2011, the United States "produced 27%t of the total carbon dioxide emissions of the world."[32] By population, 85% of today's top 10% of world carbon dioxide emitters "live in advanced countries" among which is the United States.[33] Inequity is not separable from climate change.

No single country can solve such problems and there are well-known challenges to the provision of global public goods.[34] However, there is a lot one country can do to reverse its history of inequity, to unleash the potential of the poor and the working classes, to reverse climate change, and to create a bigger economic pie for all. One way to start is to emphasize proactive comparison. Comparative administration is discussed next.

2. Comparative Administration

The act of comparing oneself, one's village, and one's country with another is not new. Despite claims by American public administration scholars that comparative administration studies began in the 1950s and 1960s, comparative administration is an older endeavor. The Greeks were influenced by the prior administrative organization of the Achaemenids of modern-day Turkey, Iran, Iraq, Lebanon, and eastern Egypt; the spread of Islam (after 613 C.E.) influenced the administrative states of North Africa, the Levant, Spain, and parts of Balkans. So, too, did Confucianism, Christianity, and Hinduism influence the world's regions. Each influence reshaped political and administrative apparatuses.

Specific to the United States, academic interest in political-administrative comparison began in the late

1800s. This includes early 20th-century studies that called for colonialism studies, not anti-colonialism studies.[35] By WWII's end, new interests arose, namely how to develop what colonial administrators had purposefully underdeveloped. Paired with this question was a Cold War in which democracy and capitalism (of the West) were pitted against authoritarianism and communism (of the then-Soviet Union). This led to new theories about modernization,[36] dependency,[37] and administrative-policy challenges of underdevelopment.[38]

It also led to academic assumptions with parallels to hegemonic intellectualism. That is, knowledge about administrative state development was assumed to be unidirectional from the West to the rest.[39] Post-WWII globalization came with new trading mechanisms (e.g., rules, treaties, organizations) and how to develop world economies. Development is more than creating markets for U.S. exports. It is about reducing poverty, increasing educational and health access, and creating a world in which all (and not just the few) can participate and prosper.

3. International Administration

Parallel to questions of "how to administratively develop" were new events, organizations, and ideas within supranational (above the state) locations. Global governance emerged without global government. This is an important distinction. There is no global government, no global executive branch, no global legislative branch, and no global judiciary.[40] This is also not "international administration" as in "any non-U.S. administrative state." Instead, it is administration by international organizations.[41]

With the creation of the United Nations in 1946, along with the International Monetary Fund and the World Bank in 1944, a new era of global governance began. The system learned from League of Nations failures and from successes like the International Telecommunications Union (1865), Permanent Court of Arbitration (1899), and the International Labour Organisation (1919), among others. Today, there are more than 540 international (governmental) organizations (IOs).[42] By definition, IOs must have three or more member-states, a headquarters, a permanent staff (called international civil servants), and standard operations.[43] For example, the U.S.-Canada Boundary Commission is an international body but not an IO as it has only two member-states. But the United Nations, for example, with 193 member-states, is an IO. The United States is represented at the UN by a U.S. Ambassador who is appointed by the U.S. president and confirmed by the U.S. Senate. Most IOs have U.S. representation either by an ambassador or interaction with federal departments or a U.S. embassy located in the IO's headquarters country.

IOs are headquartered in more than 120 countries and most include the United States as a member-state. Dues are often minimal. For example, the budget of the United Nations in 2022 was $3.12 billion. This is 1/17 of the $55.2 billion spent annually on U.S. foreign aid.[44] Politicians suggest that the United States spends too much on foreign aid but numbers cannot lie. America's annual foreign aid budget is less than 0.22% of its gross national income (GNI), which is far below the OECD-recommended amount of 0.7% of GNI.

Other organizations such as Interpol (international police coordination body) or the Bank of International Settlements (BIS, central bank coordinating body) look like IOs but are informal IOs. They have a headquarters, permanent staff, and operating standards, but they do not have member-*states*. It is not the *state* that is represented at Interpol or BIS but representatives from our national police agency (e.g., the FBI) for Interpol and the U.S. Federal Reserve for BIS. Interpol is a coordinating body, but it is not a police force, and it has no power of arrest. The power to arrest lies solely within each state. BIS and its 63-member central banks can suggest an improved capital asset ratio, for example, for commercial banks, but they cannot require it.

4. Global Civil Society

Global civil society actors are transnational forces that seek policy change in multiple countries. Since the creation of anti-slavery movements in the 1830s, the Red Cross in 1863, suffragette movements and labor unions in the early 1900s, and non-governmental organizations (NGOs) like Save the Children in 1919, transnational civil society has dramatically expanded. [45] Today there are tens of thousands of NGOs with international, global, and transnational foci. NGOs may be headquartered in one country (e.g., Transparency International in Berlin, Germany), but their ideas (e.g., anti-corruption) and their influence are global.

Other global civil society actors include NGOs, private associations, foundations, think tanks, transnational advocacy networks, and transnational social movements. A few examples illustrate their diversity: NGOs include the Coalition for Human Rights in Development. It is a California-based organization of 100 members in 50 countries that advocate for human rights within international development. Private associations include the World Business Council for Sustainable Development with the leaders of more than 200 global corporations as members. Member corporations follow international guidelines for sustainability and many guidelines exceed country-specific requirements. Foundations like the Gates Foundation have significant influence not only on the health and educational practices of foreign countries but on the United States too. For think tanks, there are 11,175 think tanks (2020) in the world of which 1,871 are in the United States.[46] The International Campaign to Ban Landmines is a Swiss-based transnational advocacy movement that earned the 1997 Nobel Peace Prize. With more than 80% of the world's states (164) as Mine Ban Treaty signatories, the Campaign encourages states to implement the Treaty while encouraging non-signatory countries to sign. As of 2023, the United States is not a signatory. The transnational social movement #MeToo started as U.S.-focused, but has since spread worldwide, contextualizing to each country's unique gender barriers.

5. Transnational Administration (and Global Policy)

Global governance is transnationally administered.[47] At a basic level, this means that policies and administrative ideas are dispersed, deconcentrated, devolved, and decentralized from a traditional "owner" (the state) to global governance actors, who have policy power. It is not global *public* policy but instead, global (without public) policy.[48] It is only global *public* policy if the administrative state or the IO, as public actors, create the policy and its administration for global audiences.[49] Today, lines between exclusively state-based policy/administration and supranational and global policy and its administration are increasingly blurred.[50] If the pre-Cold War and Cold War eras engaged global governance via states, IOs, and certain NGOs, the post-Cold War era has witnessed an explosion in transnational actor categories. There are at least 24 with transnational influence.[51] Eight of the 24 have already been mentioned: informal IOs and seven actor types within global civil society. All 24 actors are non-state and non-IO actors that desire to alter one or more state-specific and/or globally relevant laws, regulations, and policies. Many specialize in one or two sectors and/or parts of the world.

Several are IO-adjacent or state-adjacent. They include global consortiums of IOs (e.g., International Consortium on Combating Wildlife Crime), informal clubs (e.g., G7 Group of Nations), informal IOs within a formal IO (e.g., Quint Group within NATO), quasi-judicial actors (e.g., Inspection Panel of the World Bank), transgovernmental networks (e.g., International Competition Network), transnational public-private partnerships (e.g., GAVI Vaccine Alliance), transnational regulatory regimes outside of IOs (e.g., Kimberley Process Certification Scheme), transnational regulatory regimes within IOs (e.g., Global Reporting Initiative), hybrid intergovernmental-private relationships (e.g., ICANN, which is a California-based actor that assigns and monitors domain names like .gov, .edu, .cn, .fr, and so on.), and hybrid intergovernmental-state arrangements (e.g., Svalbard Global Seed Vault, which holds duplicates of 1.2 million seeds from nearly all countries).

Five transnational actors are adjacent to global civil society. This includes expertise networks (e.g., WHO Expert Committee on Developing Global Standards for Governance and Oversight of Human Genome Editing), individual global citizen activists (e.g., Greta Thunberg), global commissions (e.g., World Commission on Dams), global forums (e.g., Global Forum on Migration and Development), global task forces (e.g., Panel of Eminent Persons on UN-Civil Society Relations), and hacktivists (e.g., Anonymous). For example, Greta Thunberg's initial environmental protest in Sweden became a global movement of children wanting a positive climate future. The Human Genome Editing Committee heard from experts from dozens of countries before releasing a report on best-practice governance standards.

To use cities as an example, there is much more than the Sister Cities movement. Global cities, in particular, do more than administer their own city but have also become global actors with influence. Multiple transnational actors have arisen to link cities together. Examples include the World Conference of Mayors, state-driven offices of international trade (e.g., Wisconsin Economic Development Corporation), sector-specific global networks (e.g., Local Governments for Sustainability (ICLEI)), OECD interaction with cities, UN-Habitat's work on homes and communities, and hybrid organizations like Cities Alliance. Countries are not their members; mayors, cities, and local departments or ministries are the membership. The conversation of equity, diversity, and inclusion is not a U.S.-specific enterprise. In today's world, administrative and policy "borders" are porous, and best practice emanates not only from states and IOs but multiple transnational actors, where each seeks to address slices of development challenges.

In Conclusion: Now What?

This chapter is intended for American readers who have limited exposure to the administrative and policy world outside of the United States. For students with global families and/or prior international travel, this chapter may be a review. Regardless of one's positionality, the chapter suggests that America does not exist on a metaphorical island separated from the rest of the world. Nor are the United States and the West the sole sources of administrative and/or policy knowledge. There was diffusion of knowledge for millennia before the Western Hemisphere was "discovered" by Europeans. However, knowledge can be incomplete, gendered, non-inclusionary, non-diverse, and unaware of administrative spaces outside its own. *In its very best form, knowledge is a global, diverse, inclusionary, multidisciplinary, and multidirectional kaleidoscope of contextualized interaction.* When done well, knowledge reduces inequities, increases diversity, and encourages inclusion.

This chapter makes clear that social equity conversations within the United States are not immune to influences, events, and actors from outside. Countries are embedded in the global environment. Challenges faced by the United States are rarely unique. While some are specific to the United States (e.g., high prison population, insufficient health care, predilection to arm civilians, and shortcomings during COVID-19), its other challenges are not unique. The act of comparison is an act of knowledge creation, learning, and exchanging information. It is humbling to learn that somewhere else does it better than one's own administrative state.

Not only is knowledge transfer endemic to human experience, so too are interactions outside one's community and country. Whether via trade, cultural exchange, or even war, information is exchanged. The globalization of our world—from its earliest exchanges over land and sea, to the industrial revolution, to today's interconnected world—has created new actors and new conversations. While IOs and NGOs are mid-to-late 19th-century inventions, transnational actors and their policy power are post-Cold War phenomena. Each creates space for administrative and policy discussions about how to improve social equity. The answer to this section's "now what" question is, at a minimum, engagement, active listening, observation, reading, comparing, and thinking transnationally.

Summary of Key Points

Equity, diversity, and inclusion are global challenges.

Travel (in person or metaphorically) helps one get out of an Americanist bubble, to learn from others, and to engage in administrative and policy comparison.

Active listening, observing, and reading are repeatable exercises with significant benefits to U.S.-based students and practitioners.

Equity knowledge is deepened via comparative knowledge and understanding international administration, global civil society, and transnational administration.

Discussion Questions

1. Look at syllabi for other courses you are taking. Which countries are taught and/or who is the first author (gender, ethnicity, university location) of your readings? Answer the following:
   a) Are most case studies largely American?
   b) Are most first authors affiliated with American universities?
   c) Are most first authors male and/or White?
   d) What might happen to your "doors" if you learned about public administration from the voices, people, and places in which other perspectives exist?
2. Think of your career interests (health, education, transportation, public finance, human resource management, etc.) and then answer this: How do your interests interact with the world outside of America? *Hint*: If your answer is "none," think again.
3. Find examples of three transnational actor categories at the global level then answer the following:
   a) What is similar about each actor? What is different?
   b) What is their purpose? How does the purpose vary from your other actor examples?
   c) How might your examples interact with the administrative state (local, state, federal) of the United States?
4. Choose one organization in the last two paragraphs of section 5 (Transnational Administration (and Global Policy) and/or find one that is not listed. Then answer these questions:
   a) Does it have "members?" Who are the "members?"
   b) If it is a para-diplomatic city actor, which cities are "represented?" What happens in their meetings and conferences? Can you find a discussion of those meetings or actors on the city websites?
   c) If it is a transnational public-private partnership, how much of the partnership is influenced by public actors versus private actors? How is it funded?
   d) More generally, who is the organization's audience?
   e) How would you determine if the organization is accountable, transparent, and legitimate?

Additional Resources

1. Access "7 Ways to Improve Your Active Listening Skills," at https://health.clevelandclinic.org/active-listening/ (2023).
2. Thomas Davies, *NGOs—A New History of Transnational Civil Society*. (London: C. Hurst & Co. Publishers Ltd, 2014).
3. Morgen Johansen, ed., *Social Equity in the Asia-Pacific Region: Conceptualizations and Realities*. Cham: Springer International Publishing, 2019.
4. Moloney, Kim, Meng-Hsuan Chou, Philip Osei, and Yonique Campbell. "Methodological Americanism: Disciplinary Senility and Intellectual Hegemonies in (American) Public Administration." *Administrative Theory & Praxis* 44, no. 4 (2022): 261–276.
5. Diane Stone and Kim Moloney, eds. *The Oxford Handbook of Global Policy and Transnational Administration* (Oxford: Oxford University Press, 2019).

Notes

1. Nilima Gulrajani, and Kim Moloney, "Globalizing Public Administration: Today's Research and Tomorrow's Agenda." *Public Administration Review* 72, no. 1 (2012): 78–86.
2. Esteban Leonardo Santis, "Otherness: An Unfinished Project in Public Administration." *Administrative Theory & Praxis* 44, no. 2 (2022): 133–42.
3. Muhammad Azfar Nisar, "Decolonization and Public Administration: Frustrated Ramblings of a Spoilsport." *Administrative Theory & Praxis* 45, no. 2 (2023): 147–157.
4. Meng-Hsuan Chou, Kim Moloney, Philip Osei, and Yonique Campbell, "Methodological Nationalism and Epistemological Diversity in (American) Public Administration," 2023, https://doi.org/10.5281/zenodo.7969442; Kim Moloney, Meng-Hsuan Chou, Philip Osei, and Yonique Campbell, "Methodological Americanism: Disciplinary Senility and Intellectual Hegemonies in (American) Public Administration," *Administrative Theory & Praxis* 44, no. 4 (2022): 261–276, https://doi.org/10.1080/10841806.2022.2140387
5. Kim Moloney, Pablo Sanabria-Pulido, and Mehmet Akif Demircioglu, "Interrogating Hegemonic Embraces: Representative Bureaucracy, Methodological Whiteness, and Non-West Exclusions." *Public Administration Review* 83, no. 1 (2023): 195–202, https://doi.org/10.1111/puar.13512; Paul P. van Riper. "Some Anomalies in the Deep History of U.S. Public Administration." *Public Administration Review* 57, no. 3 (1997): 218–222.
6. Aroon P. Manoharan, and Nandhini Rangarajan, "Public Administrators as Storytellers: Nurturing Narrative Competence to Enrich Their Professional Identity." *Administrative Theory & Praxis* 45, no. 2 (2023): 158–169, https://doi.org/10.1080/10841806.2022.2086753
7. Personal stories are unusual for academic chapters but with editor encouragement, the chapter starts with stories.
8. Meng-Hsuan Chou, Kim Moloney, Philip Osei, and Yonique Campbell, "Methodological Nationalism and Epistemological Diversity in (American) Public Administration," (2023): 8, https://doi.org/10.5281/zenodo.7969442
9. Brian Bourke, "Positionality: Reflecting on the Research Process," *The Qualitative Report* 19, no. 33 (2014): 2, https://doi.org/10.46743/2160-3715/2014.1026
10. Bourke, "Positionality," 3.
11. Schnequa N. Diggs, "The Delusion of Privilege," *Administrative Theory & Praxis* 44, no. 2 (2022): 105–112, https://doi.org/10.1080/10841806.2021.1984102; Santis, "Otherness."
12. Bourke, "Positionality," 2.
13. There are 193 member-states of the United Nations, not including territories and non-independent locales.
14. International Monetary Fund, "Download Entire World Economic Outlook Database, April 2023." https://www.imf.org/en/Publications/WEO/weo-database/2023/April/download-entire-database
15. Emily A. Shrider, Melissa Kollar, Frances Chen, and Jessica Semega, "Income and Poverty in the United States: 2020," The United States Census Bureau (United States Census Bureau, September 14, 2021), https://

www.census.gov/library/publications/2021/demo/p60-273.html.
16. John Creamer, Emily Shrider, Kalee Burns, and Frances Chen, "Poverty in the United States: 2021," (United States Census Bureau, September 13, 2022), https://www.census.gov/library/publications/2022/demo/p60-277.html
17. World Bank, "GDP per Capita, PPP (Current International $) | Data," 2023, https://data.worldbank.org/indicator/NY.GDP.PCAP.PP.CD?most_recent_value_desc=true&year_high_desc=true
18. SIPRI, "World Military Expenditure Passes $2 Trillion for First Time," SIPRI, April 25, 2022, https://www.sipri.org/media/press-release/2022/world-military-expenditure-passes-2-trillion-first-time
19. Organisation for Economic Co-operation and Development, "Intergenerational Mobility in Education," Organisation for Economic Co-operation and Development, 2023, https://stats.oecd.org/Index.aspx?QueryId=79431
20. Morgen Johansen, ed., *Social Equity in the Asia-Pacific Region: Conceptualizations and Realities* (Cham: Springer International Publishing, 2019).
21. Sara R. Collins, Munira Z. Gunja, and Gabrielle N. Aboulafia, "U.S. Health Insurance Coverage in 2020: A Looming Crisis in Affordability," Commonwealth Fund, 2020, U.S. Health Insurance Coverage in 2020: A Looming Crisis in Affordability—Findings from the Commonwealth Fund Biennial Health Insurance Survey, 2020; Katherine Keisler-Starkey, and Lisa N. Bunch, "Health Insurance Coverage in the United States: 2021," United States Census Bureau, September 13, 2022, https://www.census.gov/library/publications/2022/demo/p60-278.html
22. Munira Z. Gunja, Evan D. Gumas, and Reginald D. Williams II, "U.S. Health Care from a Global Perspective, 2022: Accelerating Spending, Worsening Outcomes," The Commonwealth Fund, January 31, 2023, https://www.commonwealthfund.org/publications/issue-briefs/2023/jan/us-health-care-global-perspective-2022
23. Munira Z. Gunja, Evan D. Gumas, and Reginald D. Williams II. "U.S. Health Care from a Global Perspective, 2022: Accelerating Spending, Worsening Outcomes."
24. Ty Haqqi, "5 Largest Cement Companies in the World," *Insider Monkey*, 2020, https://www.insidermonkey.com/blog/5-largest-cement-companies-in-the-world-889187/?singlepage=1
25. Organisation for Economic Co-operation and Development, *Key Indicators on the Distribution of Household Disposable Income and Poverty, 2007, 2018, and 2019 or Most Recent Year* (Paris: OECD, 2023).
26. Karl T. Muth, "The Potential and Limits of Administrative Sovereignty," In *The Oxford Handbook of Global Policy and Transnational Administration,* ed. Diane Stone and Kim Moloney, (Oxford, UK: Oxford University Press, 2019), 59–74.
27. In 1648, Europe's emergent states agreed that states have exclusive sovereignty over their territory and, the sovereignty of states is equal, among other ideas. The Treaty of Westphalia is a tenet of international law and is the basis of a modern international order. At the time, Westphalia (part of today's Germany) was still part of the Roman Empire.
28. Jen McCaffery, and Lela Nargi, "14 Facts about Animals That Have Gone Extinct in the Last 100 Years," *Reader's Digest*, November 28, 2022, https://www.rd.com/list/animals-extinct-last-100-years/
29. Sascha Pare, "Antarctic Currents Supplying 40% of World's Deep Ocean with Nutrients and Oxygen Slowing Dramatically." Space.com, May 27, 2023, https://www.space.com/antarctic-ocean-currents-slowing-dramatically
30. Nabil Ahmed, Anna Marriott, Nafkote Dabi, Megan Lowthers, Max Lawson, and Leah Mugehera, "Inequality Kills," Oxfam International, January 17, 2022, https://www.oxfam.org/en/research/inequality-kills
31. Nabil Ahmed, Anna Marriott, Nafkote Dabi, Megan Lowthers, Max Lawson, and Leah Mugehera, "Inequality Kills," 7.
32. Mengpin Ge, Johannes Friedrich, and Thomas Damassa, "6 Graphs Explain the World's Top 10 Emitters," World Resources Institute, November 25, 2014, https://www.wri.org/insights/6-graphs-explain-worlds-top-10-emitters
33. Laura Cozzi, Olivia Chen, and Hyeji Kim, "The World's Top 1% of Emitters Produce over 1000 Times More CO2 than the Bottom 1%—Analysis," International Energy Agency, February 22, 2023, https://www.iea.org/commentaries/the-world-s-top-1-of-emitters-produce-over-1000-times-more-co2-than-the-bottom-1
34. As examples, see the following. Inge Kaul, and Donald Blondin, "Global Public Goods and the United Nations," In *Global Governance and Development*, ed. José Antonio Ocampo (Oxford, UK: Oxford University Press, 2016), 32–65; Nico Krisch, "The Decay of Consent: International Law in an Age of Global Public Goods," *The American Journal of International Law* 108, no. 1 (January 2014): 1–40, https://doi.org/10.5305/amerjintelaw.108.1.0001
35. Albert J. Beveridge, "The Development of a Colonial

Policy for the United States," *Annals of the American Academy of Political and Social Science* 30, no. 1 (1907): 3–15.

36. Walter W. Rostow, *The Stages of Economic Growth: A Non-Communist Manifesto* (Cambridge: Cambridge University Press, 1960).
37. Raul Prebisch, *The Economic Development of Latin America and Its Principal Problems* (New York: United Nations, 1950).
38. David Morawetz, *Twenty-Five Years of Economic Development, 1950 to 1975* (Washington, DC: World Bank, 1977).
39. Moloney, Kim, Meng-Hsuan Chou, Philip Osei, and Yonique Campbell, "Methodological Americanism: Disciplinary Senility and Intellectual Hegemonies in (American) Public Administration," *Administrative Theory & Praxis* 44, no. 4 (2022): 261–276. Anshuman Prasad, "Toward Decolonizing Modern Western Structures of Knowledge: A Postcolonial Interrogation of (Critical) Management Studies," In *The Routledge Companion to Critical Management Studies*, ed. Anshuman Prasad, Pushkala Prasad, Albert J. Mills, and Jean Helms Mills (New York: Routledge, 2015): 185–122.
40. Kim Moloney, and David H. Rosenbloom. "Creating Space for Public Administration in International Organization Studies." *American Review of Public Administration* 50, no. 3 (2020): 227–243. Further, there is no global legislature. The closest is the European Parliament, but its powers are far less than a parliament in a democratic state. There is no global judiciary. There are international judicial bodies (e.g., International Criminal Court, International Court of Justice) but their powers over states and individuals remain limited. There is also no global executive branch. The UN and its 20+ IOs are just 5% of the world's total number of supranational regional and international organizations.
41. Michael W. Bauer and Christoph Knill, *Management Reforms in International Organizations* (Nomos Verlagsgesellschaft Mbh & Company, 2007); Michael W. Bauer, Christoph Knill, and Steffen Eckhard (eds). *International Bureaucracy: Challenges and Lessons for Public Administration Research* (London: Palgrave Macmillan UK, 2017).
42. Jon C.W. Pevehouse, Timothy Nordstrom, Roseanne W. McManus, and Anne Spencer Jamison, "Tracking Organizations in the World: The Correlates of War IGO Version 3.0 Datasets," *Journal of Peace Research* 57, no. 3 (2020): 492–503.
43. Kelly-Kate S. Pease, *International Organizations: Perspectives on Global Governance.* (London: Routledge, 2018).
44. Organisation for Economic Co-operation and Development, "Total Flows by Donor," OECD.org (Organisation for Economic Co-operation and Development, n.d.), https://stats.oecd.org/Index.aspx?DataSetCode=Table1; United Nations, "Secretary-General Unveils $3.12 Billion Budget Proposal for 2022 to Fifth Committee, Stressing Organization Must Remain Flexible amid Recent Surges in COVID-19," United Nations, October 13, 2021, https://press.un.org/en/2021/gaab4372.doc.htm
45. Thomas Davies, *NGOs—A New History of Transnational Civil Society* (C. Hurst & Co. Publishers Ltd, 2014).
46. James G. McGann, *2020 Global Go to Think Tank Index Report* (Philadelphia: University of Pennsylvania, 2020).
47. Kim Moloney, "Deconcentrated Global Governance, Transnational Administration, and the Public Administration Discipline," *Global Public Policy and Governance* 1, no. 2 (2021): 175–201.
48. Diane Stone, *Making Global Policy* (Cambridge: Cambridge University Press, 2019).
49. Diane Stone, and Kim Moloney, eds. *The Oxford Handbook of Global Policy and Transnational Administration* (Oxford: Oxford University Press, 2019).
50. Diane Stone, and Stella Ladi, "Global Public Policy and Transnational Administration," *Public Administration* 93, no. 4 (2015): 839–855, https://doi.org/10.1111/padm.12207
51. Kim Moloney, and T. Legrand, "In Loco Civitatis? Accountability, Transnational Actors, and Global Governance," unpublished manuscript.

3 DOING EQUITY WORK "EQUITABLY": HOW AN INTERSECTIONAL APPROACH HELPS

Meghna Sabharwal and Rashmi Chordiya

From the Editors

Everyone has multiple identities: race, color, gender identity, sexuality, and more. This is why our administrative approaches to achieving social equity should be more nuanced. Each identity on its own, and each combination of identities, comes with different experiences of privilege or marginalization. Sabharwal and Chordiya explore how intersectionality informs public administration in the contexts of health care, education, and workplace dynamics. They note how Targeted Universalism—a five-step, goal-oriented equity approach focused on establishing common goals for everyone—can be used to promote fairness.

"There is no such thing as a single-issue struggle because we do not live single-issue lives."

—Audre Lorde[1]

What Is Intersectionality and Why Does It Matter?

Building on contributions from Black, Indigenous, and other racialized people of color, Kimberlé Crenshaw coined the term "intersectionality" in 1989. In her acclaimed TED talk on "the urgency of intersectionality," she notes, "we all know that, where there's no name for a problem, you can't see a problem, and when you can't see a problem, you pretty much can't solve it."[2] Intersectionality reveals how multiple forms of oppression overlap and intersect due to socially constructed hierarchies of superiority and inferiority. The concept operationalizes structured and systemic ways in which interlocking systems of oppression affect the lives of multiply[3] marginalized people of color.[4]

The Framework of Intersectionality: Key Teachings

Crenshaw's contributions mark the beginning of a way to understand how identities intersect.[5] As a theoretical framework, intersectionality explains how multiple social categories (e.g., race, ethnicity, gender, sexual orientation, socioeconomic status, age) combine at the level of individual experience and result in interlocking systems of privilege or oppression at the societal level (e.g., racism, sexism, heterosexism)."[6]

As articulated in the powerful quote by Audre Lorde (above), intersectionality teaches us to interrupt and replace single-issue consciousness with an intersectional consciousness.[7] Single-identity consciousness prioritizes one marginalized identity over others and ignores multiply marginalized identities. Single-identity approaches in equity work create win-lose solutions and unhelpful debates about who has it worse (i.e., Oppression Olympics).[8] Conversely, intersectional consciousness highlights the inseparability of race, gender, disability, sexuality, caste, and class in the lives of marginalized individuals. Intersectionality requires us to acknowledge diversity within groups and the multidimensionality of inequities. It also encourages us to question the socially constructed nature of our identities and to recognize how marginalization, privilege, and oppression are embedded in institutions and systems. Intersectionality also helps us understand how societal norms shape power dynamics and perceptions of identity.[9] An example of intersectional consciousness arises in the centering of low-income queer, racialized people of color within the Disability Justice movement.[10]

Intersectional consciousness requires public administrators to be aware of the impact of multiple systemic disadvantages on multiply marginalized individuals. Consider the experiences of a Black transgender woman needing welfare assistance. While navigating the welfare system, she will experience challenges and administrative burdens that are not solely rooted in poverty or being Black or transgender. Rather, her experiences emerge from the interplay of these intersecting identities within the context of multiple, interlocking forms of oppression, and racism. Instead of focusing on a single issue of welfare assistance, a welfare officer can take an intersectional approach that acknowledges and addresses the complexities of her lived experience as a Black transgender woman with low income.

One of the key teachings of intersectionality is to acknowledge the whole personhood of those we serve, rather than superficially compartmentalizing them.[11] Adopting a holistic approach allows administrators to address the complexities of people's lives.[12] Intersectionality is a way of thinking that empowers marginalized communities and avoids their erasure.[13] It emphasizes the socially constructed nature of identities and cautions against oversimplifying social identity categories.

Intersectionality as a Liberatory Tool

In the context of social inequities, where oppression often works through divide-and-conquer strategies, intersectionality serves as a liberatory tool.[14] This is because its practice necessitates working in solidarity to interrupt and end cycles of oppression and domination.[15]

Intersectionality helps to build awareness of how oppression co-opts members of marginalized communities, pitting them against each other by placing some in privileged categories (e.g., by income or education) and others in disadvantaged categories (e.g., by race, gender, or disability). Intersectionality helps us understand that oppression is systemic and structural and it affects us all; at the same time, it affects each differently. It teaches us that, while our differences are real, it is not our differences that separate us. Rather, it is our refusal to engage with differences that get in the way of solidarity.[16]

Oppression is an "us" problem, not a "them" problem that we "experts" are trying to remedy or solve. The liberatory work of building solidarity is about not reproducing colonial behaviors of supremacy, where behaviors are embedded in a savior complex. Rather, the work of solidarity is rooted in the assumption that our liberation is interdependent and that struggles and aspirations are interconnected.[17] As administrators and public servants, intersectionality offers the clarity we need to engage in social equity work in ways that shift power and anchor leadership in love, shared humanity, interdependence, reciprocity, repair, and healing.

Seeing Social Inequities Through an Intersectional Lens

This section applies the framework of intersectionality to operationalize difference and shed light on how oppression and power structures compound the disempowerment of communities that are at the margin of margins. Health care, education, and workplaces are the contexts examined.

Health Care

In health care, we recognize that people's access to care and their health outcomes are influenced by their unique identities as well as social factors. Someone's race, ethnic background, gender, socioeconomic status, geographical location, disability, sexual orientation, Indigenous identity, and/or caste affect how they access care. Policy debates center on the problem of access to care for those who are uninsured and those who are members of marginalized groups. While the Affordable Care Act is a positive step forward, health insurance alone cannot fully address the factors that contribute to poor health outcomes and persistent inequalities.[18]

One's health depends on more than access to medical care. It is influenced by intersecting factors, including race, gender, sexuality, disability, geography, and class. These factors combine with education, income, access to nutritious food, safe housing, and lifestyle. These dynamics are interconnected so analyzing health outcomes by intersectional categories reveals patterns that otherwise go unnoticed.[19,20]

Medical sociologists have used an intersectional approach to link health outcomes to systems of racism, sexism, classism, and ableism and to understand population health.[21] For example, there is substantial evidence that when Indigenous cultures are objectified and labeled as "other," attributing health and social disparities to them without consideration of context fosters a blame-oriented perspective toward Indigenous Americans.[22]

Another example comes in studies that employ intersectional analysis of race and gender. In comparison studies, individuals and groups that are disadvantaged or lower in the social hierarchy (e.g., Black, Indigenous, and women of color), fare worse than those on the higher rungs (white men of higher socioeconomic status), who enjoy significantly better health outcomes.[23] This contrast shows that to improve the health of marginalized groups, it is crucial to dismantle overlapping layers of inequity rather than addressing one form of inequity alone.

Education

Education is another policy domain where an intersectional approach is advantageous. Education is a powerful tool for reducing economic and social disparities because it acts as a leveler in society. Intersectionality makes us aware that students have diverse identities, backgrounds, and contexts that shape their experiences, readiness for learning, and needs as they progress through the system. By recognizing these intersections, educators are better equipped to establish inclusive and nurturing learning environments that are responsive to the needs of all students.

Despite integration as mandated by *Brown v. Board of Education* (1954), the U.S. education system continues to marginalize Black, Indigenous, and students of color. These students are often subjected to fewer resources for instruction and a lack of support for their learning and development.[24] Studies consistently demonstrate that schools with a significant concentration of low-income and Black, Indigenous, and students of color receive fewer resources compared to other schools in the same district. [25]

The content students are taught is another way that inequities occur. By whitewashing what is taught, alternative voices and experiences are obscured. Omitting a true account of history ill-equips students to understand why things are as they are. A remedy is to foster inclusive educational systems and to do this, representation matters. A study of U.S. colleges and universities from 2002–2014 found that matching faculty members' sex-race-ethnicity with that of the students yielded positive outcomes for Black males, Latinos, and Latinas.[26] The study provides support for the value of students being taught by those with whom they identify.

In addition to teachers who are representative of their students, organizational factors and power dynamics contribute to disparities in leadership. For example, one study found that women and men of color are less likely to be promoted to the position of principal compared to white men.[27] This persists even though the pipeline for assistant principals is diverse. The failure of Black and Brown assistant principals to be promoted reflects power dynamics that favor Whites. Moreover, some studies explore who is influential in shaping decisions versus those who are relegated to a mere token role. This type of research applies an intersectional lens of race and gender to provide a clearer view of who is, and is not, advantaged by the status quo.[28]

Workplace

The employment environment is another place where intersectionality has a powerful effect. Each employee's identity profoundly influences their experiences at work. Factors such as race, gender, caste, age, religion, disability, and sexuality impact pay equity, promotion opportunities, and workplace discrimination. An intersectional lens enables a deeper understanding of the complexities and interconnectedness between various forms of advantage and disadvantage. In turn, greater appreciation for intersectional identities enables more equitable workplace policies, practices, and interventions that appeal to the unique needs and experiences of workers.

Workers use narratives to explain why some employees are heroes and some are villains. Listening to these reveals more than the story. It is an effective way to understand how the organization acknowledges and explains intersectionality. Stories help to center race and gender with other forms of identities like disability, sexual orientation, religion, class, caste, and age. Narratives reveal how combinations of identities become a source of advantage or disadvantage.[29] Take the case of a transgender woman of color. The intersections of race, gender, and sexual identity create a complex web of discrimination. Narratives explaining why she was, or was not, promoted will reveal the biases thought to be "acceptable."

A recent study conducted by Butz and Gaynor focused on the experiences of transgender women of color and social welfare offices.[30] The authors found that "trans WOC are more likely to report avoiding public assistance offices and Social Security offices than other transgender identifying respondents, including when compared exclusively against white trans women."[31] The study concludes that the intersection of marginalized identities, identifying as a trans woman and a person of color, has a compounding impact. It is associated with both the tendency to avoid applying for public benefits and an increased likelihood of being discriminated against when interacting with social welfare employees. The evidence gathered in the study demonstrates that trans women of color have a higher tendency to avoid accessing public welfare benefits because they must navigate multiple oppressive systems (marginalized gender, class, and racial identities).

Whether trans-sexual, homosexual, or heterosexual, women of color consistently face challenges in the workplace. In fact, they endure higher levels of incivility compared to men of color.[32] This incivility occurs in disrespectful treatment from co-workers and superiors, skepticism toward their work, and lack of interest in the ideas they contribute. These findings are consistent with other studies that highlight subtle biases that inhibit the career progression of women of color.[33] Both gender and race hinder their advancement and when they achieve success, they endure comments expressing surprise and being "impressed" that they were able to rise to the occasion. Studies also find that women of color and LGBT (lesbian, gay, bisexual, and transgender) employees experience greater exclusion and find their places of work less supportive, less open, and less fair.[34]

While COVID-19 may be behind us, its effects in the workplace are still being felt. The pandemic worsened disparities for some employees, especially women of color, women with disabilities, immigrant women, and women with younger children.[35] When women opt for flexible work arrangements, they often face lower salaries and limited access to health insurance. Outdated human resource policies fail to account for these unequal burdens on women.

In the absence of corrective policies, women are further left behind, reinforcing systemic barriers to their upward mobility. Hoang and colleagues[36] argue that human resource managers need to rethink policies and practices, including how to design family-friendly policies, and how to ensure the workplace provides equal opportunity for all workers to participate, be visible, and have promotion opportunities. Applying an intersectional lens and creating inclusionary policies is long overdue and an intersectional perspective is better than a one-size-fits-all approach. It recognizes the complexities of intersecting identities and helps address disparities faced by underrepresented employees.

Intersectionality as a Key to Developing Holistic Understanding of Social Inequities

Inequities are influenced by a complex interplay of factors, including past injustices, discrimination, economic disparities, and limited access to essential services. Intersectionality helps us understand and confront inequities across policy domains, such as health, education, housing, policing, workplace discrimination, and many more. It recognizes that each person's experiences are deeply influenced by their unique identities.

To confront inequities a comprehensive approach is needed, involving policy changes, resource allocation, education transformation, and community empowerment. Intersectionality helps us understand and address inequities by recognizing the interconnectedness of social identities and systems of inequality.[37] It requires self-awareness and acknowledges the influence of race, class, gender, sexual orientation, disability, and religion on one's identity. An intersectional lens uncovers hidden disparities and inspires practical solutions. In the following section, we discuss how intersectionality is key to equitable problem-solving approaches.

Intersectionality as a Pathway to Action

Most public service jobs involve some degree of discretion and discretion provides an opportunity to redress oppression. The liberatory tool of intersectionality makes it possible to identify inequities and injustices in policies, programs, and processes. Progress can be made by excavating and illuminating patterns in persons' lived experiences that result from deeply buried inequities. For example, approaching education policy reform from an intersectional perspective goes beyond a narrow focus on school-based solutions or test scores to tackle the achievement gap. It acknowledges the significance of linking education outcomes to the context of people's lives and takes into account factors like living conditions, job security, access to food, transportation and housing, and health insurance. This more comprehensive understanding of individuals' circumstances requires actively listening to their experiences and recognizing the multiple barriers they encounter. In turn, this opens the door to targeted interventions designed to improve educational outcomes. This is how an intersectional lens helps identify and address the interconnected forces that shape every aspect of education.[38]

Awareness of intersectionality also helps us to identify constructive relationships and workable solutions. Relationships anchored in empowerment, trust, and mutuality between administrators and those they serve can be powerful agents of change. In the next section, we explore targeted universalism as a pathway for action and an approach that operationalizes intersectionality and addresses social and economic problems.

Targeted universalism teaches us that, when we create systems that are ameliorative for those closest to the margins, we also create systems that are more equitable for all.[39] The lens of intersectionality is integral to targeted universalism because it helps to identify the right problems; ask the right questions; include, empower, and shift power to the people and the communities most impacted by inequities; and to cocreate and coinnovate solutions.

Targeted Universalism (TU)

Targeted universalism is a collective, goal-oriented approach to equity that involves working in broad coalitions to establish universal goals. The following paragraphs discuss key principles of targeted universalism (TU) and introduce its five broad steps. We also reflect and discuss how TU is deeply intersectional in its identification and framing of social inequities as well as in its problem-solving approach.

The TU approach is clear about who must be included in the decision-making process and how decisions should be made. The process necessitates deep and purposeful coalition building to ensure inclusion and partnership with those most affected by the problem. Groups that have been historically excluded from the decision-making process should be meaningfully included. The TU approach means meaningful, purposeful, empowered, structured inclusion and partnership. Intentional time and effort should be dedicated to foreground the leadership and perspectives of multiply marginalized communities. This coalition also includes those affected by change strategies, those implementing the intervention/project, those documenting the implementation process, and those with a strong experienced or expert understanding of the problem or issue. Throughout the process, evidence should inform the decisions. Targeted universalism invites us to think about universal or meta-goals and then find equitable pathways to achieve them. Instead of measuring progress based on disparities among subgroups within a target population, the TU approach focuses on getting all groups closer to the universal goal and measuring each group's progress relative to the universal goal.

For example, in the context of pay equity, TU involves arriving at a collective, broad-based agreement on universal goals. An example of a universal goal for pay equity could be to ensure equal pay for work of equal value to the organization. Equal pay for work of equal value can be determined through inclusive job evaluation methods that account for male and female-dominated job demands in regard to skills and qualifications, job responsibilities, job efforts, and work environments.[40] Progress would be measured not in terms of whether women of color are reaching the salary of white men. Rather, progress would be measured in terms of whether subgroups of people of color as well as white people are receiving equal pay for work of equal value across job types, occupations, and organizational functions. TU avoids making assumptions about the needs and challenges of social groups within the target population. To achieve progress, TU focuses on creating systems and structures that are aligned with the goal and on removing systemic and structural barriers that get in the way of achieving it.

The Five-Step Process for Developing Targeted Universalism (TU) Approaches

Step 1: Universal or Meta Goal Setting

A clear and concrete articulation of a universal goal is the first step in the TU framework. The articulation derives from a shared recognition of the problem and collective aspiration. The goal guides subsequent policy development, program evaluation, and benchmarks of success. "Universal" refers to generic universalism as much as it relates to the policymaking institution/organization's jurisdiction. As discussed earlier, universal goal-setting is carried out through a collective process involving a coalition of community groups, organizations, partners, and collaborators. The scope or unit of analysis and implementation could be an organization, a department, a city, a county, a state, a nation-state, and so on. Universal goals must be defined through a collective process and contextualized as they relate to a broadly agreed problem or need within a given policy jurisdiction (e.g., an organization, a department, a municipality, a county, a state, a nation-state or at a global level). It is important to have concrete working definitions of both "universal" as well as what the scope or unit is for policy response and implementation.

Step 2: Assessment of General Population Performance Relative to the Universal Goal

With the direction and vision of a universal goal in place, the second step in implementing targeted universalism is gathering evidence to understand how well the overall population fares relative to the universal goal. The performance of the general population relative to the goal reveals the extent and scope of the problem. Performance of the overall population provides context for understanding the extent and depth of the problem/need. This assessment informs both the operational direction of the work as well as serves as a measure of continued progress/performance/impact in terms of goal achievement.

Step 3: Identify Groups and Places That Are Performing Differently with Respect to the Goal and Disaggregate Them

The third step within the TU framework is to conduct a more granular or layered assessment of how subgroups within a given population perform relative to the universal goal. This step allows decision-makers to account for diversity in social demographics as well as geographical locations.

Step 4: Assess and Understand the Structures That Support or Impede Each Group or Community from Achieving the Universal Goal

Step 4 deepens our analysis of the variation in performance outcomes among diverse subgroups within a given jurisdiction/scope/unit with respect to the universal goal. It requires an examination of the systems and structures that shape these outcomes for subgroups. It is essential that the quantitative and qualitative information/evidence/data in this step include representation and perspectives from diverse stakeholders who are impacted by the problem/need. It is important to acknowledge power structures and the biases implicit and explicit that sculpt the information that is gathered about structures and systems that impede each group from achieving the universal goal. Questions and contradictions are likely to emerge based on diverse perspectives and insights. Furthermore, the phases of information gathering are nonlinear; insights gathered from one phase of data collection shape insights from another phase. The information and understanding helps reach the source of the problem/need and informs the strategies that emerge.

Step 5: Develop and Implement Targeted Strategies for Each Group to Reach the Universal Goal

In this final step, strategies are designed, keeping the needs and contexts of subgroups in mind. There is rarely a "one size fits all" solution. Thus, development and implementation of a set of strategies is the likely outcome. This step also calls for appreciation that, while we may be focused on reaching a common universal goal, each group is located differently within existing power structures so their needs and circumstances vary, with some being more acute and extreme than others. Therefore, any approach to implementation of targeted strategies must include weighing the intensity of priorities for the groups involved. Similarly, rather than an even distribution of resources across all groups, there is a need to prioritize greater support for groups farthest away from the universal goal.

An Intersectional Targeted Universalism: A Call for Empowerment, Trust, and Relationality

Targeted universalism is deeply intersectional in terms of both framing and practice. It is rooted in the assumption that social and economic problems have uneven effects across the population. TU interrupts, and seeks to transform, traditional top-down approaches to decision-making that involve participation from communities in extractive and superficial ways. TU demonstrates intersectionality in its processes because it employs intentional efforts to build coalitions and collectively problem-solve.

TU calls for shifting and sharing power and building trust while connecting diverse communities, particularly those who have been marginalized within existing power structures. A core assumption of targeted universalism is that it moves the marginalized from the margins to the center.

As a relational approach to equity work, TU necessitates liberatory skills such as balancing fierceness and tenderness, self-care and collective care, patience, courage, empathy, and compassion for self and others. These skills are necessary to do the work of repairing and building trust with those who have experienced harm due to past policies and decisions that have the effect of exclusion, exploitation, and marginalization. It requires us to cultivate a trauma-informed public service, one that begins with an acknowledgment of the historical, intergenerational, persistent trauma that has brought hurt and harm to multiply marginalized communities.[41] The work requires us to engage in long-term, vulnerable work of repairing distrust and building trust. It necessitates commitment to transformative change in the form of dismantling oppressive systems that caused harm in the first place. Furthermore, to cocreate and coinnovate equitable and liberatory systems, requires cultivating coalitions, collectives, and shared equity leadership. Most importantly, it requires a concrete and intentional investment of time, space, and resources to trust and follow the leadership of people and communities most affected by inequities and injustices.

Summary of Key Points

To summarize, intersectionality provides a framework for understanding how different aspects of our identity intersect and shape our experiences and opportunities. It is an ongoing exploration that requires us to critically examine identity categories, going beyond simplistic interpretations and challenging oppressive systems. It acknowledges the historical impacts of colonialism. Targeted universalism is a pathway for action and an operational approach to effectively tackle social and economic problems.

Targeted universalism offers an intersectional approach to addressing social and economic problems by acknowledging that these issues impact different segments of the population differently. It recognizes that the intensity of experiences of harm and marginalization vary based on the intersecting identities of individuals. TU acknowledges the need to consider these intersectional experiences and tailor solutions accordingly, in order to ensure that the most marginalized and impacted groups receive targeted support and interventions. By embracing an intersectional lens, TU can be used to create more equitable and inclusive outcomes for all members of society.

Discussion Questions

1. Identify a theory, idea, or concept that has been personally resonant or helpful to you. Describe its significance in fostering intersectional analysis within the realm of social equity and justice work.
2. Were any of your existing assumptions challenged or validated by the chapter? Describe.
3. Are there any limitations or contradictions in the chapter that you would like to name?
4. Did the ideas, reflections, or analysis in this chapter bring to your attention questions, contradictions, or organizational dynamics related to intersectionality and social equity? (We invite mindfulness and intentional practice about consent and confidentiality in the sharing of stories, lived experiences, and discussion around these experiences.)

Additional Resources

1. Patricia Hill Collins, *Intersectionality as Critical Social Theory* (Durham, NC: Duke University Press, 2019).
2. john a. powell, Stephen Menendian, and Wendy Ake, "Targeted Universalism: Policy & Practice: (Berkeley: Haas Institute for a Fair and Inclusive Society at UC Berkeley, 2019). Access at https://belonging.berkeley.edu/

Notes

1. Audre Lorde, *Sister Outsider* (New York: Penguin Random House, 2007).
2. Kimberlé Crenshaw, "Transcript of 'The Urgency of Intersectionality,'" TED Ideas Worth Spreading, accessed July 26, 2023, https://www.ted.com/talks/kimberle_crenshaw_the_urgency_of_intersectionality/transcript. At 7 minutes, 54 seconds
3. We use "multiply" (muhl-ti-plee) as an adverb to mean, "in several different ways or respects." "Multiply marginalized" describes several different ways oppression was experienced by those with more than one socially disadvantaged identity. Also, see Patricia Hill Collins, *Black Feminist Thought, 30th Anniversary Edition: Knowledge, Consciousness, and the Politics of Empowerment* (New York: Routledge, 2022).
4. Kimberlé Crenshaw, "Demarginalizing the Intersection of Race and Sex: A Black Feminist Critique of Antidiscrimination Doctrine, Feminist Theory and Antiracist Politics," *University of Chicago Legal Forum*, no. 1 (1989), https://chicagounbound.uchicago.edu/uclf/vol1989/iss1/8; Kimberlé Crenshaw, "Transcript of 'The Urgency of Intersectionality,'" TED Ideas Worth Spreading, accessed July 26, 2023, https://www.ted.com/talks/kimberle_crenshaw_the_urgency_of_intersectionality/transcript; Kimberlé Crenshaw, Ashton Applewhite, and J.R. Fleming, "10. Age Against the Machine: The Fatal Intersection of Racism & Ageism in the Time of Coronavirus Intersectionality Matters with Kimberlé Crenshaw," SoundCloud, accessed July 26, 2023, https://soundcloud.com/intersectionality-matters/10-age-against-the-machine-the-fatal-intersection-of-racism-ageism-in-the-time-of-coronavirus
5. Ange-Marie Hancock, *Solidarity Politics for Millennial: A Guide to Ending the Oppression Olympicss* (New York: Springer, 2011).
6. Lisa Bowleg, "The Problem with the Phrase Women and Minorities: Intersectionality—An Important Theoretical

Framework for Public Health," *American Journal of Public Health* 102, no. 7 (2012): 1267. Also: Nira Yuval-Davis, "Intersectionality and Feminist Politics," *European Journal of Women's Studies* 13, no. 3 (2006): 193–209.

7. Hancock, *Solidarity Politics for Millennials,* p. 103.
8. Hancock, *Solidarity Politics for Millennials;* john a. powell, Stephen Menendian, and Wendy Ake, *Targeted Universalism: Policy & Practice* (Berkeley: Haas Institute for a Fair and Inclusive Society at UC Berkeley, 2019), https://belonging.berkeley.edu/
9. Hancock, *Solidarity Politics for Millennials.*
10. Sins Invalid, "Skin, Tooth, and Bone: The Basis of Movement Is Our People, A Disability Justice Primer," accessed July 26, 2023, https://www.sinsinvalid.org/disability-justice-primer
11. Victor Ray, Pamela Herd, and Donald Moynihan, "Racialized Burdens," *Journal of Public Administration Research and Theory* 33, no. 1 (2023): 139–152.
12. Nuriel Heckler and Anthony Starke, "At the Intersections of Identities," In *Achieving Social Equity: From Problems to Solutions* (1st ed.), ed. Mary E. Guy and Sean A. McCandless (Irvine, CA: Melvin & Leigh, 2020), 53–64; Leslie McCall, "The Complexity of Intersectionality," *Signs: Journal of Women in Culture and Society* 30, no. 3 (2005): 1771–1800.
13. Hancock, *Solidarity Politics for Millennials.*
14. Emancipation refers to freedom from legal and political restraint; it involves transfer of ownership or control from one party to another such as in the case of the Emancipation Proclamation of 1863. However, emancipation is not liberation. The transfer of ownership from the oppressor to the oppressed does not necessitate liberation. Someone who has been granted full ownership of themselves in a legal sense could still be oppressed (Living 2021). Liberation is the work of transformation to remove social, political, and economic constraints in order to achieve freedom and equality for all. Pojmann provides a distinction: "Emancipation means working from within existing systems and trying to change them, whereas liberation implies a complete overthrow of the *status quo*" (74). See Victorious Living, "The Difference Between Emancipation and Liberation," Victorious Living (blog), June 17, 2021, https://www.patheos.com/blogs/victoriousliving/ 2021/06/the-difference-between-emancipation-and-liberation/; Wendy Pojmann, "Emancipation or Liberation?: Women's Associations and the Italian Movement," *The Historian* 67, no. 1 (2005): 73–96; Cara Page and Erica Woodland, *Healing Justice Lineages: Dreaming at the Crossroads of Liberation, Collective Care, and Safety* (Berkeley, CA: North Atlantic Books, 2023).
15. Angela Y. Davis, and Elizabeth Martínez, "Building Coalitions of People of Color," accessed July 26, 2023, https://culturalstudies.ucsc.edu/inscriptions/volume-7/angela-y-davis-elizabeth-martinez/; Hancock, *Solidarity Politics for Millennials.*
16. Hancock, *Solidarity Politics for Millennials*; Patty Krawec, *Becoming Kin: An Indigenous Call to Unforgetting the Past and Reimaging Our Future* (Minneapolis: Broadleaf Books, 2022); Audre Lorde, *Sister Outsider*; Amanda Morris, "Weaving Intersectional Rhetoric: The Digital Counternarratives of Indigenous Feminist Bloggers," *ENTHYMEMA* 19 (2017): 235–251; Katie Boudreau Morris, "Decolonizing Solidarity: Cultivating Relationships of Discomfort," *Settler Colonial Studies* 7, no. 4 (2017): 456–473.
17. Rashmi Chordiya and Adana Protonentis, "Healing from White Supremacy Culture and Ableism: Disability Justice as an Antidote," *Journal of Social Equity and Public Administration* 2, no. 1 (2024): 127–152; Lilla Watson, "About," Lilla: International Women's Network (blog), October 15, 2008, accessed July 26, 2023, https://lillanetwork.wordpress.com/about/
18. Olena Hankivsky and Renee Cormier, "Intersectionality and Public Policy: Some Lessons from Existing Models," *Political Research Quarterly* 64, no. 1 (2011): 217–229; powell et al., *Targeted Universalism.*
19. Hankivsky and Cormier, "Intersectionality and Public Policy"; powell et al., *Targeted Universalism.*
20. James E. Wright II, Stephanie Dolamore, and RaJade M. Berry-James, "What the Hell Is Wrong with America? The Truth about Racism and Justice for All," *Journal of Public Management & Social Policy* 29, no. 1 (2022): 6–28.
21. Patricia A. Homan, Tyson H. Brown, "Sick and Tired of Being Excluded: Structural Racism in Disenfranchisement as a Threat to Population Health Equity," *Health Affairs* 41, no. 2 (2022): 219–227.
22. Krawec, *Becoming Kin.*
23. Jennifer A. Ailshire, and James S House, "The Unequal Burden of Weight Gain: An Intersectional Approach to Understanding Social Disparities in BMI Trajectories from 1986 to 2001/2002," *Social Forces* 90, no. 2 (2011): 397–423, https://doi.org/10.1093/sf/sor001; Patricia Homan, Tyson H. Brown, and Brittany King, "Structural Intersectionality as a New Direction for Health Disparities Research," *Journal of Health and Social Behavior* 62, no. 3 (2021): 350–370.
24. *Brown v. Board of Education,* 1954, 347 U.S. 483; *Plessy v. Ferguson,* 1896, 163 U.S. 537.
25. Linda Darling-Hammond, "Teacher Education and the American Future," *Journal of Teacher Education* 61, nos. 1–2 (2010): 35–47; Heather G. Peske and Kati Haycock,

Teaching Inequality: How Poor and Minority Students Are Shortchanged on Teacher Quality (Washington, DC: Education Trust, 2006), accessed July 26, 2023, https://eric.ed.gov/?id=eD494820

26. Daniel L. Fay, Alisa Hicklin Fryar, Kenneth J. Meier, and Vicky Wilkins, "Intersectionality and Equity: Dynamic Bureaucratic Representation in Higher Education," *Public Administration* 99, no. 2 (2021): 335–352.
27. Edward Fuller, Liz Hollingworth, and Brian P. An, "Exploring Intersectionality and the Employment of School Leaders," *Journal of Educational Administration*, 57, no. 2 (2019): 134–151.
28. Fuller et al., "Exploring Intersectionality;" Natasha Codiroli Mcmaster, and Rose Cook, "The Contribution of Intersectionality to Quantitative Research into Educational Inequalities," *Review of Education* 7, no. 2 (2018): 271–292.
29. Cynthia J. Barboza-Wilkes, Thai V. Le, and William Resh, "Deconstructing Burnout at the Intersections of Race, Gender, and Generation in Local Government," *Journal of Public Administration Research and Theory* 33, no. 1(2023): 186–201; Samantha June Larson, "Actions for Queering American Public Administration," *Administration & Society* 54, no. 1 (2022): 145–163; Gregory B. Lewis and M. Blake Emidy, "Sexual Orientation and Organizational Justice in the Federal Service: Exploring Differences through an Intersectional Lens," *Journal of Public Administration Research and Theory* 32, no. 3 (2022): 489—508; Mohamed Mousa, "From Intersectionality to Substantive Representation: Determinants of the Representation of Women Faculty in Academic Contexts," *International Journal of Public Administration* 46, no. 2 (2023): 97–106; Meghna Sabharwal, Helisse Levine, Maria D'Agostino, and Tiffany Nguyen, "Inclusive Work Practices: Turnover Intentions among LGBT Employees of the U.S. Federal Government," *American Review of Public Administration* 49, no. 4 (2019): 482–494.
30. Adam M. Butz and Tia Sherèe Gaynor, "Intersectionality and Social Welfare: Avoidance and Unequal Treatment among Transgender Women of Color," *Public Administration Review* 82, no. 3 (2022): 433–445.
31. Butz and Gaynor, "Intersectionality and Social Welfare," 7.
32. Ellie Smith, Beth Sundstrom, and Cara Delay, "Listening to Women: Understanding and Challenging Systems of Power to Achieve Reproductive Justice in South Carolina," *Journal of Social Issues* 76, no. 2 (2020): 363–390.
33. Maria D'Agostino, Helisse Levine, Meghna Sabharwal, and Al C. Johnson-Manning, "Organizational Practices and Second-Generation Gender Bias: A Qualitative Inquiry into the Career Progression of U.S. State-Level Managers," *American Review of Public Administration* 52, no. 5 (2022): 335–350.
34. Anna Clark Fountain, Jiwon Suh, and Kwang Bin Bae, "Protected, but Not Included? The Role of Workplace Inclusion for Sexual and Gender Minorities in the Federal Service," *Journal of Public and Nonprofit Affairs* 8, no. 3(2022): 323–348; Madinah F. Hamidullah and Norma M. Riccucci, "Intersectionality and Family-Friendly Policies in the Federal Government," *Administration & Society* 49, no. 1 (2017): 105–120; Trang Hoang, Jiwon Suh, and Meghna Sabharwal, "Beyond a Numbers Game? Impact of Diversity and Inclusion on the Perception of Organizational Justice," *Public Administration Review* 82, no. 3 (2022): 537–555; Ashley Nelson and Jaclyn Piatak, "Intersectionality, Leadership, and Inclusion: How Do Racially Underrepresented Women Fare in the Federal Government?" *Review of Public Personnel Administration* 41, no. 2 (2021): 294–318; Sabharwal et al., "Inclusive Work Practices."
35. Thanh Thi Hoang, Ravin R. Cline, and Meghna Sabharwal, "Women Falling through the Cracks: Intersectionality during Crisis and Implications for Human Resource Management." In *Intersectionality and Crisis Management*, ed. Hilary J. Knepper, Michelle D. Evans, and Tiffany J. Henley, (New York: Routledge, 2023), 59–80. Also: Prudence L. Carter and Kevin G. Welner, *Closing the Opportunity Gap: What America Must Do to Give Every Child an Even Chance* (Oxford: Oxford University Press, 2013).
36. Hoang et al., "Beyond a Numbers Game," 75.
37. Nancy López, Gadsden, Vivian L., "Health Inequities, Social Determinants, and Intersectionality," *NAM Perspectives* 6, no. 12 (2016): 1–15.
38. Hankivsky and Cormier, "Intersectionality and Public Policy."
39. powell et al., T*argeted Universalism*; Adana Protonentis, Rashmi Chordiya, and ChrisTiana ObeySumner, "Centering the Margins: Restorative and Transformative Justice as Our Path to Social Equity," *Administrative Theory & Praxis* 43, no. 3: 333–354.
40. Rashmi Chordiya and Larry Hubbell, "Fostering Internal Pay Equity through Gender Neutral Job Evaluations: A Case Study of the Federal Job Evaluation System," *Public Personnel Management* 52, no. 1 (2023): 25–47.
41. Resmaa Menakem, *My Grandmother's Hands: Racialized Trauma and the Pathway to Mending Our Hearts and Bodies* (Las Vegas: Central Recovery Press, 2017); Cara Page and Erica Woodland, *Healing Justice Lineages: Dreaming at the Crossroads of Liberation, Collective Care, and Safety* (Berkeley, CA: North Atlantic Books, 2023).

4 GENDER EQUITY IN THE WORKPLACE

Michelle D. Evans and Hillary J. Knepper

From the Editors

Gender inequity is as present now as it was generations ago. While its effects are sometimes obscured, they are obvious in the wage gap, job segregation, and the politics of privilege. Those who identify as men are on the winning side of the ledger and those who identify as women or as nonbinary are on the losing side. Gender inequities arise in all aspects of life, both public and private. They are particularly easy to observe and remediate in the workplace so this chapter focuses on human resource management and describes pathways to action.

To examine gender equity through a social equity lens, we start with definitions that serve as the foundation for the remainder of the chapter. As discussed in chapter 1, social equity is a term used to consider fairness and justice in terms of opportunity, access, and full inclusion of everyone in society. *Gender* is a fluid and evolving term with a definition shaped by a range of factors, including an individual's personal, political, or religious beliefs; educational background; cultural or ethnic background; age; and countless other influences.[1]

Definitions

The term *gender* is frequently used interchangeably with *sex*. In reality, gender has a much different meaning. Sex is a binary description of the biological male or female designation assigned at birth. Gender is a concept that includes a trio of conditions pertaining to identity, fluidity, and transgender. More specifically, gender identity refers to how individuals describe themselves. It may or may not match the sex assigned at birth.

Gender fluidity denotes no fixed binary gender or a gender identity that changes over time. Transgender refers to individuals whose gender identity does not match the binary sex assigned at birth and/or an identity that does not conform to societal expectations. As this discussion makes obvious, gender labels apply to a range of identities based on behavioral and psychological traits as well as sociocultural norms and expectations.[2]

As appreciation for intersectionality grows, understandings about gender continue to expand. *Intersectionality* is a term used to describe the presence of multiple identities, often resulting in compounding layers of identity that too often produce compounding layers of discrimination.[3] As such, intersectionality also factors into gender equity. Legislative and policy changes that pertain to gender are equally relevant for all women, but many result in disparate impacts on Black or Indigenous women in comparison to White women.

Meanings for the word "gender" are not limited to personal identity. The word is also used to capture behavioral norms and expectations, much as the French language uses *la* and *le* to denote masculine or feminine concepts, constructs, objects, or persons. In organization design, structures are sometimes assigned a gender, with traditional, top-down structures labeled as masculine while flattened networks and collaborations are labeled as feminine. Rewards and organizational culture reify the terminology.

Gender equity is about fairness, respect, and freedom from discrimination regardless of one's gender identity. Gender equity, just as with other matters related to equity, can be identified and addressed by focusing on issues of access, opportunities, advancement, and pay. Using these issues makes it possible to see the difference between equity and equality. Equality is sameness, while equity focuses on fairness in opportunities and outcomes. In the workplace, gender equity encompasses not just legal rights, but also pay equity, elimination of discrimination in terms of hiring and promotions, elimination of sexual harassment, removal of job segregation, and less rigid gender roles and expectations for everyone.

Gender inequity is not unique to the United States. It is an issue worldwide. For example, the United Nations (UN) encourages all nations to fully include women in economic development and quality-of-life initiatives. To advance gender equity, the UN includes gender equality as its fifth in a list of 17 Sustainable Development Goals. While progress has been made, significant challenges to achieving gender equity remain. In the workplace, both domestically and abroad, roadblocks to equity arise in the form of power dynamics, occupational segregation based on gender, and fewer promotion opportunities for those discriminated against.

The Workplace Mirrors Cultural Values

Employees arrive at work each day carrying the values they learn at home, at school, and in religious teachings. The workplace is a microcosm of cultural values, so gender dynamics arise on the job just as they do in leisure activities and family roles. These values are made manifest by who gets hired for which jobs, how salaries are set, who gets promoted, and who holds decision-making power. These facets of human resource management provide us with a framework for analyzing challenges that exist for women, in terms of glass ceilings, glass walls, and sticky floors, and for creating a more gender equitable workforce.

Discussion begins by examining gender equity from its emergence as an issue of concern in the public service workforce through today's continuing challenges. This is followed by an exploration of the evolving understanding of gender in the context of history, legal action, and socio-political factors. Then, in order to achieve transformative change, managerial competencies are identified and pathways to action are presented. The chapter concludes with recommendations for how to break down barriers and create a more representative, skilled public administration workforce where competencies, not gender, are the driving force.

History, Context, and Scope

The increasing role of women in the paid workforce was not the result of a sudden change in cultural values or legal emancipation. Rather, it was a more gradual movement away from unpaid labor in the home as rural lifestyles declined, urban opportunities arose, and economics demanded that women join men in the paid workforce. Urbanization and industrialization combined to increase the need for a larger labor pool, particularly in fields such as textile manufacturing and office work. This allowed women to venture into job markets previously closed to them. Workforce shortages during the two world wars, Dust Bowl/drought-type disasters, and economic depressions accelerated the trend toward women seeking paid employment. These changes coincided with shifts in workforce power dynamics, such as weakening trade union power, increased use of apprenticeships, prohibitions against child labor, and workplace safety improvements.

Workplace equity awareness had its beginnings in the early work of abolitionists in the United States as they advocated against slave labor. It was not until after the Civil War that the federal government formally addressed labor needs in a substantive way. This increased attention to labor considerations and resulted in the establishment of the U.S. Department of Labor in 1913, followed by the creation of the Women's Bureau in 1920. Both of these administrative organizations raised awareness of gender equity in the workplace. Attention at the federal level was instrumental in creating policies to address the employment and advancement of women, to improve their working conditions, and to draw attention to pay equity.

Although women's standing in the workforce has improved substantially since the mid-1800s when it was thought proper to pay women half of whatever men earned for the same work, equity has yet to be achieved.[4] To explain the slow journey, we trace the interaction between employment law, organizational structures, the political process, and human resource management, all of which are influenced by greater representation of women and an increasingly intersectional lens. All of these elements affect one another and are controlled by systems that privilege existing power bases and afford them advantage to access, resources, and reinforcement of cultural stereotypes. First, we turn to legal accelerants that codified women's rights and provided prohibitions against some forms of discrimination.

Legal Advances

To understand the scope of legislative efforts regarding gender equity, we review a multitude of legal protections designed to create a firewall that outlaws discrimination. These include U.S. policies and laws as well as international efforts that have global implications. Many of these efforts focus on allowing women the same rights as men, while others focus on overcoming discrimination and historical inequities with the aim of providing substantive equality.

Our attention is first drawn to 1920 with ratification of the Nineteenth Amendment to the U.S. Constitution. It extended suffrage to women and meant that, at least theoretically, women had access to full participation and representation in the electoral process. However, it should be noted that suffrage, as well as many other legal/judicial highlights in this section, were focused on improving equity mainly for white women, with protections for others often taking decades and additional legal/judicial efforts.

Shifting social and cultural dynamics in the 1960s and 1970s saw a proliferation of laws and court rulings impacting women and gender equity. Civil rights activities led to enforcing racial desegregation in the wake of the 1954 *Brown v. Board of Education* decision. Civil rights initiatives extended to efforts aimed at eliminating discrimination against women, including the Equal Pay Act of 1963 followed by the Civil Rights Act of 1964. The Civil Rights Act prohibits discrimination on the basis of race, color, religion, sex, or national origin. Interestingly, the insertion of the word "sex" in the legislation was controversial because, at the time, many in Congress thought protection for women was ludicrous. Nevertheless, enough supported the bill that the wording prevailed and the Act passed.

The 1960s brought not only the extension of civil rights protections to women but also freedom to reliably control their reproduction. In 1960 the U.S. Food and Drug Administration (FDA) approved birth control pills. This meant that, for the first time, women had the ability to control the size and timing of their families. As the years progressed, the 1970s brought significant improvements that afforded women some of the rights men took for granted. For example, 1972 brought the transformative passage of Title IX, which bans sex discrimination in federally funded education programs. Title IX is best known for its impact on women in terms of access to school-sponsored sports and protections against sexual harassment and sexual violence.

During the 1970s, legislation also included the Equal Rights Amendment of 1972, which passed in the House and Senate but has never been ratified by enough states to make it a reality. The wording of the amendment is straightforward: "Equality of rights under the law shall not be denied or abridged by the United States or by any State on account of sex." That not enough states are willing to ratify this to make it a reality is damning proof of the liminal space within which women reside.

The 1970s also brought court rulings that expanded women's privacy rights and autonomy over their reproductive choices, which increased their economic security and career opportunities. The best known of these is the 1973 *Roe v. Wade* decision, which paved the way for safe, legal abortions. Shortly thereafter, the Pregnancy Discrimination Act of 1978 built on protections guaranteed in the Civil Rights Act of 1964 by including protections in hiring, promotions, job termination, and pay inequity in connection to pregnancy. Progress continued with the passage of the Civil Rights Act of 1991 which allowed victims of sex discrimination the same access to financial compensation as victims of racial discrimination. This meant that it was finally worth civil rights lawyers' time to bring legal action. This had the effect of opening the floodgates to litigation benefiting women. This was followed by the Family Medical Leave Act (FMLA) in 1993. This Act provides up to three months of unpaid leave after the birth of a child or to care for family illness without fear of losing a job. Benefits accrue to caregivers, regardless of their gender.

Because the workplace reflects cultural values and because employment is monetized, laws and workplace processes are a logical pairing. Substantive change in the workplace leads to social change and vice versa. This includes erasing negative stereotypes; improving socioeconomic status; increasing participation in politics, policy, and decision-making; removing gendered job segregation; and acknowledging that family responsibilities impact everyone, not just women. For instance, universal access to health care, child/elder care assistance, parental leave, disability assistance, and living wages, are central to the gender equity fight. These policies improve personal freedom, safety, and economic mobility; decrease vulnerability to domestic violence and sexual harassment; and increase personal autonomy.

Around the globe, progress is uneven. UN Women[5] estimates that more than a quarter of the world's population has no access to the types of policies enacted in the United States. The legal landscape for gender equity varies considerably in other nations. Progress is often accomplished, or at least spearheaded, through the United Nations and through human rights treaties, diplomatic efforts, and non-governmental organizations, as well as through globalized corporate efforts. In many ways, the United States has been a leader in equity issues, in terms of legislation aimed at gender equity and in support and advocacy for greater gender equity throughout the world. The United States, and Eleanor Roosevelt in particular, were a major force in the creation and adoption of the U.N.'s Universal Declaration of Human Rights in 1948, which codified and served as a core foundation of rights for women in battles for equity and inclusion.

Pushback

As laws and court decisions make obvious, the last 60 years have brought cultural shifts in the social construction of gender and with regard to LGBTQ+ rights. Acknowledging the difference that gender makes, and allowing women to have equivalent agency over their bodies that men have always enjoyed, are initiatives that are applauded by advocates and protested against by opponents. In fact, the 2022 *Dobbs v. Jackson Women's Health* decision turned the clock back 50 years in the United States by removing women's right to abortion. The *Dobbs* decision goes further than simply overturning long-standing rights for women; it sets the stage for additional rollbacks of gender equity.

The *Dobbs* ruling foreshadows potential reversals in terms of birth control, health care autonomy, LGBTQ+ rights, and marriage equality. All these dimensions of gender impact workplace opportunities and protections, which, in turn, affect socioeconomic status. Similarly, the growing pushback to diversity, equity, and inclusion (DEI) programs and similar policy efforts aimed at removing historical workplace disadvantages, reflects a desire to return to a time where the status quo was one of men's advantage and women's disadvantage.

As in a choreography of three steps forward followed by two steps backward, advances toward gender equity are like climbing a slippery slope. Legislative changes and judicial rulings, while significant, do not automatically translate into significant changes in the workplace. It takes far longer to change attitudes and behavior than it does to issue a court decree or pass a law and opposition is intense long after laws are in place.

Political Dimensions

Discussion turns now to the role that politics plays in achieving gender equity. Politics focuses on issues of governance, power, and debates over who gets what. This vision of politics extends beyond politicians and political parties to include businesses, nonprofits, media, civil society, and individuals. Politics are grounded in values, customs, and social norms amidst a constantly evolving understanding of identity.

The purpose of politics is to settle disagreements with consensus or compromise rather than guns. However, structural inequities make it difficult to access the ruling coalitions and to gain traction in promoting change. For instance, consensus implies broad support, but it often results in blocking the voices of marginalized communities because they have insufficient numbers, power, or access to be heard when decisions are made.[6] This, in turn, means they are overlooked when resources are allocated. This exclusion results in perpetual cycles of inequitable benefits and burdens. Notwithstanding, skills in navigating conflicting norms and values are invaluable when the goal is to form coalitions around shared interests. For example, attempts to level the playing field for gender equity—as in debates over bodily autonomy—are often viewed as encroachment into patriarchal notions of privilege.[7] Women's rights get pitted against men's rights as if autonomy is a zero-sum game. It is not. The change is that autonomy for all genders takes away the power of one to dominate the other. This illuminates a fundamental power differential. Those who benefit from inequity, whether by choice or by happenstance, view change as a negative because it threatens the advantage to which they have grown accustomed.

Nonprofit organizations are increasingly powerful players in political decision-making as they give voice to the interests of those who are marginalized. They also provide a focal point for consolidating activities for change. As movers and shakers across the gender equity landscape, for example, the National Organization for Women, Time's Up, Planned Parenthood, Human Rights Watch, or Gay Men's Health Crisis, each reflects the evolving understanding of gender and LGBTQ+ issues.

While nonprofits are advocates in issues connected to gender equity, they are not without their own internal challenges. The nonprofit workforce is overwhelmingly female (66%–75%), yet executive and board leadership is far less so (45% women), particularly in large nonprofits with budgets over $25 million.[8] But the good news is that the nonprofit sector has a higher percentage of women executives and a smaller pay equity gap than either the public or private sectors.

The Politics of Privilege

A common approach used by those in power is to frame policies and structures from neutral, objective, or diversity "blind" perspectives. These approaches are billed as attempts at fairness and equity, but in reality, they perpetuate historical privilege. This myth of neutrality creates a system whereby power elites are able to control eligibility, access, organizational processes, and evaluation of outcomes. This means they determine what hoops must be jumped through, how one should behave while jumping through them, and how to assess performance while jumping through them in a "neutral" system of merit.[9] While lauding neutrality, systems end up creating practices, protocols, rules, and measurements that meet the needs of the few, whether the few are the elite or the center, without addressing needs of the outliers, the newcomers, the marginalized, or those simply categorized as "others."

Political behavior with regard to gender equity is driven by definitions and understandings of gender, with corresponding actions influenced by expectations around gender norms. Indeed, as we learn more about the interconnection between physiology, psychology, and sociology, questions abound regarding the degree to which gender is binary versus a continuum, socially constructed or biologically determined, or some combination. Societal, legal, and political realms converge with regard to gender and this convergence is reflected in human resource management.

Human Resource Management

Workplace policies reflect social norms regarding gender; disadvantage is manifested in the form of less discretion, lower wages, and fewer opportunities for promotion. This is why human resource management (HRM) is a frequent target for legal action. This section discusses some of the most pressing HRM topics, including pay inequity and its relationship to job segregation, power dynamics, and advancement challenges.

Pay Equity

Wage gaps based on gender are common around the globe regardless of the economic status of the nation. Progress has been made, but it is spotty. For example, the wage gap for women in the United States has closed somewhat over the last 40 years. In 1980 women earned about 64% of men's wages, by 2020 women earned just over 82% of men's wages.[10] While the gender pay gap in the United States still feels like a chasm to women, it is narrower than in many other nations. Internationally, the overall worldwide wage for women is 77% of men's earnings.[11]

Women's income is important because they are often the primary wage earner in a household. Nearly one-third of global households and nearly half of U.S. households are headed by women. Moreover, a significant portion of the remaining households also rely on women's income. Table 4.1 displays gender wage gap statistics provided by the Organisation for Economic Co-operation and Development. As the table shows, pay equity ranges from a low of less than 69% in Korea to a high of nearly 99% in Belgium.

Greater progress at closing wage gaps has occurred in lower-wage jobs than in higher-wage jobs. This is true even in nations that have more legal protections for gender equality. Why? Because occupations remain segregated by gender. Some industries are thought to be more appropriate for men and higher-level posts are thought to be more appropriately filled by men. It is no coincidence that these positions pay more than those dominated by women.

Power Dynamics

Power differentials continue to exist between women and men in the workplace because these differentials also exist in society at large. Structural inequities are demonstrated by the fact that men occupy more of the decision-making posts in organizations and earn higher wages. Indeed, these structural arrangements, thought to be "normal," perpetuate unequal outcomes, reinforce existing power dynamics, and continue inequities in pay and job segregation. These inequities place women in double jeopardy because they have less protection when economic recessions and domestic crises occur. When women fall further down the socioeconomic ladder, the climb back for them is even steeper than it is for men.

Table 4.1. Women's Pay as Percentage of Men's Pay Around the Globe

Latin America	%	Europe	%	Asia/Pacific	%	Other	%
Argentina	93.8	Belgium	98.8	Australia	90.1	Canada	83.3
Brazil	90.9	Bulgaria	97.5	Japan	77.9	Israel	76.0
Chile	91.4	France	85.0	Korea	68.9	United States	83.1
Colombia	96.8	Norway	95.4	New Zealand	93.3		
Costa Rica	94.8	Sweden	92.8				
Mexico	87.5	UK	85.7				

Source: Organisation for Economic Co-operation & Development, "Gender Wage Gap," accessed May 29, 2023. https://data.oecd.org/earnwage/gender-wage-gap.htm#indicator-chart

Advancement Challenges: Glass Ceilings, Glass Walls, Sticky Floors

Table 4.1 highlights challenges in pay equity, but statistics overlook the key causes of gender pay disparities. The challenge goes beyond comparable worth, where women and men performing jobs should be paid the same. The challenge comes also with glass ceilings, glass walls, and sticky floors. These metaphors reflect three obstacles that confront women: *Glass ceilings* refer to the appearance of fairness and equal opportunity for advancement when, in fact, organizations simply refuse to promote women above a given level. *Glass walls* refer to the appearance of equal opportunity across jobs when, in fact, employers refuse to hire women into categories of jobs thought "more appropriate" for men. In other words, glass walls are about occupational segregation. Despite women surpassing men in terms of educational achievement, women disproportionately are employed in education, health care, and service-dominated fields, a trend replicated across government, nonprofits, and business. For instance, women were first allowed to join the U.S. military during WWI, but in limited capacities. It wasn't until 1994 that policy changes allowed women access to approximately 80% of military jobs, with full occupational equity achieved in 2016 when combat-related positions finally opened to women.[12]

Glass walls are not just an issue that impacts women; they also affect and constrain men's opportunities. As American society evolves, it is now socially acceptable for women to explore career paths previously closed to them, such as in military combat and law enforcement. Men, on the other hand, also face challenges with gendered role expectations, especially with regard to jobs that require nurturance and support, which are jobs thought of as "women's jobs." Few men apply for jobs as elementary school teachers and few men pursue careers in nursing.

Sticky floors refer to what happens when women and men compete for promotions and women lose because their prior experience is in lower-status jobs that provide fewer opportunities for them to demonstrate autonomy and decision-making prowess. In other words, because of glass walls and glass ceilings, women are prevented from building a résumé that demonstrates the types of skills required for promotion to top levels.

These barriers to full workforce integration—glass ceilings and walls, and sticky floors—pose challenges that have been addressed in small part by laws and political activism, but they are so deeply rooted in social norms that they defy easy fixes. This is the status quo. Nevertheless, there is a way forward and the next section enumerates some actions.

Pathways to Action

It has been nearly 40 years since West and Zimmerman[13] noted the power of gender as an "ideological device, which produces, reduces, and legitimates'" to constrain opportunity and to reinforce societal and institutional expectations. Today, public administration struggles with these same tenacious challenges in building greater gender equity. Women in public service are neither represented nor compensated equally to men and this results in constraints on their voices and influence. This deprives the nation of a cadre of skilled employees.

There are no easy fixes when it comes to gender equity. The challenges of lower pay, limited advancement opportunities, and limited autonomy on the job are complicated by work-life balance issues related to women's caregiving responsibilities. Pathways to action involve adjusting employment practices to accommodate all workers rather than expecting workers to accommodate to whatever practices already exist. More specifically, we explore actions necessary for building a more gender equitable public sector work environment. Second, we explore the core competencies necessary to activate gender equity.

Be Global and Learn From Others

Other nations provide examples of how to improve gender equity. Finland, for instance, supports parents with up to 320 working days of parental leave once the baby is born (or adopted).[14] For single parents, all 320 days are available, whereas with two parents, each may take up to 160 days. After this period ends, childcare leave is available until the child turns three years old. Parental and childcare leave come with a financial allowance to protect economic stability.

Steps Toward Equity

There are several actions that, when applied intentionally, help to push gender equity forward. These include conducting an inclusivity audit and learning from its results, balancing work demands with life demands, and ensuring that women are paid for the work they perform.

A first step toward building greater gender equity in the workplace is to conduct an inclusivity audit. This involves analyzing the degree of gender diversity, pay differentials, opportunities for advancement, representation at each rank in the hierarchy, and employee perceptions of the work environment. Information gained from the audit is then used to learn where obstacles exist, to raise awareness of them, and to remove them.

A second step is improving work-life balance. Flexible scheduling and hybrid work structures give promise but, for many women, the flexibility of remote options is tainted with the deleterious effects of balancing domestic responsibilities and caregiving while also working for the employer. This wrinkle has yet to be resolved. Beyond flexible work schedules and generous parental and caregiving leave, educational stipends can be used to better meet the needs of employees and to improve recruitment, retention, and development efforts. Flexible training through self-paced courses offers the promise of providing professional development opportunities that do not interfere with caregiving responsibilities.

A third step is to ensure that women employees do not get snagged by "leading in place."[15] This is a term that captures the work experience of stepping up, without formal authority, to achieve workplace goals. While this leading in place "can be deployed to further both women's careers and to promote healthier attitudes about women's contributions to organizations and communities,"[16] it must not be used as a mechanism to increase workload and responsibility without compensation, in other words, to perform unpaid service.

A fourth step is to ensure that workplace culture is friendly for all genders, such that there is zero tolerance for harassment and that "others" are welcomed rather than shunned. This refers to individuals who are of a minority gender, such as women in senior executive positions, men in nursing, or nonbinary individuals.

A fifth step is mentoring. Mentors and mentees should be matched in a nuanced manner where employees feel seen, recognized, and valued. Mentors and job coaches are effective at helping workers develop a vision, set career goals, and share insights into cultural and workplace pitfalls. Mentors and job coaches should be reflective of the needs of employees, particularly women, at whatever stage they are in their careers and should be willing to share their knowledge.

Successful mentoring and job coaching relationships exist in a triad, with three different types of mentors (or coaches) for each employee. These relationships ebb and flow and are not linear. The first mentor would be another administrator who is in the same department or program and helps orient the mentee to the workplace culture and provides guidance to processes and policies. A second mentor or coach could be someone further removed from a mentee's job duties, perhaps in a more senior position or in a related department. Matching mentor-mentees builds alliances across programs or departments. The third mentor/coach establishes an aspirational relationship by intentionally matching high-ranking individuals to junior mentees whose career goals are consistent with the senior mentor's accomplishments.

A sixth step is to improve transparency. This requires a *process* re-evaluation that examines policies and practices regarding promotion protocols, performance reviews that account for all the duties performed, not just the simplistic list in the job description, and job listings that are accurately worded, specify competencies required, and do not include pronouns that are biased toward one gender.

These six steps—inclusivity audit, work-life balance strategies, removing unpaid work, removing harassment, mentoring, and improving transparency—will not erase gender inequity but they enable progress toward it and remove some obstacles. Further, many other "best practices" of human resource management and organizational leadership are applicable. Competent administrators, regardless of the issues they face, should be adept at active listening and critical analysis; promote inclusive practices and center justice, equity, and diversity in the workplace; build alliances with and among those who share a passion for equity; engage in transformative leadership that supports workers, removes barriers, stimulates them intellectually, trusts them, and gives them what they need to succeed; and advocates for policy change.

In sum, expectations of a new generation of workers, and the post-COVID-19 reckoning with what a workweek is and whether in-person, hybrid, or remote work is the best route, present opportunities for an evolutionary leap in rethinking how public administrators support their contemporary workforce.

These influences could dramatically alter how we structure our workplace policies, environments, and employee expectations to everyone's benefit.

Conclusion

The times demand an inclusive, gender equitable workplace. It matters for the socioeconomic status of women, the respect due to everyone regardless of their gender identity, representativeness throughout the bureaucracy, and organizational productivity.

Gender equity inside the workplace means reexamining and reimagining equity outside the workplace. Traditional workplace norms were established a century ago when it was assumed that men would work outside the home and women would manage the home and care for family members. That model is no longer the norm. Both women and men engage in paid employment, yet workplace practices are slow to move beyond the male worker/female homemaker model. Policies that enable harmony between work life and personal life are an elusive but possible goal. Human resource management and leadership are crucial in these efforts.

For true change to occur, operational changes in the workplace must be paired with macro-level changes in social expectations for fairness, along with recognition and understanding of how notions of gender are socially constructed. This chapter has reviewed the historical, legal, political, and human resource management landscape of gender equity. We have pointed out pathways to action and made recommendations from a competencies perspective.

While a number of laws exist that prohibit gender discrimination, the fact remains that discrimination remains. Gendered social norms pave an uneven road, resulting in outcomes that are inequitable across the gender landscape. Gender equity begins with not only increasing opportunities for women into formerly male-dominated positions but also encouraging and supporting men in female-dominated occupations. And it extends to more deeply appreciating the life experiences and skills of those who identify as neither male nor female.

Pay equity goes hand in hand with valuing the work that is thought to be "essential women's work," meaning the labor that goes into expressing empathy, nurturance, and supportiveness.[17] Relying on women to go the extra mile and "lead in place" to smooth ruffled feathers, unite teams, and ensure work units collaborate in a constructive way, while male peers are excused for not being capable of doing that part of the work, is emblematic of gender inequity. Job descriptions should accurately reflect the responsibilities of the job—both cognitive and emotive—with pay being commensurate with duties.

The good news is that the job market is competitive and favors those agencies that insist on equitable workplace initiatives that shatter glass walls and ceilings. Everyone wins when there is gender equity. Women's skills are better utilized. Men's skills are better utilized. The pay gap disappears. Fresh voices are welcomed to decision-making meetings. The outcome is worth the work it takes to achieve it.

Summary Of Key Points

Gender inequities bring challenges and either constrain or expand each person's life experience.

Understanding the power dynamics surrounding, and the social and structural barriers to, gender equity is the beginning point for creating change.

Opportunities for shattering glass walls, glass ceilings, and sticky floors involve addressing power and pay differentials.

There are actions and administrative competencies that accelerate more gender equitable workplaces.

This unique juncture in history—post-COVID-19, competitive job market, changing generational leadership—provides a window of opportunity for transformative change.

Gender equity today means taking advantage of all the intersecting attributes that employees bring with them into the workplace (i.e., gender identity, race, [dis]ability, socioeconomic status, and more).

Discussion Questions

1. How can public administrators use the pathways to action to foster gender equity?
2. List three challenges public administration professionals may confront as they navigate gender inequity in the workplace.
3. Analyze glass ceilings, glass walls, and sticky floors as discussed in this chapter and identify additional action steps and/or competencies to overcome them.

Additional Resources

1. The Biden-Harris administration developed strategic initiatives aimed at targeting gender parity with specific attention to gender nonconforming and intersectional identities. Consult the U.S. National Strategy on Gender Equity and Equality[18] to review them.
2. Scroll through the website of the International City/County Management Association.[19] It has developed multiple initiatives, such as SheLeadsGov,[20] that are aimed at increasing women's leadership in municipal government and reducing pay inequity.
3. Consult the European Union (EU) Directive 2022/2381.[21] The EU has been a world leader in laws promoting workplace equity, such as quotas requiring gender balance in senior/board leadership, incentives to develop senior female leadership and narrow gendered pay gaps.
4. For a history of the wage gap, read Claudia Goldin's book, *Understanding the Gender Gap: An Economic History of American Women* (New York: Oxford University Press, 1990).
5. To learn about federal guidance in regard to sexual harassment, visit https://www.mspb.gov/studies/studies/Sexual_Harassment_in_Federal_Workplaces_Understanding_and_Addressing_the_Problem_1987037.pdf

Notes

1. Nancy Burns and Katherine Gallagher, "Public Opinion on Gender Issues: The Politics of Equity and Roles," *Annual Review of Political Science* 13 (2010): 425–443.
2. Zoë Klobus, Michelle D. Evans, and Hillary J. Knepper. "Gender and Public Administration Scholarship." In *Handbook on Gender and Public Administration,* ed. Patricia Shields and Nicole M. Elias (Edward Elgar Publishing: Cheltenham, UK, 2022), 364–382.
3. See Hillary J. Knepper, Michelle D. Evans, and Tiffany J. Henley, "Considering Intersectionality and Its Implications for Crisis Management." In *Intersectionality and Crisis Management: A Path to Social Equity,* ed. Hillary J. Knepper, Michelle D. Evans, and Tiffany J. Henley (Routledge: New York, 2023), ch. 1.
4. Paul Van Riper, *History of the U.S. Civil Service* (New York: Row, Peterson, 1958)

5. U.N. Women, "Progress of the World's Women 2015–2016: Transforming Economies, Realizing Rights," U.N. Women, 2015. https://progress.unwomen.org/en/2015/download/index.html#report
6. Schnequa N. Diggs, Rosa Castillo Krewson, and Sean A. McCandless, "Intersectional Disparities During Crisis: Improving Social Equity Through Public and Nonprofit Management." In *Intersectionality and Crisis Management: A Path to Social Equity,* ed. Hillary J. Knepper, Michelle D. Evans, and Tiffany J. Henley (New York: Routledge, 2023), ch. 5.
7. Sohela Nazneen and Sam Hickey, "How Does Politics Shape the Negotiation of Gender Equity in the Global South?" In *Negotiating Gender Equity in the Global South,* ed. Sohela Nazneen, Sam Hickey, and Eleni Sifaki (UK: Taylor & Francis Group, 2019), 209.
8. Michelle D. Evans and Hillary J. Knepper, "Gender and Nonprofit Administration: Past, Present and Future." In *Handbook on Gender and Public Administration*, ed. Patricia Shields and Nicole M. Elias (Cheltenham, UK: Edward Elgar Publishing, 2022), 195–211.
9. Shannon Portillo, Domonic Bearfield, and Nicole Humphrey, "The Myth of Bureaucratic Neutrality: Institutionalized Inequity in Local Government Hiring," *Review of Public Personnel Administration* 40, no. 3 (2019): 516–531.
10. U.S. Bureau of Labor Statistics, "Labor Force Statistics from the Current Population Survey: Demographics," accessed August 3, 2022. https://www.bls.gov/cps/demographics.htm#women
11. U.N. Women, "Progress of the World's Women 2015–2016: Transforming Economies, Realizing Rights." https://progress.unwomen.org/en/2015/download/index.html#report
12. Jennifer Silva, "Women in the Military: Through the Decades," accessed May 30, 2023. https://newsroom.woundedwarriorproject.org/Women-in-the-Military-Through-the-Decades
13. Candace West and Don H. Zimmerman, "Doing Gender," *Gender and Society* 1, no. 2 (1987): 125–151.
14. Kela—Social Insurance Institution of Finland. 2023. "The Parental Allowance System Was Reformed," accessed July 30, 2023. https://www.kela.fi/family-leave-reform-2022
15. Rita M. Hilton and Rosemary O'Leary, *Leading in Place: Leadership Through Different Eyes* (New York: Routledge, 2018).
16. Ibid., 135.
17. Mary E. Guy and Meredith A. Newman, "Women's Jobs, Men's Jobs: Sex Segregation and Emotional Labor," *Public Administration Review* 64, no. 3 (2004): 289–298.
18. The White House. 2021. "National Strategy on Gender Equity and Equality," The White House, accessed July 23, 2023. https://www.whitehouse.gov/briefing-room/statements-releases/2021/10/22/fact-sheet-national-strategy-on-gender-equity-and-equality/
19. International City/County Management Association [ICMA], "Leadership Development Programs," accessed July 23, 2023. https://icma.org/page/leadership-development-programs
20. Ibid. "SheLeadsGov," accessed July 29, 2023. https://icma.org/sheleadsgov
21. Rosemarie Lally, "EU Directive on Gender-Balanced Boards Supports Workplace Equality," Society for Human Resource Management [SHRM], accessed July 29, 2023. https://www.shrm.org/resourcesandtools/hr-topics/global-hr/pages/eu-directive-gender-balanced-boards.aspx

5 LGBTQ+, RACE, AND THE PURSUIT OF SOCIAL EQUITY

Cornel Grey and Kareem K.M. Willis

From the Editors

This chapter focuses on LGBTQ+ persons who are Black. Like a stack of blocks, each marginalized characteristic—sexual identity, gender identity, Blackness—compounds discrimination, inequities, and harm. Using an intersectional lens, Grey and Willis explain how inequities arise and how laws, policies, and processes reduce or permit discrimination. They offer pathways for acknowledging inequity, understanding the difference that race makes, and partnering with allies to overcome obstacles. Laced throughout the discussion is the role that intersectionality plays in compounding or minimizing discrimination.

Despite decades of legal advancements and changes in societal acceptance, lesbian, gay, bisexual, trans, queer, and other sexualities as well as gender diverse (LGBTQ+) communities living in North America continue to face inequities. Across all four dimensions of social equity—access, processes, quality, and outcomes—LGBTQ+ communities disproportionately face inequities, whether concerning health care, housing, discrimination on the job, or bias experienced throughout societal interactions.[1]

When studying inequities experienced by LGBTQ+ communities and developing solutions, it is important to remember three characteristics. First, LGBTQ+ communities are highly intersectional. These communities intersect with all other communities, whether concerning racial and ethnic identity, gender identity, socioeconomic class, geographic origin, and many more. Second, the term "LGBTQ+" belies enormous complexity. For instance, "lesbian, gay, and bisexual" refer to *sexuality* (sometimes called sexual orientation), which refers to sexual attractions and behaviors toward others. These terms are highly intersectional with gender identity, and the complexity grows when factoring in other dimensions like race, ethnicity, and more. Third, "transgender" is a broad, complex term that refers largely to gender identity, namely "to describe people whose gender identity is different from the gender they were thought to be when they were born."[2] As such, while the experiences of LGBTQ+ communities differ from non-LGBTQ+ communities, there can and are enormous differences experienced *within* these communities as well. Such is the reality of intersectionality and the need for anyone working in public service to examine equity from an intersectional lens.

Not surprisingly, LGBTQ+ equity has historically been discussed as a single equity domain, largely referring to sexuality (lesbian, gay, and bisexual) and only later to gender identity (transgender). A complicating factor is that the experiences of white male gay individuals have dominated discussions and social movements meant to foster LGBTQ+ equity. The experiences of LGBTQ+ people of color, especially Black LGBTQ+ people, have themselves been marginalized within already marginalized communities. Thus, an intersectional lens leads to a deeper understanding of the causes and solutions to LGBTQ+ inequities.

We tackle this issue by centering the lived experiences of Black LGBTQ+ people. As documented below, systems of oppression compound for people who exist at the intersection of multiple marginalized identities. Even in discussions that seek to highlight these disparities, the experiences of Black LGBTQ+ people are often mobilized by researchers, health care providers, and nonprofit organizations to illustrate the severity of the problem, such as the impact of HIV in Black communities. At other times, the experiences are treated as an afterthought, or offered as a fruitful subject for future consideration rather than present analysis.

This chapter offers a more robust examination of Black queer life, drawing on a Black feminist and queer theoretical framework to broaden the discussion of how power and its misuse, as well as lack of access, influences outcomes for certain groups. We delve into the experiences of Black queer communities, shedding light on the discrimination they face in various aspects of life. By examining the impacts of discrimination on Black LGBTQ+ communities across multiple dimensions of public life (including education, employment, health care, criminal justice, and everyday life), we demonstrate how Black queer people disappear from public policies that are intended to improve quality of life because of what George Lipsitz refers to as a "possessive investment in whiteness."[3] The term refers to the ongoing ways in which white individuals and groups have benefited from and maintained their privileged social, economic, and political positions through, the reinforcement of their racial identity. Throughout, we borrow from Black feminist thinkers and collectives like the Combahee River Collective who declared "[i]f Black women were free, it would mean that everyone else would have to be free since our freedom would necessitate the destruction of all the systems of oppression."[4]

Intersectional Discrimination

Intersectionality was coined by Kimberlé Crenshaw,[5] drawing on a rich legacy of Black feminist theorizing of power, such as Sojourner Truth's speech "Ain't I a Woman,"[6] Frances M. Beal's description of "double jeopardy,"[7] and Patricia Hill Collins's discussion of "matrix of domination."[8] Each of these Black feminists offered a nuanced analysis of power and its impacts on the bodies and lives of multiple marginalized people, specifically Black women. Using this literature as a guide, "intersectional discrimination" refers to the experience of individuals who face discrimination based on multiple aspects of their identity. It occurs when someone is subjected to prejudice and bias due to the combination of two or more characteristics, such as race, gender, sexuality, religion, disability, or socioeconomic status. Combinations compound the effects of each form of discrimination, leading to challenges and barriers for those affected.

Discrimination based on a single characteristic of sexuality and gender identity is usually the focus when someone examines LGBTQ+ equity. However, intersectionality prompts a deeper look. For example, an individual who identifies as a woman and belongs to a racial or ethnic minority group may experience discrimination based on *both* gender and race. Another example is how a transgender person of color may experience discrimination not only based on their gender identity but also due to their racial background. When marginalization and exclusion combine, the unique challenges that result are too often overlooked by policymakers and administrators. Double discrimination manifests in access to opportunities; unequal treatment in employment, education, housing, and health care; and social marginalization.

Intersectional discrimination occurs in the workplace, educational institutions, the criminal justice system, and social interactions. Women of color, for example, face systemic barriers that hinder their professional advancement, such as stereotypes and biases that prevent them from reaching leadership positions despite their qualifications. Similarly, individuals with disabilities who identify as LGBTQ+ experience discrimination from both ableist and homophobic/transphobic attitudes, resulting in inequitable access to resources and social exclusion. The consequences of intersectional discrimination are far-reaching, leading to feelings of isolation, diminished self-esteem, mental health challenges, and reduced opportunities for personal and professional growth. Moreover, the cumulative effects of discrimination perpetuate cycles of poverty and social exclusion for marginalized groups, further entrenching inequalities.

The Role of Public Administration

Public administration fails Black communities.[9] This is evident in neighborhood sustainability, policing,[10] social welfare,[11] disaster response after hurricanes,[12] and health care, as the incidences of HIV and COVID-19 reveal.[13] These disparities lead to questions of social equity: Who are the intended beneficiaries of public policy? Who is the "public" in public policy? Intersectionality provides the lens for administrators to better answer these questions. As a way of thinking about how power functions, it is more meaningful than simply using an additive strategy whereby one counts race + gender + class + sexuality. Because societal structures shape how our identities are experienced, intersectional analysis, in bell hooks' words, offers thoughtful analyses of "white supremacist capitalist patriarchy."[14]

Black LGBTQ+ people face multiple forms of discrimination and intersecting oppression based on their race, sexual orientation, and gender identity. These oppressions result in social exclusion, rejection by family or community, and limited access to supportive networks. It is common for Black people to be imagined as separate from the LGBTQ+ community altogether. For example, in 2016 a protest conducted by Black Lives Matter–Toronto at Toronto Pride was described in the media as a "hijacking," with many attendees shouting that discussions about racism do not belong at Pride. According to a 2020 study conducted by the Center for American Progress, 33% of Black LGBTQ+ people reported experiencing discrimination in the past year.[15] Despite narratives that construct the LGBTQ+ community as a safe and inclusive space for everyone, Black LGBTQ+ folks regularly face discrimination from non-Black people within the community.[16] Black people within the LGBTQ+ community consistently report worse outcomes than their white counterparts when describing police interactions, working conditions, economic challenges, and health.[17]

How Discrimination Compounds and Intersects

An intersectional lens invites questions of how discrimination compounds and intersects for LGBTQ+ communities. As discussed next, these inequities are notably acute with regard to health care and legal protections.

Health

There are few areas that showcase the importance of fair access, processes, quality, and outcomes for LGBTQ+ communities more than health care. LGBTQ+ communities are often at higher risk of suicidal thoughts, anxiety, and substance abuse. In terms of physical health, LGBTQ+ people experience greater risk concerning chronic conditions, such as cancer.[18] Further, LGBTQ+ people are less likely to receive regular health care and to have health insurance. And they are more likely to question the cultural competence of health care providers. The root causes of these disparities are linked to the minoritized status of LGBTQ+ communities, lack of training and cultural competency by health care workers, restrictive benefits, stigma, and institutional biases.[19]

Health inequities are profoundly intersectional. The stresses of bias, prejudice, and discrimination are compounded by race, ethnicity, and socioeconomic class. Despite claims that public health crises like COVID-19 and HIV are over, Black people continue to be impacted.[20] Even though data show the impact of racism, and though race-based data were collected during the COVID-19 pandemic in Canada and the United States, Black populations were consistently underserved, despite knowledge of the disproportionalities.[21]

The social determinants of health shed light on inequities experienced by Black LGBTQ+ people. Structural determinants point to how issues of quality of life, mental health, and physical health reach far beyond one's immediate circumstances. Rather, the structures and institutions one encounters can and do impact health. For one, Black LGBTQ+ people, especially Black transgender women, are disproportionately likely to experience discrimination in the workplace and in societal interactions as well as to experience violence. Structural racism adds to the impacts of other inequities. For instance, when accessing health care, Black LGBTQ+ people encounter a system that is largely white and not culturally competent enough to understand and take their health concerns seriously. Further, poverty makes it challenging to access quality health care, yet poverty itself is a consequence of oppression.[22]

Further, and problematically, public health scholarship on sexual minorities has largely focused on risk-taking practices and poor health outcomes, particularly among gay men.[23] This is where an intersectional lens is again helpful. While Black gay, bisexual, queer, and other men who have sex with men (GBQM) are less likely to engage in high-risk practices, they nonetheless have an extraordinarily high chance (50%) of contracting HIV in their lifetime.[24] This makes it obvious that any serious intervention to curb HIV rates and improve health outcomes for GBQM must grapple with factors beyond sexual behavior.

These inequities do not "just occur." Rather, they result from stigmatization of Black queer populations. It is not unusual for professionals working at the frontlines to engage in racist, homophobic, and transphobic discrimination.[25] While it is clear that gender and sexual minorities (GSM) are affected by heterosexism, homophobia, and barriers to care, there are few mentions of how race factors into individuals' experiences. For instance, some studies examine hate crimes experienced by gay men, yet authors rarely examine differences based on race as well.[26] At times, the framing is problematic, such as when studies report that many victims of GSM homicide are trans women, with many being women of color. Race, and specifically blackness, is in the narrative as a point of reference but points to the problem that the unique experiences of Black LGBTQ+ communities are not sufficiently understood, nor are they thought to be worthy of consideration.

Lack of Legal Protection

In both Canada and the United States, there have been significant legal advancements concerning LGBTQ+ equity. In Canada, several advancements are evident. For one, societal acceptance of LGBTQ+ people is among the highest in the world. Further, in 1995, the Supreme Court of Canada held in *Egan v. Canada* that sexual orientation is protected under the Canadian Charter of Rights and Freedoms. Transgender rights are growing, with discrimination based on gender identity or expression being illegal under Canadian law.[27] In the United States, societal acceptance of LGBTQ+ communities has grown, albeit not to the extent as in Canada. The U.S. Supreme Court ruled in a 2015 decision, *Obergefell v. Hodges*, that marriage discrimination is unconstitutional and then ruled in a 2020 decision, *Bostock v. Clayton County*, that people cannot be fired solely for their sexual orientation and/or gender identity.

Despite these advancements, there have been legal setbacks, particularly in the United States. In fact, 2021–2023 set records for the number of anti-LGBTQ bills introduced. While many never became law, this nevertheless points to the uneven path toward LGBTQ+ equity.[28] For instance, in 2022, Florida's governor signed into law the so-called "Don't Say Gay or Trans bill," which "prohibits instruction about sexual orientation or gender identity in grades K–3 and bans instruction about sexual orientation or gender identity in grades 4–12" if such material is deemed not age- or developmentally appropriate."[29] Another prominent example has been the increase in policies targeting trans-identified people, including limiting transgender health care, banning transgender participation in sports, targeting drag performances, and more. The majority of resistance to transgender equity is in politically conservative states like Texas, Florida, Alabama, and Kentucky. For example, the Kentucky legislature recently introduced several bills targeting the trans community, including H.B. 253 and S.B. 84. These bills would prevent trans youth from receiving gender-affirming care such as hormone therapy and transition procedures, and physicians providing gender-affirming care would be subject to disciplinary action.

Furthermore, Black LGBTQ+ individuals face legal disparities. For example, while some jurisdictions have enacted laws protecting LGBTQ+ individuals from employment discrimination, many Black LGBTQ+ individuals still lack comprehensive legal protection. This leaves them vulnerable to discrimination, harassment, and unfair treatment in the workplace based on their sexual orientation, gender identity, and race. This is especially true of Black trans women and gender-nonconforming individuals who experience barriers to employment and heightened discrimination in their workplaces.

Legal disparities affect health care access for Black LGBTQ+ individuals. In some cases, laws or policies may allow health care providers to refuse services based on religious or moral objections, raising the likelihood of discrimination. Black LGBTQ+ individuals also face legal disparities within the criminal justice system, as they experience disproportionate rates of discriminatory policing, profiling, and harsher sentencing. In turn, this results in their overrepresentation in the prison system, as well as discrimination and mistreatment within correctional facilities.[30]

Liberation for All—Pathways to Action

Liberation for oppressed communities requires a diversity of strategies. We offer these suggestions as pathways to action for current and future public administrators. While these strategies are by no means exhaustive, they offer a point of entry for interventions.

Acknowledge the Problem

The murder of George Floyd, an African American man living in Minneapolis, by a police officer in 2020 sparked global conversations about the nature of anti-Black racism. These conversations were not limited to the role of the police. University administrators engaged in conversations about the recruitment and retention of Black staff and faculty, the experience of Black students on campus, and the extent to which existing curricula offered sufficient opportunities to engage in analyses of race. Politicians debated the existence of racism, and public health experts examined disproportionate impacts of COVID-19 on Black communities. Private and public organizations sent statements condemning anti-Black racism. Some made vague commitments to do better. While it remains to be determined if these responses were sufficient and/or successful, such actions are important first steps toward dialogue. Being open to a difficult conversation means that the door to change is open. The next step is to learn and reflect on how anti-Black racism and homophobia are embedded in the very structure of each organization and to take steps to transform the environment.[31]

Decenter Whiteness

Even though LGBTQ+ persons exist across all racial and ethnic groups, the conversation around queer liberation still excludes, to a great extent, individuals from minoritized races and ethnicities. The responses to LGBTQ+ discrimination by policymakers, service providers, and advocacy organizations reinforce and perpetuate the dominance of white perspectives and experiences. Therefore, promoting equity requires that a new starting point be established to effect true change. Jasbir Puar's articulation of homonationalism, for example, offers a way to understand how the mobilization of LGBTQ+ rights and inclusive policies have largely benefited the lives of cisgender, white gay men.[32] Those charged with pursuing the public good must go beyond this to address all communities' needs, with special attention to the needs of the most vulnerable. Decentering whiteness is a critical step.

While the North American gay rights movement draws on the vocabulary and strategies of the Black civil rights movement,[33] Blackness has largely been absent from contemporary discourses about gay rights and LGBTQ+ health.[34] In fact, anti-Black racism is presumed to have been solved or has seemingly been positioned as irrelevant to the LGBTQ+ community.[35] Black LGBTQ+ people find themselves underserved by LGBTQ+ advocacy organizations, and such organizations do little to support Black LGBTQ+ equity beyond performative displays of community service as rationales for (continued) funding. Further, LGBTQ+ organizations continue to be dominated by white men. For example, a 2015 investigation by the Pipeline Project found that the workplace culture at Human Rights Watch (a nongovernmental human rights abuses watchdog) was akin to a "White Men's Club."[36]

Another example is how the priorities of LGBT organizers narrowed over time to focus on personal pride, achieving visibility, and lobbying for individual equality within existing institutions.[37] Furthermore, the issues with which historically marginalized communities—especially Indigenous people and people of color—were particularly concerned (i.e., housing, health care, affirmative action) were described as "non-gay issues." The construction of gay organizations as white, male, and middle-class is motivated by a commitment to whiteness as a form of social and political capital. White gay men engage in "gay whitening practices," such as embodying whiteness as a strategy to connect with powerful stakeholders, portraying gayness as white, and excluding people of color from LGBT organizations.[38]

Decentering whiteness is a concept rooted in critical race theory and social justice movements. It represents a deliberate effort to challenge and dismantle the dominant position and influence of whiteness in social, cultural, and institutional contexts. In many societies, whiteness has been positioned as the norm or the standard against which other racial and ethnic groups are measured. This privileging of whiteness has resulted in systemic racism, discrimination, and unequal power dynamics. Decentering whiteness disrupts this power imbalance to create a more equitable society. The concept involves recognizing and challenging the ways in which whiteness shapes institutions, norms, and collective consciousness. It calls for actively examining and questioning how whiteness is normalized and enforced as the default or ideal standard in education, media, politics, and cultural representation.

Decentering whiteness involves several important steps. It requires individuals, particularly those who benefit from white privilege, to reflect on their own privilege and how it influences their perspectives, experiences, and interactions with others. It involves intentionally amplifying and prioritizing the voices and experiences of marginalized communities, allowing their perspectives to shape narratives, policies, and decision-making processes. Decentering whiteness requires questioning and challenging the assumptions and biases that underpin systems and institutions, aiming to dismantle structures that perpetuate racial inequalities. It involves actively creating spaces and opportunities that embrace diversity, representation, and inclusion. This includes diversifying leadership positions, curricular content, media representation, and cultural narratives.

It is important to note that decentering whiteness does not mean disregarding or devaluing white individuals or their experiences. Rather, it aims to challenge the dominance of whiteness as the norm and to create a more inclusive, just, and equitable society where all racial and ethnic groups are respected and valued.

Reimagine Policies and Laws as Vehicles for Positive Change

The findings discussed in this chapter underscore how policy workers must consider the specific needs of the Black LGBTQ+ community when pursuing efforts to promote equity. Public policy informs the direction of resources and plays a crucial role in securing access to services for marginalized communities. Social equity is about framing Black LGBTQ+ people as equal subjects of care, entitled to the same privileges afforded to the rest of the population. Laws, policies, and procedures are essential in securing human rights as they codify human rights into legally binding principles, ensuring that individuals are protected from discrimination, abuse, and violations.

While public policy to date has failed to protect Black LGBTQ+ people, public policy remains a powerful tool to promote equity. Policies, when rooted in anti-racist and anti-oppressive practices, play a vital role in creating a just society for Black LGBTQ+ people. As such, public administrators should have these questions at the front of their minds: How can policies and programs alleviate suffering for those who exist at the intersection of multiple marginalized identities? And, how can policies be designed to effectively address past harms and prevent future ones for these communities?

Addressing legal disparities for Black LGBTQ+ individuals requires enacting comprehensive anti-discrimination laws and policies, beyond those mentioned earlier, that explicitly and thoroughly protect LGBTQ+ individuals from discrimination based on sexual orientation, gender identity, and race. Promoting policies and legal protections helps to reduce disparities experienced by Black LGBTQ+ individuals when they must navigate the criminal justice system. Training for legal professionals, increasing diversity in the judiciary, and reforming discriminatory laws support efforts to address bias and discrimination within the legal system.

Public administration can learn from Black feminism, namely that the administration of public policy should minimize, as much as possible, barriers that prevent access to services. Those who know they are likely to face racism and homophobia are reluctant to deal with bureaucracy and the obstacles its rules erect. Their reluctance is compounded by processes that involve administrative surveillance and administrative burdens.

Practice Radical Allyship

Allyship is a practice where a person "gives voice" to the marginalized. Promoting equity requires allies willing to yield space so that individuals can be agents of change for their own communities. A question for allies to ask themselves is this: "what am I willing to risk supporting this community?" The answer requires reflection on their own commitment to the community they want to support. It does not take much to attend an event, to invite someone to speak at an event or to consult for a project. However, it requires courage on the part of the ally (specifically white allies) to speak up when someone makes an offensive remark (under the guise of jest) or to advocate for a colleague. Administrators can have various attitudes toward allyship, whether as commitment, or unspoken requirement, or performative, or even as an opportunity to build a stronger relationship with a colleague. Allies should be clear about *why* they claim allyship.

Allies promote equity even when under pressure, and racialized and queer people in the workplace must never be treated as if they should be grateful for simply being treated with respect and dignity. Allies make mistakes, but allies should remember that marginalized colleagues are often put in positions where they must manage the bruised feelings of someone trying to make things better. It is an extra burden for Black and queer administrators when everyday navigation of prejudice is complicated by white affect.[39]

Summary of Key Points

Addressing any disparity requires a comprehensive approach that addresses systemic inequities, improves cultural competency, and promotes inclusive policies and practices. As this chapter discussed, this is also the case for LGBTQ+ equity, a dimension of social equity that requires an intersectional lens. The work requires administrators to understand the history of issues, investigate causes and effects, and pursue equity for all. It is not unusual for a new, more equitable path forward to cause some discomfort. That is not a sufficient reason for not doing it.

Fortunately, approaches already exist for revolutionizing systems of oppression. Largely developed and popularized by members of marginalized and disenfranchised groups, critical perspectives provide practitioners with insights that enable them to reshape policies and processes in a way that is more emancipatory, inclusive, and liberating. Critical theories challenge the status quo, highlight where oppression is built into the system, and provide ways to foster positive change. By using critical perspectives to guide administrative action, practitioners can craft innovative solutions that redress injustice, repair harm, and harness democratic power from the ground up. This is a creative, critical reimagining of what justice, life, and liberty for all should and could look like.

Discussion Questions

1. What are the historical roots and contemporary manifestations of violence and discrimination against Black LGBTQ+ individuals, and what strategies can be implemented to promote their safety, dignity, and well-being?
2. What are the ethical considerations and challenges to meaningfully engaging with Black LGBTQ+ populations, and how can public administrators deploy culturally sensitive and inclusive strategies that respect the diversity and agency of participants?
3. What are some emerging policy debates and legal advancements concerning the rights and protections of Black LGBTQ+ individuals, and what role can public administrators play in advancing these agendas?

Additional Resource

Access results from the Center for American Progress's survey of LGBTQ+ people of color. Results show the effects of the compounded harm that results from experiencing multiple forms of discrimination in the workplace, health care systems, and police interactions. The harm leads to gaps in economic advancement and poor mental and physical health outcomes. Access the report here: https://www.americanprogress.org/article/discrimination-experiences-among-lgbtq-people-us-2020-survey-results/#Ca=10. Learn about the Rainbow Railroad by visiting https://www.rainbowrailroad.org/about

Notes

1. Lorenda A. Naylor, *Social Equity and LGBTQ Rights: Dismantling Discrimination and Expanding Civil Rights* (New York: Routledge, 2021).
2. National Center for Transgender Equality, "Understanding Transgender People: The Basics," *National Center for Transgender Equality*, January 27, 2023, https://transequality.org/issues/resources/understanding-transgender-people-the-basics
3. George Lipsitz, *The Possessive Investment in Whiteness: How White People Profit from Identity Politics* (Philadelphia: Temple University Press, 2006).
4. Combahee River Collective, "A Black Feminist Statement," *Off Our Backs* 9, no. 6 (1979): 6–8.
5. Kimberle Crenshaw, "Demarginalizing the Intersection of Race and Sex: A Black Feminist Critique of Antidiscrimination Doctrine," *University of Chicago Legal Forum*, 1989, 139–167.
6. Sojourner Truth, "Ain't I A Woman?" (Women's Rights Convention, Akron, Ohio, 1851).
7. Frances M. Beal, "Double Jeopardy: To Be Black and Female," *Meridians: Feminism, Race, Transnationalism* 8, no. 2 (2008): 166–176.
8. Patricia Hill Collins, *Black Feminist Thought: Knowledge, Consciousness, and the Politics of Empowerment*, 2nd ed. (New York: Routledge, 1999).
9. Mario A. Rivera and James D. Ward, "Institutional Racism, Diversity and Public Administration," in *Diversity and Public Administration: Theory, Issues, and Perspectives*, 2nd ed. (Armonk, New York: M.E. Sharpe, 2010), 81–95; Matthew T. Witt, "A Noteworthy Absence: How and Why Race and Racism Is Ignored by Public Administration Scholarship," *History Compass* 9, no. 7 (2011): 549–561; Maren B. Trochmann et al., "Resistance or Reinforcement? A Critical Discourse Analysis of Racism and Anti-Blackness in Public Administration Scholarship," *Administrative Theory & Praxis* 44, no. 2 (2022): 158–177, https://doi.org/10.1080/10841806.2021.1918990
10. Parastou Saberi, "Toronto and the 'Paris Problem': Community Policing in 'Immigrant Neighbourhoods,'" *Race & Class* 59, no. 2 (2017): 49–69; Rinaldo Walcott, "Time for White Left to Speak Up on Anti-Black Racism," *NOW Toronto*, May 24, 2017, https://nowtoronto.com/news/time-for-white-left-to-speak-up/; Robyn Maynard, *Policing Black Lives: State Violence in Canada from Slavery to the Present* (Halifax: Fernwood Publishing, 2017); Maynard; Michelle Alexander, *The New Jim Crow: Mass Incarceration in the Age of Colorblindness* (New York: New Press, 2010).no. 2 (October 1, 2017
11. Julilly Kohler-Hausmann, "'The Crime of Survival': Fraud Prosecutions, Community Surveillance and the Original 'Welfare Queen,'" *Journal of Social History* 41, no. 2 (2007): 329–354; Carly Hayden Foster, "The Welfare Queen: Race, Gender, Class, and Public Opinion," *Race, Gender & Class* 15, no. 3/4 (2008): 162–179.
12. Camilla Stivers, "'So Poor and So Black': Hurricane Katrina, Public Administration, and the Issue of Race," *Public Administration Review* 67, no. s1 (2007): 48–56.
13. Pascal Djiadeu et al., "Barriers to HIV Care among Francophone African, Caribbean and Black Immigrant People Living with HIV in Canada: A Protocol for a Scoping Systematic Review," *BMJ Open* 9, no. 1 (2019): e027440, https://doi.org/10.1136/bmjopen-2018-027440; Apondi J. Odhiambo et al., "Legislatively Excluded, Medically Uninsured and Structurally Violated: The Social Organization of HIV Healthcare for African, Caribbean and Black Immigrants with Precarious Immigration Status in Toronto, Canada," *Qualitative Health Research* 32, no. 5 (2022): 847–865; Apondi J. Odhiambo et al., "Structural Violence and the Uncertainty of Viral Undetectability for African, Caribbean and Black People Living with HIV in Canada: An Institutional Ethnography," *International Journal for Equity in Health* 22, no. 1 (2023): 33, https://doi.org/10.1186/s12939-022-01792-4; Zinzi Bailey et al., "Racism in the Time of COVID-19," *IAPHS—Interdisciplinary Association for Population Health Science* (blog), April 8, 2020, https://iaphs.org/racism-in-the-time-of-covid-19/; Cornel Grey et al., "Unpacking Racism during COVID-19: Narratives from Racialized Canadian Gay, Bisexual, and Queer Men," *International Journal for Equity in Health* 22, no. 1 (2023): 152, https://doi.org/10.1186/s12939-023-01961-z; Crista E. Johnson-Agbakwu et al., "Racism, COVID-19, and Health Inequity in the USA: A Call to Action," *Journal of Racial and Ethnic Health Disparities*, November 16, 2020, https://doi.org/10.1007/s40615-020-00928-y\\uc0\\u8221{} {\\i{}BMJ Open} 9, no. 1 (30 2019
14. bell hooks, *Feminism Is for Everybody: Passionate Politics* (Cambridge, MA: South End Press, 2000).
15. Lindsay Mahowald, "Black LGBTQ Individuals Experience Heightened Levels of Discrimination," *Center for American Progress* (blog), July 13, 2021, https://www.americanprogress.org/article/black-lgbtq-individuals-experience-heightened-levels-discrimination/

16. Elizabeth A. McConnell et al., "Multiple Minority Stress and LGBT Community Resilience among Sexual Minority Men," *Psychology of Sexual Orientation and Gender Diversity* 5, no. 1 (2018): 1–12; Soon Kyu Choi, Bianca D.M. Wilson, and Christy Mallory, "Black LGBT Adults in the US: LGBT Well-Being at the Intersection of Race," (UCLA School of Law, Williams Institute, January 2021), https://williamsinstitute.law.ucla.edu/publications/black-lgbt-adults-in-the-us/
17. Mahowald, "Black LGBTQ Individuals Experience Heightened Levels of Discrimination."
18. Baker, Kellen. "Cancer in LGBT Populations: Differences, Disparities, and Strategies for Change," (2020), https://cebp.aacrjournals.org/content/29/12_Supplement/IA12, accessed December 17, 2023.
19. Cigna Healthcare, "LGBTQ+ Health Disparities," *Cigna Healthcare,* accessed December 14, 2023, https://www.cigna.com/knowledge-center/lgbt-disparities#:~:text=LGBTQ%2B%20people%20are%20less%20likely%20to%20have%20a%20regular%20health%20care%20provider.&text=Lesbian%20and%20bisexual%20women%20have,women%20are%20at%20greater%20risk.&text=LGBTQ%2B%20people%20have%20higher%20rates,related%20cervical%20or%20anal%20cancers
20. Rinaldo Walcott, "Nothing New Here to See: How COVID-19 and State Violence Converge on Black Life," *TOPIA: Canadian Journal of Cultural Studies* 41 (2020): 158–163, https://doi.org/10.3138/topia-019; Rinaldo Walcott, "A History of Violence," *Critical Studies in Improvisation / Études Critiques En Improvisation* 14, no. 1 (2021), https://doi.org/10.21083/csieci.v14i1.6507
21. Walcott, "Nothing New Here to See"; Rinaldo Walcott, "Data or Politics? Why the Answer Still Remains Political." *The Royal Society of Canada* (blog), November 12, 2020, https://rsc-src.ca/en/covid-19/impact-covid-19-in-racialized-communities/data-or-politics-why-answer-still-remains
22. National LGBTQIA+ Health Education Center, *Understanding and Addressing the Social Determinants of Health for Black LGBTQ People: A Way Forward for Health Centers* (Boston, MA: National LGBTQIA+ Health Education Center, 2019).
23. K. Bryant Smalley, K. Bryant Warren, and K. Nikki Barefoot, "Gender and Sexual Minority Health: History, Current State, and Terminology," in *LGBT Health: Meeting the Needs of Gender and Sexual Minorities,* ed. K. Bryant Smalley, Jacob C. Warren, and K. Nikki Barefoot, (New York: Springer Publishing, 2018), 3–15.
24. National Center for HIV/AIDS, Viral Hepatitis, STD, and TB Prevention, "Lifetime Risk of HIV Diagnosis," (Centers for Disease Control and Prevention, February 23, 2016), https://www.cdc.gov/nchhstp/newsroom/2016/croi-press-release-risk.html
25. Grey et al., "Unpacking Racism during COVID-19: Narratives from Racialized Canadian Gay, Bisexual, and Queer Men."
26. Rebecca L Stotzer, "Comparison of Hate Crime Rates Across Protected and Unprotected Groups—An Update," (The Williams Institute, January 2012); Zachary McClain, Rosemary Thomas, and Baligh R. Yehia, "Sociocultural and Systemic Barriers to Health for Gender and Sexual Minority Populations," in *LGBT Health: Meeting the Needs of Gender and Sexual Minorities*, ed. K. Bryant Smalley, Jacob C. Warren, and K. Nikki Barefoot, (New York: Springer Publishing, 2018), 15–25.
27. An Act to Amend the Canadian Human Rights Act and the Criminal Code, S.C. 2017, c.13 (2017), https://laws-lois.justice.gc.ca/eng/AnnualStatutes/2017_13/page-1.html; *Egan v. Canada,* 2 SCR 513 (1995); Asher & Lyric, "The 203 Worst & Safest) Countries for LGBTQ+ Travel in 2023,*" Asher & Lyric,* accessed December 14, 2023, https://www.asherfergusson.com/lgbtq-travel-safety/
28. Gay and Lesbian Alliance against Defamation, "GLAAD Media Guide: State Legislation About LGBTQ People," *GLAAD,* accessed December 14, 2023, https://glaad.org/reference/state-legislation/?gad_source=1&gclid=Cj0KCQiA7OqrBhD9ARIsAK3UXh1a5p9kqHHdhEcnzjO-Beb7OI0S2GQ_Edkw-oZhk5V8dVDtCftgUE8aAtKmEALw_wcB; Laurel Powell, "2021 Becomes Deadliest Year on Record for Transgender and Non-Binary People," *Human Rights Campaign,* November 9, 2021, https://www.hrc.org/press-releases/2021-becomes-deadliest-year-on-record-for-transgender-and-non-binary-people
29. Lambda Legal, FAQ: Florida's "Don't Say Gay or Trans Bill": What LGBTQ+ People Should Know, *Lambda Legal,* September 27, 2022, https://lambdalegal.org/publication/ fl_20220927_faq-dont-say-gay-or-trans/
30. Alexi Jones, "Visualizing the Unequal Treatment of LGBTQ People in the Criminal Justice System," *Prison Policy Initiative,* March 2, 2021, https://www.prisonpolicy.org/blog/2021/03/02/lgbtq/; National Black Women's Justice Institute, "LGBTQ People in the Criminal Legal System," *NBWJI,* June 28, 2021,

https://www.nbwji.org/post/lgbtq-people-in-the-criminal-legal-system

31. José Fernando Serrano Amaya, "Challenging or Reshaping Heteronormativity with Public Policies? A Case Study from Bogotá, Colombia," *IDS Working Papers* 2011, no. 361 (2011): 1–41; RaJade M. Berry-James et al., "Stepping Up to the Plate: Making Social Equity a Priority in Public Administration's Troubled Times," *Journal of Public Affairs Education* 27, no. 1 (2021): 5–15; Brandi Blessett and Tia Sherèe Gaynor, "Race, Racism and Administrative Callousness: Using Critical Race Theory for a Race-Conscious Public Administration," *Public Integrity* 23, no. 5 (2021): 455–458; Nicole Humphrey, Domonic A. Bearfield, and Shannon K. Portillo, *The Myth of Bureaucratic Neutrality: An Examination of Merit and Representation*(New York: Routledge, 2022); Samantha June Larson, "Actions for Queering American Public Administration," *Administration & Society* 54, no. 1 (January 1, 2022): 145–163.Racism and Administrative Callousness: Using Critical Race Theory for a Race-Conscious Public Administration,\\uc0\\u8221{} {\\i{}Public Integrity} 23, no. 5 (September 3, 2021
32. Jasbin K. Puar, *Terrorist Assemblages: Homonationalism in Queer Times* (Durham, NC: Duke University Press, 2007).
33. Michael Joseph Gross, "Gay Is the New Black?," November 16, 2008, http://www.advocate.com/news/2008/11/16/gay-new-black; Amy L. Stone and Jane Ward, "From 'Black People Are Not a Homosexual Act' to 'Gay Is the New Black': Mapping White Uses of Blackness in Modern Gay Rights Campaigns in the United States," *Social Identities* 17, no. 5 (2011): 605–624; Gary Younge, "Gay Is the New Black," *The Guardian*, June 16, 2003, sec. World news, https://www.theguardian.com/world/2003/jun/16/gayrights.usa; Michelle Kelsey Kearl, "'Is Gay the New Black?': An Intersectional Perspective on Social Movement Rhetoric in California's Proposition 8 Debate," *Communication and Critical/Cultural Studies* 12, no. 1 (2015): 63–82; Elena Kiesling, "The Missing Colors of the Rainbow: Black Queer Resistance," *European Journal of American Studies* 11, no. 3 (2017), https://doi.org/10.4000/ejas.11830\\uc0\\u8221{} November 16, 2008, http://www.advocate.com/news/2008/11/16/gay-new-black; Amy L. Stone and Jane Ward, \\uc0\\u8220{}From \\uc0\\u8216{}Black People Are Not a Homosexual Act\\uc0\\u8217{} to \\uc0\\u8216{}Gay Is the New Black\\uc0\\u8217{}: Mapping White Uses of Blackness in Modern Gay Rights Campaigns in the United States,\\uc0\\u8221{} {\\i{}Social Identities} 17, no. 5 (September 1, 2011
34. Allan Bérubé, "How Gay Stays White and What Kind of White It Stays," in *The Making and Unmaking of Whiteness*, ed. Birgit Brander Rasmussen et al. (Durham: Duke University Press, 2001), 234–65, https://read.dukeupress.edu/books/book/530/chapter/123635/How-Gay-Stays-White-and-What-Kind-of-White-It
35. Kiesling, "The Missing Colors of the Rainbow."
36. Chris Geidner, "Internal Report: Major Diversity, Organizational Problems at Human Rights Campaign," *BuzzFeed News* (blog), June 3, 2015, https://www.buzzfeednews.com/article/chrisgeidner/internal-report-major-diversity-organizational-problems-at-h
37. Bérubé.
38. Ibid.
39. Mamta Motwani Accapadi, "When White Women Cry: How White Women's Tears Oppress Women of Color," *College Student Affairs Journal* 26, no. 2 (2007): 208–215; Daphne Jeyapal and Liz Grigg, "The Crying White Woman and the Politics of Emotion in Anti-Oppressive Social Work Education," in *Teaching Social Work: Reflections on Pedagogy and Practice*, ed. Rick Csiernik and Susan Hillock (Toronto: University of Toronto Press, 2021).

6 RIGHTS AND RESILIENCE: INDIGENOUS AMERICANS AND SOCIAL EQUITY

John C. Ronquillo

From the Editors

Even though Indigenous Americans—Native Americans, Alaska Natives, and Native Hawaiians—face an array of inequities at the hands of the American government, the issues they face are among the least discussed. From the time of European colonization and forced removals up to recent issues such as the Dakota Access Pipeline and court cases pertaining to sovereignty, Indigenous Americans have been forced into a subordinate, ward-like status. Ronquillo shows how history, laws, and attitudes converge to overlook equity issues. The chapter offers strategies to improve equity, starting with greater awareness and extending to economic development, allyship, greater representation, and collaboration.

Social injustices wrought upon Indigenous populations throughout the history of the United States are well-documented. While public administration has devoted increasing treatment to better understanding social equity, and has adopted social equity as one of the four normative pillars of the field, too often, the issues faced by Native Americans—the *first* Americans—are among the *last* to be discussed.

H. George Fredrickson, widely recognized for integrating the concept of social equity into the discourse of public administration, noted: "There is an irony in the diminishing equality among Americans across various spheres of social, economic, and political life." Fredrickson rejected a detached or "clean hands" approach to addressing social equity.[1] Instead, he advocated for active engagement, urging administrators to grapple with the issue of inequality, get involved despite complexities, and passionately work towards implementing social equity. He stressed the necessity to confront inequality head-on, feel the outrage, show determination, and take action to apply social equity principles within administrative frameworks. This is the right call because too little attention has been given to the disparities faced by Native communities.

This chapter focuses on equity challenges faced by Native populations. The first section provides context while subsequent sections present strategies to promote social equity moving forward.

Indigenous Americans and Public Administration: A History of Social Inequity

The composition of Native communities confounds those unfamiliar with the history of colonization. Thus, the first step is to clarify terms and provide historical context.

Clarifying Terminology

In terms of identity, *Native Americans* or *American Indians*[2] refer to people from Indigenous tribal communities in the contiguous United States. *Alaska Natives* refer to the Indigenous inhabitants of the State of Alaska, which formally came under the purview of the U.S. government in 1867 after Secretary of State William H. Seward negotiated the purchase of the land from Russia. *Native Hawaiians* refer to aboriginal[3] Polynesians who descend from the original Polynesians who settled the Hawaiian Islands in ancient times.

These populations exhibit considerable variation in their political identities. Native populations share various elements of indigeneity, and there is a contemporary solidarity among many of these communities. However, attempting to categorize these diverse groups under a unified "pan-Indigenous" label fails to capture the distinctive traits and characteristics of each community. Understanding social equity concerning Native American issues demands recognition of the extensive diversity and richness inherent in Indigenous cultures and tribal affiliations. For instance, more than 570 tribes have obtained federal recognition, with several others acknowledged by various state governments. Meanwhile, additional groups are striving to secure some form of formal government acknowledgment.

Historical Context

The Americas have been populated for thousands of years, and there are many who ignore or forget the contributions of native populations. At the very least, they have never been properly educated about the first "American" civilizations. "The Americas were not an unpopulated wilderness in 1491," says Kevin Gover (Pawnee), Under Secretary for Museums and Culture at the Smithsonian and former Director of the National Museum of the American Indian.

> these continents were full of technology and knowledge and awareness and philosophy and mathematics and science, and as many people as there were in Europe at the time. And, you know, it's a convenient erasure to say the Americas were a wilderness . . . I mean, even at the Smithsonian you'll hear that kind of thing. But that's how deeply engrained the wilderness narrative is. And if I could change that one thing, it would be to get people to understand there were a lot of people here in 1491, and ask themselves, what happened to them? . . . what better thing can a Smithsonian Museum at the foot of Capitol Hill do than really teach a better version of history than is commonly known?[4]

During the pre-Columbian period—the period before European colonization signified by the arrival of Christopher Columbus—Native peoples and societies flourished. Their communities were accomplished in architecture, the arts, governance, and sustainable living. The arrival of European colonizers in the late 15th century changed these ways of life. Through armed conflicts and the transmission of communicable diseases, Native civilizations were decimated. European imperialist powers saw the so-called "New World" and its resources as ways to expand upon their own fortunes in the "Old World." Thus, European powers frequently viewed Native populations as no more than being obstacles in their way.

As soon as European colonizers made contact, Native Americans were forcibly displaced from their ancestral lands, initiating inequalities that persist today. This trend was apparent during the 19th century and was epitomized by "manifest destiny." This doctrine propagated the belief that the United States, its people, and its institutions were inherently superior, emphasizing the duty of white settlers to expand across North America and reshape it according to their vision. Their expansive ambition disregarded and violated the rights of Indigenous peoples, leading to the violent seizure of Native lands. Among the most infamous occurrences was the Trail of Tears, a series of forced relocations occurring from the 1830s to the 1850s, where Native Americans from the southeastern United States were coerced to relocate to areas west of the Mississippi River. This event resulted in the obliteration of centuries-old homelands, histories and traditions, causing numerous deaths and irreparable losses.[5]

The damage done by colonization did not end in the mid-19th century. It continued with the 1959 admissions of Alaska and Hawaii as states. In Alaska, for instance, highly advanced cultures have existed for thousands of years. Yet starting as early as the 17th century, Alaska Natives found themselves in increasing contact with European settlers, first with the Russian Empire and later with Western European powers. Russia claimed sovereignty over Alaska, and in 1867, the United States purchased Alaska from the Russian Empire for $7.2 million. Alaska was ruled as a territory until its admission to the union. Conversely, following the unification of the Hawaiian Islands under King Kamehameha I in the late 18th century, the Kingdom of Hawai'i[6] flourished as an independent monarchy for nearly 100 years before pro-U.S. white militias overthrew the government.[7] The overthrow was followed by the short-lived Republic of Hawai'i (1894–1898) followed by U.S. annexation in 1898.[8] Thus, both Alaska's and Hawaii's admissions perpetuated colonization well into the 20th century.[9]

The relationship between the American government and Native American communities has been characterized by continual displacement and dispossession. The forced assimilation of tribal communities, particularly children, was pervasive well into the 20th century. Through "manifest destiny," racist rhetoric propagated the idea that Native Americans needed to be "civilized" and compelled to adopt white culture for their presumed betterment. For instance, Richard Henry Pratt, a U.S. Army General advocating for the "Americanization" and "civilization" of Native Americans, coined the phrase "Kill the Indian . . . and save the man." Pratt established the Carlisle Indian Industrial School in 1879 as an embodiment of this philosophy. This boarding school aimed to assimilate Native children into "white culture" and eradicate their tribal identities. Carlisle served as a model for boarding schools nationwide that forcibly separated Native children from their heritage, imposing a culture foreign to their own.

As noted by Rosita Worl (Tlingit), a Harvard-trained anthropologist and President of the Sealaska Heritage Foundation in Juneau Alaska, "I was kidnapped by a social welfare person and put into a home. An orphanage up in Haines."[10] Further,

> I remember driving past the shrimp cannery where my grandparents were picking shrimp. And the cab driver said, "Shouldn't we stop and tell the grandparents?" And I remember the [woman who took me] said, "No, drive on." And that's when I knew something was wrong. And so I tried to fight and get away. I couldn't get away. I was six years old. . . . and there . . . the policy was "civilize and Christianize."

It took Rosita Worl three years before her family could get her out of that orphanage. The "civilize and Christianize" ideology persisted well into the 20th century. Although too extensive to enumerate here, further impacts affect Native communities to this day.

Constitutional and Case Law Dimensions

Understanding the context of these inequities requires a look into how U.S. law treats Native populations. Historically, Native nations were viewed as sovereign entities by colonizers who sought to establish a presence in the early stages of nation-building and expansion in North America.[11] These considerations influenced the earliest constitutional and legal provisions regarding Native populations.

The U.S. government's highest guiding document is the Constitution. Despite the protections afforded by it to both citizens and noncitizens, U.S. law largely consigns Native populations to a subordinate status. Indians and tribes are *overtly* mentioned in the Constitution twice. Native populations are cast *not quite* as foreign nations but also not entirely as wards of the state:

> **Article I, Section 2, Clause 3:** Representatives and direct Taxes shall be apportioned among the several States which may be included within this Union, according to their respective Numbers, which shall be determined by adding to the whole Number of free Persons, including those bound to Service for a Term of Years, and excluding Indians not taxed, three-fifths of all other Persons.

> **Article I, Section 8:** Congress shall have the Power [...] To regulate Commerce with foreign Nations, and among the several States, and with the Indian Tribes.

Additionally, Supreme Court cases have shaped Native Americans' status. Volumes could discuss the complexity of these rulings, but several cases are particularly important. The first three cases make up the "Marshall Trilogy" named after Supreme Court Chief Justice John Marshall. These cases provided both greater legal standing for Native populations and their sovereignty while simultaneously making Native populations subordinate to the federal government. In *Johnson v. McIntosh* (1823), the Supreme Court found that private citizens could not purchase Native American lands. This case laid some of the groundwork for the doctrine of "aboriginal title," or the recognition of a right to occupancy if Native Americans and their ancestors had continuous and long-term occupation of land, although Congress has the right to extinguish such titles.[12] In *Cherokee Nation v. Georgia* (1831)—brought to the Supreme Court by the Cherokee Nation to obtain a federal injunction against the state of Georgia for stripping members of their rights and lands in the lead-up to the Trail of Tears—the court asserted that the Cherokee nation was sovereign but in a ward-like relationship under the guardianship of the United States.[13] A later ruling in *Worcester v. Georgia* (1832) found, in part, that the federal government alone had the sole right to deal with Indian nations.[14]

Laws Defining Relations with Native Americans

Relatedly, statutory laws have changed the status of Native Americans. While not a comprehensive list, eight are particularly important. The first was the 1871 Indian Appropriations Act. This Act had several consequences, most significant of which was that it cast any Native American group as dependent nations or wards of the U.S. federal government. It provided that agreements with tribes would no longer be conducted through treaties, as was normal for agreements between coequal nations. Instead, agreements would be by statute. This doctrine was expanded by several other laws, which the Supreme Court upheld in its ruling in *United States v. Kagama* (1886).[15]

The second is the Indian Removal Act of 1830. This Act authorized the president to negotiate with southern Native populations to remove them from the South and move them west of the Mississippi. The third was the Dawes Severalty Act of 1887, which authorized the President to create subdivided allotments of tribal holdings. This fundamentally converted Native property ownership into a Westernized model of private property. The fourth, the 1921 Hawaiian Homes Commission Act, followed the overthrow and annexation of Hawaii. It stipulates that those with at least 50% Hawaiian blood were eligible for a 99-year residential, agricultural, or pastoral homestead lease for an annual rental of $1.00.[16]

The fifth was the 1924 Indian Citizenship Act, which granted Indigenous peoples U.S. citizenship. Previously, they had been excluded under an interpretation of the Fourteenth Amendment that defined citizens as persons born in the United States and subject to its jurisdiction. This law also lessened the exclusive federal focus on Indian affairs and gave significant powers in Native affairs to state governments.[17] The sixth was the Indian Reorganization Act of 1934.[18] This Act contributed to the formation of reservations as they are known today, although most American Indians do not live on reservations. The seventh is the 1971 Alaska Native Claims Settlement Act (ANCSA). Although there is only one reservation[19] in Alaska, the law, the largest Native land claims settlement in U.S. history, sought to address Alaska Native land claims and transferred authority of land claims to Alaskan Native regional and local village corporations. Today, those land claims are held by 13 Alaska Native regional corporations and over 200 village and urban corporations.[20] Finally, in 2020, to in part rectify the federal appropriation of some tribal lands, Congress acted at the urging of Interior Secretary Deb Haaland, the first Native American serving as a Cabinet secretary, and passed the Montana Water Rights Protection Act. The law returns land management from the U.S. Fish and Wildlife Service to the Confederated Salish and Kootenai Tribes.[21]

This exceptionally brief summation of legal dimensions, especially concerning property rights, reveals how U.S. policy has displaced Native populations, constricted their power, and consigned them to a ward-like status that continues to this day.

Contemporary Issues at the Intersection of Social Equity and Public Administration

Given the legally enforced subordinate status of Native Americans, numerous issues implicate government policies and procedures. Most notable are issues pertaining to child welfare, water rights, impacts of government shutdowns, and law enforcement and criminal jurisdiction.

The Indian Child Welfare Act and Child Welfare Issues

Until the late 1970s, Native children were forcibly removed from their homes and placed in non-Native homes; this is known as the "Indian Adoption Era." Under the guise of improving child welfare, removals occurred due to a lack of cultural awareness about Native American life, involved due process violations and economic incentives for removing children, and were an uninformed attempt to improve socioeconomic conditions in Native communities. To stop the misguided policy, Congress passed the Indian Child Welfare Act (ICWA) in 1978. Among other things, it sought to improve standards for child welfare placements, prevent breaking up Indian families, and empower tribal governments in custody cases.[22] Yet ICWA is not without controversy. The documentary *Blood Memory* highlights several problems with it, including cultural dilution and erasure, displacement, child welfare policies, and blood quantum (that is, defining Native American identity by ancestry percentages).[23] These are all areas where social equity and public policy intersect.

Blood Memory highlights people who have contested inequities of the Indian Adoption Era and ICWA. The first is Sandy White Hawk (Sincangu Lakota), the founding director of the First Nations Repatriation Institute, who argues that the ICWA does not sufficiently acknowledge and protect Native identities.[24] White Hawk was adopted by a white missionary family and removed from her community. She works to reunite displaced adoptees with their birth families and tribal communities in order to heal wounds caused by the Indian Adoption Era.

The second is Mark Fiddler (Turtle Mountain Band of Chippewa Indians), a private practice attorney, children's rights advocate, and founding director of the Indian Child Welfare Law Center.[25] Fiddler was involved in the Supreme Court case *Adoptive Couple v. Baby Girl* (2013). This case concerned a custody battle between "Baby Girl" and the "Adoptive Couple" who took custody of "Baby Girl" after her father did not consent to her adoption. Lower courts ruled that the child was an "Indian Child," and that "Adoptive Couple" did not follow ICWA's procedural directives for adoption, and that the father was entitled to custody rights. The Supreme Court, however, ruled that ICWA and its provisions to prevent the break-up of Indian families did not apply in this case.[26] In the documentary, Fiddler argues that ICWA, while perhaps well-intentioned, nevertheless leads to extensive inequities and impoverished tribal sovereignty, and he urges that it be overturned. In 2022, the U.S. Supreme Court ruled in a 7–2 decision in *Haaland v. Brackeen* (2022) that ICWA is consistent with Congress's Article I authority. The decision reversed a Fifth Circuit Court of Appeals decision that had struck down portions of ICWA. This reaffirms that when Congress exercises Article I powers, federal law preempts conflicting state family laws.[27]

The Dakota Access Pipeline and Standing Rock Water Protectors

Another salient event is the protest centered on the Dakota Access Pipeline. In April 2016, the first protesters—many of whom preferred to be called "water protectors"—established camp near where the Cannonball River meets the Missouri River in North Dakota, the northernmost clime of the Standing Rock Indian Reservation. These water protectors were joining Standing Rock elder LaDonna Brave Bull Allard to oppose Texas-based Energy Transfer LP's Dakota Access Pipeline. The pipeline would carry crude oil from the Bakken oil fields in North Dakota to southern Illinois and cross under the Missouri and Mississippi Rivers, thus threatening access to clean water, as well as lands sacred to the Native peoples of the Standing Rock reservation. Revealingly, an earlier plan for the pipeline was to have crossed the Missouri River north of Bismarck, but it was subsequently moved further south over concerns that an oil spill at that location would have contaminated the state capitol region's drinking water.[28]

The Standing Rock Sioux Tribe asserted that the pipeline violated the tenets of Article II of the Treaty of Fort Laramie wherein the land in question was

> set apart for the absolute and undisturbed use and occupation of the Indians herein named, and for such other friendly tribes or individual Indians as from time to time they may be willing, with the consent of the United States, to admit amongst them; and the United States now solemnly agrees that no persons, except those herein designated and authorized so to do, and except such officers, agents, and employees of the government as may be authorized to enter upon Indian reservations in discharge of duties enjoined by law, shall ever be permitted to pass over, settle upon, or reside in the territory described in this article. . . .[29]

Further, the Supreme Court ruled in *United States v. Sioux Nation of Indians* (1980) that tribal lands had been taken by the United States illegally and that the tribe was owed what is now estimated to be in excess of $1 billion in compensation and interest,[30] although the tribe does not want to accept payment and would rather see their land returned to them.

Protests over the pipeline continued and escalated. Law enforcement donned riot gear at meetings with protesters and employed forceful removal tactics including barricading portions of land with razor wire, deploying attack dogs, using tear gas, and spraying protestors with water cannons in freezing weather. The protests drew a number of high-profile individuals, ranging from elected officials to entertainers and activists. In fact, the Standing Rock protests constituted the largest gathering of Indigenous people in U.S. history.[31]

In December 2016, President Barack Obama, through the Army Corps of Engineers, denied an easement to allow pipeline construction to dig below the Missouri River. A later executive order by President Trump reversed this policy.[32] The number of protesters onsite gradually decreased with those remaining being evicted by the Army National Guard in February 2017 and the pipeline was completed as planned.[33] Still, the nearly 11-month protest heightened awareness of other concerns that affect Native lands, and the protest has emboldened continued action on the part of Native communities and environmental groups.

Legal battles continued throughout the Biden administration, which initiated a review of the pipeline's permitting and environmental impact assessment. As recently as September 2023, the U.S. Army Corps of Engineers was seeking public comment on their Draft Environmental Impact Statement, while being challenged in court by Energy Transfer LP.[34]

The 2018–2019 Government Shutdown and Its Effect on Native Americans

The 2018–2019 government shutdown—the longest in U.S. federal history—had numerous damaging effects, with federal employees directly affected by furloughs, no paychecks, and swaths of citizens indirectly affected through a slowdown or halting of government services. The influence of the shutdown on Native American communities was palpable, with media reports that about 9,000 Indian Health Service (IHS) employees were working without pay, and that another large percentage were being paid through alternate funding streams.[35] Some tribes had to institute hiring freezes while others were concerned about food delivery. Public safety officers on reservations were working without pay.[36] The shutdown was crippling and put lives at risk.[37]

The shutdown laid bare the subordinate status of tribal communities. In exchange for large swaths of Native land, the federal government promised tribes many services, to the point that the IHS is responsible for the care of over 2 million Native Americans and Alaska Natives. Despite the fact that the federal government's track record in honoring its obligations to tribes is uneven at best, tribes rely on federal services and are especially vulnerable when government funds are blocked. Some tribes suffered more than others because they differed economically. Since IHS is not well funded anyway, many tribes already look to other funding sources—usually their own—in order to supplement needs. Wealthier tribes with healthier reserves are better able to weather shutdowns, while poorer tribes suffer disproportionately.

The structure of the federal budgeting process exacerbates inequity. IHS was shut down because it is funded through the Department of the Interior whose funding was on hold. While IHS providers continued to provide as many services as they could without pay, it was not enough.[38] In short, because of the way that funding comes to tribal communities, even partial shutdowns cause undue harm and compound inequity.

Key Supreme Court Cases on Law Enforcement and Tribal Jurisdiction

Recent U.S. Supreme Court decisions have drawn attention to issues of sovereignty, especially as it pertains to law enforcement and criminal activity. The court's 2020 ruling in *McGirt v. Oklahoma,*[39] for example, enhances sovereignty and prohibits the State of Oklahoma from bringing charges against Native Americans for crimes committed on Native lands. In 1997, Jimcy McGirt, an enrolled member of the Seminole Tribe of Oklahoma, had previously been convicted of three sexual offenses by the State of Oklahoma. He subsequently contended that Oklahoma had no jurisdiction to prosecute him because of his tribal enrollment and because his crimes took place on the historical boundaries of the Mvskoke (Creek) Reservation. In a 5–4 ruling, the Court held that Oklahoma did not have the jurisdictional authority to prosecute McGirt, and that the land in Oklahoma apportioned to the Creek Nation in an 1866 treaty is considered "Indian Country" under the Major Crimes Act.[40] Setting apart the nature of McGirt's crimes, the Court ruled that criminal cases involving tribal members on tribal lands should not be tried in state court. The decision helped legitimize the sovereignty of tribal governments, allowing them either to oversee their own jurisprudence and criminal prosecutions or prosecute crimes involving tribally enrolled Native Americans at the federal level.

In a 2021 case, *United States v. Cooley*, the Supreme Court considered whether tribal police officers have the authority to detain and search non-Native Americans on public roads within tribal reservations.[41] In this case, a tribal police officer stopped a non-Native American, Joshua James Cooley, on a public highway within the Crow Reservation in Montana. The officer found drugs, paraphernalia, and two semi-automatic rifles in Cooley's vehicle, leading to federal charges against him. The question was whether tribal law enforcement officers possess the legal right to stop and search non-Native Americans if they suspect a violation of federal or state laws on public roads within reservations. In a unanimous decision, the Court ruled that tribal police officers do have the authority to detain and search non-Native Americans if they reasonably suspect a law is being broken. This ruling clarified the authority of tribal officers to enforce the law within the boundaries of tribal lands even when involving non-Native individuals.

A Brighter Future?

Despite the hurdles, there is promise of improvements in social equity for Native Americans, Alaska Natives, and Native Hawaiians. This promise is manifested in electoral politics, in policy implementation, and in growing awareness of social equity issues.

Politics

Improving social equity for Native populations requires that their concerns be addressed in electoral politics. Two promising avenues include greater representation of Native Americans in government and the intentional adoption of policies meant to improve social equity, both of which are now discussed.

Several political figures are gaining a voice in policy debates. Their empowerment could mean that equity for Native populations is on the road to being taken more seriously. For example, the Honorable Diane Humetewa (Hopi) was unanimously confirmed by the U.S. Senate in 2014 as a district judge for the District of Arizona, making her the first Native American woman federal judge in U.S. history, and only the third Native American to ever be appointed to this position.[42] Prior to this appointment, Humetewa served as the first Native American woman to serve as a U.S. Attorney.[43]

The 2018 elections saw Debora Haaland (Laguna Pueblo) of New Mexico and Sharice Davids (Ho-Chunk) of Kansas elected to the U.S. House of Representatives, becoming the first Native American women to serve in Congress. They joined Oklahoma representatives Tom Cole (Chickasaw) and Markwayne Mullin (Cherokee Nation) as the only four tribally enrolled Native Americans in Congress at the time. Yvette Herrell (Cherokee), elected in 2020, was the first Republican Native woman and first Cherokee woman elected to Congress, serving one term before losing her reelection bid.[44] Mary Peltola (Yup'ik) became the first Alaska Native elected to Congress in 2022, representing Alaska's at-large congressional district. Mullin was subsequently elected to the U.S. Senate in 2022, with Josh Brecheen (Choctaw) succeeding him in Oklahoma's 2nd district. Haaland subsequently made more history in 2021 when she became the first Native American to serve as a cabinet secretary when she was confirmed by the U.S. Senate to be the 54th U.S. Secretary of the Interior.[45]

Statehouses have seen more Native members in recent years, including Ponka-We Victors (Ponca/Tohono O'odham) and Stephanie Byers (Chickasaw) of Kansas, Ruth Buffalo (Mandan, Hidatsa, and Arikara Nation) of North Dakota, Arlando Teller (Diné) and Jamescita Peshlakai (Diné) of Arizona, and Paulette Jordan (Coeur d'Alene) of Idaho, who was the Democratic nominee for governor of Idaho in the 2018 election.[46] Teller was appointed as the Assistant Secretary for Tribal Government Affairs in the U.S. Department of Transportation, reflecting an increase of Native individuals serving in appointed positions in federal government. Alaska Lieutenant Governor Byron Mallott (Tlingit) was the first Alaska Native to serve in that capacity and was succeeded by Valerie Nurr'araaluk Davidson (Yup'ik), Alaska's first woman Alaska Native lieutenant governor.[47] Prior to serving as lieutenant governor, Davidson served as the Commissioner of the Alaska Department of Health and Social Services.

Further, the Biden administration began new actions to support Native communities. These include mandating uniform standards for federal agencies regarding how tribal communities are to be consulted in policies affecting their communities, annual training and guidance for federal administrators who work with tribal communities, launching best practice documents, implementing policies for co-management and co-stewardship of federal lands and waters, electric vehicle initiatives for tribal communities, a 10-year plan on Native language revitalization, among many other policies.[48]

Programs

Raising awareness of the issues that Native populations face is the first step to removing inequity.[49] While the placement of Native individuals in high-profile judicial and political positions is encouraging, more attention to Native social equity issues can be enabled by administrators. While this obviously helps Native American constituents, it also sensitizes public service professionals whose work intersects with tribal governance and it enriches understanding of the unique social equity issues Native populations face.[50] One of the main reasons these issues are missing from discussions in public administration is due to naivete about Native cultures. A social equity lens on Native issues helps to remedy this oversight.

Another way to improve social equity is to use and build upon work carried out in other disciplines.[51] Extensive interdisciplinary effort has been conducted on tribal government and leadership, justice and law, governance of Native nations, sovereignty issues, and a host of other topics. Those in public administration can push the needle forward by building on what is already known about tribal issues. These range from tribal gaming,[52] to Native education,[53] to environmental sovereignty and water rights,[54] to creating better Indigenous learning environments.[55] Public administration can add to these dimensions by studying what works and what fails in the provision of public services.

Another inroad can be made by developing a better understanding of tribal governance in terms of the treaties, laws, and cases that shape tribal relations with federal and state governments.[56] The work of Theodore W. Taylor informs this discussion through his landmark study entitled *The States and Their Indian Citizens*. Taylor notes that administrators must counter those attitudes that view Native populations merely as dependents of government. Such views, to Taylor, are detrimental to the goal of self-sufficiency. He argues that most tribes want to build up individual and tribal competence and be economically self-sufficient."[57] He also notes that lawmakers and administrators have obligations to improve education and employment for Native populations, perhaps by doubling or tripling education funds or by boosting employment programs. Further, and perhaps most important, he advises that administrators should prioritize helping Native populations develop more effective tribal governance. This requires a viable economic base and an ability to generate revenue. He recommends inter-tribal organizations that collaborate to pressure federal and state governments for greater protections. For their part, public service professionals can serve as allies, giving space and voice to these concerns, especially in terms of coordinating aid programs and supporting tribes as they seek to govern themselves.

Knowledge

Knowledge about tribes should be a staple of public administration knowledge. Administrators must remember that tribes are sovereign with jurisdiction in both civil and criminal cases. Federal recognition of a tribe is administered under the auspices of the Bureau of Indian Affairs under the U.S. Department of the Interior. The Bureau may grant additional benefits to tribes, including federally administered health care and educational programs. As tribal communities have become more self-sufficient, programs and services that were once under the authority of the federal government are being assumed by tribal governments.[58] Despite the progress, administrators have the duty to address disproportionately high unemployment, low education attainment, and high rates of adverse health effects.[59]

It is important to understand the rights, especially concerning property and water, of Native populations.[60] Natives face more poverty than any other group; issues of suicide, alcoholism, gangs, and sexual abuse coincide with these issues. These problems are rooted in the paucity of funds available to combat them and are exacerbated by the lack of full sovereignty over lands that contain resources worth upwards of $1.5 trillion. Federal laws make it difficult for tribes to develop these resources, which include radioactive material and practices like uranium mining. While providing jobs, they bring health and environmental hazards.[61]

In *Decolonizing Wealth,*[62] Edgar Villanueva offers ways to improve relations with tribal communities. He offers a seven-stage process: 1) grieve; 2) apologize; 3) listen; 4) relate; 5) represent; 6) invest; and 7) repair. The harmful effects of policies that have trapped Indigenous communities require acknowledgment. To best engage in these steps, Villanueva recommends that administrators learn about cultural norms and follow Indigenous communities' lead. Thus, if the first step is to grieve, grieve with those communities as long as necessary. Apologizing, listening, and relating require patience, openness, and learning. These stages lead to proactive steps. Investing and repairing are actions embedded in social equity and are forward-focused.

Summary of Key Points

Native issues abound in public administration, and as this coverage highlights, the field needs to better acknowledge them. The United States and many other countries have rich Indigenous heritages. Although the age of colonialism is largely in the past, its legacy continues to cause inequities. Administrators can confront these effects by taking proactive steps to, as Susan Gooden puts it, to name, blame, and claim the inequities faced by Native communities.[63]

The Bureau of Indian Affairs marks its 200th year in 2024, making it one of the oldest federal agencies in existence. This statement is neither an endorsement nor a criticism of the BIA, as views of the agency are mixed among Native communities. Rather, it is confirmation of the fact that Native affairs have been intricately tied to policies and programs long enough to deserve far more attention at the intersection of social equity and Native Americans, Alaska Natives, and Native Hawaiians. The story of these Indigenous Americans and their unique status is a story with multiple opportunities for us, as Fredrickson encouraged, to "walk the social equity talk."

Discussion Questions

1. Can the steps involved in other social equity interventions be applied to Native populations? How? What differences arise?
2. What might Villanueva's seven steps look like as concrete, actionable items?
3. How is sovereignty related to social equity? How does it work in favor of those communities who are granted it under legal precedent versus those who are not?
4. In what ways can you develop cultural awareness and cultural competencies related to Native or Indigenous communities? How might the parameters shift from an individual role to a management or leadership role on behalf of a government agency?

Additional Resource

Cornell Law School's Legal Information Institute's summary of American Indian Law: https://www.law.cornell.edu/wex/american_indian_law

Notes

1. H. George Fredrickson, "The State of Social Equity in American Public Administration," *National Civic Review* 94, no. 4 (2005): 31–38.
2. There are misconceptions that this term is offensive. Based on the author's fieldwork, it is a widely accepted term. However, many Native individuals would rather be identified by their tribal heritage or affiliation, such as Lumbee, Cherokee, Zuni, Lakota, and so forth.
3. Some Native Hawaiians prefer the term *aboriginal* to *Indigenous*, though many others embrace "Indigenous," especially in terms of showing solidarity with Indigenous peoples in North America and in other parts of the world.
4. Kevin Gover, personal interview, November 2016.
5. Roxanne Dunbar-Ortiz, *An Indigenous Peoples' History of the United States* (Boston, MA: Beacon Press, 2014).
6. The traditional Hawaiian spelling of "Hawai'i" is with the *'okina* or apostrophe, as a separator of vocalizations. The traditional spelling often refers to the Kingdom and Hawai'i Island, or the Big Island. Over the years, the 'okina was gradually lost in government document usage.
7. See U.S. Public Law 103-150 (107 Stat. 1510), https://www.govinfo.gov/content/pkg/STATUTE-107/pdf/STATUTE-107-Pg1510.pdf
8. See Jennifer A. Kagan and John C. Ronquillo, "*Ho'oponopono* and the *Kānaka Maoli*: The Elusive Quest for Social Equity in the Hawaiian Islands." In *Social Equity in the Asia-Pacific Region: Conceptualizations and Realities*, ed. Morgen Johansen (New York: Palgrave McMillan, 2019), 45–60.
9. Dunbar-Ortiz, *An Indigenous Peoples' History of the United States.* Kagan and Ronquillo, "*Ho'oponopono* and the *Kānaka Maoli*: The Elusive Quest for Social Equity in the Hawaiian Islands."
10. Rosita Worl, personal interview, October 2016.
11. Stephen Cornell and Joseph P. Kalt, "Two Approaches to the Development of Native Nations." In *Rebuilding Native Nations: Strategies for Governance and Development*, ed. Miriam Jorgensen, 3–33, (Tucson, AZ: The University of Arizona Press, 2007), 3–33.
12. *Johnson v. McIntosh* 21 U.S. (8. Wheat) 543 (1823).
13. *Cherokee Nation v. Georgia*, 30 U.S. (5. Pet.) 1 (1831).
14. *Worcester v. Georgia*, 31 U.S. (6 Pet.) 515 (1832).
15. *United States v. Kagama*, 118 U.S. 375 (1886).
16. "Hawaiian Homes Commission Act," Department of Hawaiian Home Lands, https://dhhl.hawaii.gov/hhc/laws-and-rules/
17. Theodore W. Taylor, *The States and Their Indian Citizens.* (Washington, DC: U.S. Government Printing Office, 1972), 168.
18. Leonard A. Carlson, *Indians, Bureaucrats, and Land: The Dawes Act and the Decline of Indian Farming* (Westport, CT: Greenwood Press, 1981).
19. The Metlakatla Indian Community of the Annette Islands Is the Only Reserve in the State of Alaska. See www.metlakatla.com
20. See Monica E. Thomas, "The Alaska Native Claims

Settlement Act: Conflict and Controversy." *Polar Record*, 23, no. 142 (1986): 27–36 and Jennifer LaFleur and Michael Grabell, "What Are Alaska Native Corporations?" *ProPublica* (December 15, 2010), https://www.propublica.org/article/what-are-alaska-native-corporations

21. Freddy Monares, "Native Tribes Celebrate Montana Land Ownership and Bison Range Restoration," *National Public Radio*, May 25, 2022, https://www.npr.org/2022/05/25/1100823011/native-tribes-celebrate-montana-land-ownership-and-bison-range-restoration
22. The Indian Child Welfare Act of 1978 (Pub. L. 95-608, 92 Stat. 3069).
23. See https://www.bloodmemorydoc.com/
24. See http://www.wearecominghome.com/
25. See https://www.icwafamilylaw.com/mark-d-fiddler/
26. *Adoptive Couple v. Baby Girl*, 570 U.S. 637 (2013).
27. *Haaland v. Brackeen*. Oyez, www.oyez.org/cases/2022/21-376, accessed December 2, 2023.
28. "Treaties Still Matter: The Dakota Access Pipeline," *Native Knowledge 360*, https://americanindian.si.edu/nk360/plains-treaties/dapl.cshtml
29. "Fort Laramie Treaty, 1868," *PBS, New Perspectives on the West*, https://www.pbs.org/weta/thewest/resources/archives/four/ftlaram.htm
30. *United States v. Sioux Nation of Indians*, 448 U.S. 371 (1980), https://supreme.justia.com/cases/federal/us/448/371/
31. "For the Future: Doing Indigenous History After Standing Rock," *Perspectives on History*, (March 9, 2018), https://www.historians.org/publications-and-directories/perspectives-on-history/march-2018/for-the-future-doing-indigenous-history-after-standing-rock
32. "Trump Seeks to Revive Dakota Access, Keystone XL Oil Pipelines," *Washington Post* (January 24, 2017), https://www.washingtonpost.com/news/energy-environment/wp/2017/01/24/trump-gives-green-light-to-dakota-access-keystone-xl-oil-pipelines/
33. "Police Remove Last Standing Rock Protesters in Military-Style Takeover," *The Guardian* (February 23, 2017), https://www.theguardian.com/us-news/2017/feb/23/dakota-access-pipeline-camp-cleared-standing-rock
34. See link: https://www.nwo.usace.army.mil/Media/News-Releases/Article/3519719/usace-seeks-public-comments-on-dapl-draft-environmental-impact-statement/
35. "Shutdown Puts Strain on Hundreds of Native American Tribes," *PBS NewsHour* (January 13, 2019), https://www.pbs.org/newshour/nation/shutdown-puts-strain-on-hundreds-of-native-american-tribes?fbclid=IwAR34OUf17bfP1QeS7r9BI-Wrlw-ZrvaiC_-TuyRLDc5GqUiley-n_3CKAhqA
36. "Shutdown Leaves Food, Medicine and Pay in Doubt in Indian Country," *New York Times* (January 1, 2019), https://www.nytimes.com/2019/01/01/us/native-american-government-shutdown.html
37. "Rep. Sharice Davids Talks Impact of Government Shutdown on Native Americans," *NPR* (January 6, 2019), https://www.npr.org/2019/01/06/682607990/rep-sharice-davids-talks-impact-of-government-shutdown-on-native-americans?fbclid=IwAR3lUGNp-KrDA5EMlt6VXTqkHtZPnCNqmKztvfFDJv5y-jT52sMHdCj0EkNxM
38. "FY 2019 HHS Contingency Staffing Plan for Operations in the Absence of Enacted Annual Agriculture and Interior Appropriations," U.S. Department of Health and Human Services, https://www.hhs.gov/about/budget/fy-2019-hhs-contingency-staffing-plan/index.html
39. *McGirt v. Oklahoma*, 591 U.S. __ (2020).
40. "McGirt v. Oklahoma," Oyez, https://argument2.oyez.org/2020/mcgirt-v-oklahoma/
41. *United States v. Cooley*, 593 U.S. __ (2021).
42. "Diane Humetewa, Confirmed to Federal Bench, Makes History," *Indian Country Today* (May 15, 2014), https://newsmaven.io/indiancountrytoday/archive/diane-humetewa-confirmed-to-federal-bench-makes-history-yq9JQViqdEGhOxS_adBLXQ/
43. "Humetewa, Diane Joyce," Federal Judicial Center, https://www.fjc.gov/history/judges/humetewa-diane-joyce
44. See https://www.abqjournal.com/news/local/herrell-wins-hard-fought-2nd-congressional-district-race/article_aea6a5af-4f02-562e-82b0-5258db7267db.html
45. See https://www.doi.gov/secretary-deb-haaland
46. The growth of Native American representation in state legislatures is captured best at: http://www.ncsl.org/research/state-tribal-institute/national-caucus-native-american-state-legislators.aspx
47. "Valerie Davidson, Alaska's New Lieutenant Governor, Has a Long History Fighting for Native Issues," *Anchorage Daily News* (October 16, 2018), https://www.adn.com/alaska-news/rural-alaska/2018/10/16/valerie-davidson-alaskas-new-lieutenant-governor-has-long-history-fighting-for-native-issues/
48. The White House, "FACT SHEET: Biden-"Harris Administration Announces New Actions to Support Indian Country and Native Communities Ahead of the Administration's Second Tribal Nations Sum-

mit," https://www.whitehouse.gov/briefing-room/statements-releases/2022/11/30/fact-sheet-biden-harris-administration-announces-new-actions-to-support-indian-country-and-native-communities-ahead-of-the-administrations-second-tribal-nations-summit/

49. Francis Paul Prucha, *Indian Policy in the United States: Historical Essays*. (Lincoln, NE: University of Nebraska Press, 1981). Paul Stuart, *The Indian Office: Growth and Development of an American Institution, 1865–1900.* (Ann Arbor, MI: UMI Research Press, 1979).
50. Steven E. Aufrecht, "Missing: Native American Governance in American Public Administration Literature." *American Review of Public Administration,* 29, no. 4 (1999): 370–390.
51. John C. Ronquillo, "American Indian Tribal Governance and Management: Public Administration Promise or Pretense?" *Public Administration Review*, 71, no. 2 (2011): 285–292.
52. Dolores Brosnan, "Indian Policy, Indian Gaming, and the Future of Tribal Economic Development." *American Review of Public Administration,* 26, no. 2 (1996): 213–229. Thaddieus Conner and William A. Taggart. "Assessing the Impact of Indian Gaming on American Indian Nations: Is the House Winning?" *Social Science Quarterly*, 94, no. 2 (2013):1016–1044.
53. Thaddieus Conner, "Collaboration and Indian Education: Exploring Intergovernmental Partnerships between Tribes and Public Schools." *Journal of American Indian Education*, 53, no. 2 (2014): 48–65.
54. Mellie Haider and Manuel P. Teodoro, "Environmental Federalism in Indian Country: Sovereignty, Primacy, and Environmental Protection." *Policy Studies Journal*, 49, no. 3 (2021): 887–908. Manuel P. Teodoro, Mellie Haider, and David Switzer, "U.S. Environmental Policy Implementation on Tribal Lands: Trust, Neglect, and Justice." *Policy Studies Journal*, 46, no. 1 (2018): 37–59.
55. Lorinda Riley and Morgen Johansen, "Creating Valuable Indigenous Learning Environments." *Journal of Public Affairs Education*, 45, no. 3 (2018): 387–411.
56. James Ortiz, "Tribal Governance and Public Administration," *Administration & Society*, 34 no. 5 (2002): 459–481.
57. Taylor, *The States and Their Indian Citizens*, 125.
58. Alyce S. Adams, Andrew J. Lee, and Michael Lipsky, "Governmental Services and Programs: Meeting Citizens' Needs." In *Rebuilding Native Nations: Strategies for Governance and Development*, ed. Miriam Jorgensen (Tucson, AZ: The University of Arizona Press, 2007), 223–245.
59. Adams, Lee, and Lipsky, "Governmental Services and Programs: Meeting Citizens' Needs." Laura E. Evans, *Power from Powerlessness: Tribal Governments, Institutional Niches, and American Federalism* (Oxford, UK: Oxford University Press, 2011).
60. Naomi Schaefer Riley, "One Way to Help Native Americans: Property Rights," *The Atlantic*, July 30, 2016, https://www.theatlantic.com/politics/archive/2016/07/native-americans-property-rights/492941/
61. Shawn E. Regan and Terry L. Anderson, "The Energy Wealth of Indian Nations," *LSU Journal of Energy Law and Resources* 3, no. 1 (2014): 195–223. Doug Brugge and Rob Goble, "The History of Uranium Mining and the Navajo People," *American Journal of Public Health* 92, no. 9 (2002): 1410–1419.
62. Edgar Villanueva, *Decolonizing Wealth: Indigenous Wisdom to Heal Divides and Restore Balance* (Oakland, CA: Berrett-Koehler Publishers, Inc., 2018).
63. Susan T. Gooden, *Race and Social Equity: A Nervous Area of Government* (New York: Routledge, 2014).

7 IMMIGRATION AND SOCIAL EQUITY CHALLENGES

Pamela Medina

From the Editors

Throughout U.S. history the nation has relied on immigrants at the same time it erects roadblocks to them. Medina describes the U.S. immigrant population and the various statuses they fall into under U.S. law, along with the barriers they face in terms of legal, administrative, linguistic, and cultural obstacles. She follows by suggesting promising strategies, such as immigrant integration via one-stop shops of information and services, expanded voting rights, greater bureaucratic representation, and more reliance on nonprofit partnerships that serve as a safe bridge between government and immigrants.

Border security remains one of the top issues facing parties interested in immigration reform. Although the United States is well known as a nation of immigrants, newcomers face increasing inequities at the intersection of border security and immigration inequity. Here is a case that describes the detention of bus passengers traveling within American borders:

> As a component of border security, under federal law, checks for citizenship documents can take place within 100 miles of any American land or water border. After attention caused by a series of viral videos of Customs and Border Patrol (CBP) agents boarding buses and trains, Greyhound, the nation's largest intercity bus operator, was sued by the state of Washington for allowing CBP to conduct warrantless searches on its buses. Although freedom from unnecessary search and seizure is guaranteed under the Fourth Amendment, these warrantless searches have been permitted under questionable cause for immigrants and non-immigrants alike. In Spokane alone, up to 250 passengers were detained as part of these searches. Greyhound was ordered to pay $2.2 million in restitution to passengers, and as of 2020 will no longer allow CBP to conduct immigration checks on its buses (which are private property).[1]

As political division grows, immigrant populations are subject to ever-evolving policy changes on both ends of the political spectrum. This chapter explores these social equity issues. The chapter begins with an overview of the history and context of immigrant inequities, followed by relevant laws impacting immigration issues, a brief discussion of political influences, and exploration of administrative issues contributing to immigrant inequity. The chapter concludes with pathways to action, including promising practices as well as validated and implemented practices that improve immigrant equity in the United States.

History and Context

Limitations on who and how many can legally immigrate have existed in the United States since 1790. Although much attention currently focuses on immigration from the southern border, immigration trends have varied through history as have the policies set in place to encourage and restrict it. Prior to 1965, for instance, immigration policy was generally based on a strategy of controlled growth limited by so-called "desired" nationalities, races, and political preferences. These policies emphasized migration from Great Britain, and Northern and Western Europe. Newer policies replaced the priority on national origin with an emphasis on family reunification and employment-based visas for skilled immigrants. Since then, immigration has been on the rise with immigrants accounting for 13.6% of the population, or 45.3 million people, in the United States as of 2020.[2]

As of 2021, immigration from Asia is most on the rise, with immigrants from China, India, the Philippines, Vietnam, and Korea accounting for approximately 20% of all immigrants. Despite the rise among immigrants from Asia, those from Mexico remain the largest group at 23.6% of all immigrants.[3]

While the term "immigrant" is broadly used to refer to any person residing in the United States who was not born with citizenship, policy debates, regulatory issues, and social equity approaches are further nuanced based on legal status. The current legal classifications of immigrants fall into three categories: Permanent Resident Aliens, Naturalized Citizens, and Undocumented Immigrants.

Permanent Resident Aliens, otherwise known as Lawful Permanent Residents, are issued visas by the Department of State and granted permanent resident status by the Department of Homeland Security (DHS). These statuses are not to be confused with temporary resident visas, which are granted for interim stays such as those for students and temporary workers. Visas for permanent residents, sometimes known as green cards, are only granted under strictly outlined purposes, primarily including family or employment sponsorships.[4]

Family sponsors are required to demonstrate that they can financially support their relatives, and applicants must meet all U.S. admission requirements. To gain a visa through an employment sponsorship, the employer must arrange a competitive search and demonstrate that the applicant has an extraordinary ability or skill that cannot be filled by an employee already residing in the United States. There are also a small number of diversity visas (50,000), sometimes known as the visa lottery, available to people from countries with historically low rates of immigration to the United States. In 2018, there were over 14 million qualified entries to the Diversity Visa Program, meaning less than 0.4% of applicants were awarded a visa through this program.[5]

Additional categories of special status admissions, classified under humanitarian programs, are also available and can lead to permanent resident status if approved. These are legal entries for refugees, asylum seekers, victims of human trafficking, and other special circumstances. The general purpose of these entries is to provide refuge to those who are unable to remain in, or return to, their home countries for fear of persecution.

Unlike refugees who apply for entry while in their home countries, asylum seekers make requests at official points of entry or when they are apprehended after border crossing. Because asylum seekers are legally entitled to a court hearing to present their claims, they are permitted to remain in the United States while they await adjudication. As a result, there have been recent efforts aimed at reducing the number of asylum seekers, including keeping asylum seekers in detention while they await their court date.[6] In 2018, 41.4% of asylum cases were denied, 20.5% were granted, and the remaining cases were closed for a variety of reasons.[7]

Refugees and asylum seekers are the bulk of immigrants who are granted visas through humanitarian programs, although there are a number of other programs within this category. These programs include, for example, the Cuban Family Reunification Program and the Filipino World War II Veterans Parole Program.[8] In 2017, family visas accounted for approximately 66% of all lawful permanent resident visas, while refugees and asylum seekers (13%), employment visas (12%), and diversity visas (5%), represented smaller shares.[9]

After earning permanent resident status, immigrants are eligible to apply for citizenship through a process of naturalization. In order to qualify, an applicant undergoes a criminal background check conducted by the Federal Bureau of Investigation (FBI), attends a naturalization interview, and must pass a civics exam demonstrating a level of understanding of American history and government. With some exemptions,[10] applicants must also demonstrate working knowledge of the English language. This application process is currently estimated to take 10 months after permanent resident status is met per requirements outlined in the previous section. In 2021, the United States naturalized 809,100 applicants.[11] Naturalization is not required for permanent residency except for those under certain humanitarian circumstances.

The final category of immigrants consists of those entering or remaining in the United States without governmental approval. Reflecting their lack of legal status, they are labeled as undocumented, unlawful, unauthorized, or illegal. Included in this category are those who cross borders illegally, asylum seekers who do not attend their court hearings, and overstays of temporary visas. Of the approximately 45 million immigrants residing in the United States in 2019, 28% were lawful permanent residents, 45% were naturalized citizens, and 23% were undocumented.[12]

Scope of Social Equity Issues

As an inherently diverse group, immigrants face diverse challenges in their journeys to the United States, as well as in their establishment as new residents and beyond. Differential treatment of immigrants stems from a variety of reasons, from xenophobia and racism, to poor cultural competence, to lack of understanding of unique needs, to administrative barriers that produce inequitable outcomes. The following section reviews examples of some of these challenges as they relate to access, process, quality, and outcomes.

Benefit Eligibility

Immigrants—even those who are undocumented—pay federal, state, and local taxes. Nevertheless, many public programs exclude both lawful and undocumented immigrants in their eligibility requirements. For instance, only 29 states allow legal resident children and pregnant women to qualify for Medicaid and the Children's Health Insurance Program (CHIP) without a five-year waiting period. Legal Permanent Residents are also ineligible to receive Supplemental Security Income (SSI) and Temporary Assistance for Needy Families (TANF) benefits.

In another materialization of this issue, immigrants are often hesitant to use benefits for which they are eligible, lest they be considered public charges. For instance, one study found that immigrants were so "fearful to access recovery aid after Hurricane Harvey in the Fall of 2017 [that they were] often living in horrific conditions as a result, even though any household with a U.S. citizen or green card holder is eligible for FEMA assistance."[13]

Civic Engagement

Since 1996 it has been a crime for non-citizens to vote in federal elections and only in a small number of communities are noncitizens permitted to vote in local elections. This has unique implications for immigrant inclusion because it means that political candidates and elected officials have little incentive to reach out to them. While other forms of civic engagement are available, such as volunteering, signing petitions, and joining civic groups, these have their own barriers. For instance, some undocumented immigrants are fearful of being asked about their legal status, or they fear their engagement in politicized events will be held against them when they become eligible to pursue a path to citizenship.

Civic engagement becomes a habit early in life for native youth but not for immigrant youth. For example, a 2008 study comparing immigrant and native youth engagement found that young immigrants tended to be less engaged in civic activities, including volunteerism.[14] This implies that immigrants face challenges in accessing and engaging with public officials and civil society in their youth and it is likely this carries on into adulthood.

Language Barriers

Immigrants from all countries and of all identities confront additional challenges related to access, regardless of their legal status. Language is one such challenge. Data from 2017 estimate that only 52% of the foreign-born population in the United States are English proficient.[15] This creates barriers to both access and service quality. A 2012 study by the U.S. Department of Health and Human Services (HHS) noted that administrators were in urgent need of more bilingual staff so they could better serve immigrants.[16]

Although Spanish is becoming more common, English continues to dominate service delivery information, especially online. The demand for more diverse, multilingual staff, and multilingual materials continues. It is not unusual for service providers to rely on untrained interpreters, such as friends or children, to communicate with immigrant clients.[17] This raises issues with information accuracy, as well as privacy, particularly in health-related interactions.

Transportation and program eligibility are also areas where language challenges arise. Immigrants often rely on friends or family to provide transportation, particularly among undocumented immigrants who live in states that require proof of legal status to obtain driver's licenses. Furthermore, for public programs they may be eligible for, immigrants with limited language proficiency must navigate complex eligibility requirements that are challenging even for native English speakers. Just becoming aware of programs that could help them is a challenge. Awareness of such programs is often gained through word of mouth, which can be problematic for immigrants who are recent arrivals or for those for whom there are few others who speak their language.[18]

Cultural Barriers

Providing culturally competent service remains an important charge for service providers, particularly because such services help to build trust within the immigrant population. For example, a study of police officers indicated communication difficulties when serving immigrants. These are related to both verbal and nonverbal behavior, including eye contact and expectations surrounding gender norms.[19] Because immigrants are often fearful of law enforcement, building trust through cultural competency is important to ensure these communities feel safe reporting crimes when they occur.

Access, quality, and procedural inequities, coupled with individual challenges that led immigrants to leave their home countries, produce disparities in outcomes that vary across immigrant groups. For instance, Mexican immigrants are the least likely of all immigrants to achieve a bachelor's degree or higher (6%), while immigrants from South and East Asia are more likely (52%) than natural-born citizens (32%) to attain a bachelor's degree or higher.[20] Furthermore, immigrants, particularly those living in suburbs, experience higher rates of poverty than do natural-born citizens.[21] Taken together, these factors and variabilities contribute to inherent disparities in social equity.

Laws and Politics

The immigration debate largely stems from border security, economic impact, and humanitarian concerns. According to a 2021 Gallup poll, 75% of surveyed Americans believed that immigration was good for the United States, while a majority also believed that illegal immigration is a significant threat to national security. These dueling perceptions highlight the tensions in the immigration debate.[22] Immigration laws are made at the federal level and Congress has been unable to reach a consensus on what laws should allow and what they should restrict. This congressional impasse has stalled any omnibus immigration legislation since 1986 when President Reagan granted the last legal amnesty to undocumented residents. More focused laws and executive orders have created a patchwork of legal attempts to address immigration issues. Examples of these measures include:

- Title VII of the Civil Rights Act of 1964 prohibits discrimination in hiring based on national origin; The Immigration and Nationality Act prohibits discrimination against not only U.S. citizens, but also legal permanent residents and temporary residents, refugees, and asylees with legal authorization to work.
- REAL ID Act "establishes statutory guidelines for removal cases, expands the terrorism-related grounds for inadmissibility and deportation, (and) includes measures to improve border infrastructure." The REAL ID Act also requires verification of legal status before a driver's license or personal identification card can be issued that would be accepted for federal purposes.
- 2012 Deferred Action for Childhood Arrivals (DACA) allows deferred action for two years for people who came to the United States as children. It allows them to remain and request work authorization after meeting certain guidelines.
- Executive Order 13769 (in effect from January 27 2017 to March 6, 2017) known as the Trump travel ban, lowered the number of refugees admitted into the United States and suspended entry from certain Muslim-majority countries.
- E-Verify is an internet-based system comparing an employee's employment eligibility information to information in records stored by the U.S. Department of Homeland Security and the Social Security Administration. Use of E-Verify is required in some states and not in others.

Furthermore, case law influences the enforcement of immigration laws at the state level. In the case of *Arizona v. United States* (2012), the state of Arizona attempted to pass a law giving state officers the authority to make warrantless arrests of aliens presumed to be deportable. In hearing the case, the U.S. Supreme Court ruled that this was not within the scope of responsibility for a state government without instruction from the federal government. Furthermore, the Court ruled that officers requesting immigration documentation could not consider race, color, or national origin in their requests for documents.[23]

Courts have also been instrumental in setting the basis for detention and deportation regulations. For instance, in *Jennings v. Rodriguez* (2018), the court determined that immigrants held in detention awaiting deportation proceedings do not have a statutory right to periodic bond hearings.[24] In *Maslenjak v. United States* (2017), the Supreme Court ruled that naturalized citizens could be stripped of their citizenship for making false statements to government officials, if these statements influenced the process of obtaining citizenship.[25]

A number of other cases have also determined the crimes under which lawful permanent residents (LPRs)can be deported. These provide precedents for defining federal immigration statutes that permit deportation for noncitizens who commit aggravated felonies. For example, both burglary and driving under the influence fall outside of the scope of "aggravated felonies" in specific circumstances.[26] These cases, all decided after the year 2000, demonstrate the ways that immigrant rights are nuanced by particular circumstances.

At the state level, politics influence perceptions of immigrants, the availability of state resources, as well as enforcement of penalties. An example is found in Florida Senate Bill 1718 which takes strict action against employers who knowingly hire undocumented immigrants. It also creates harsh penalties for those using false identification, adds a citizenship question in hospital admissions where Medicaid is accepted, and does not allow undocumented immigrants with out-of-state driver licenses to drive in the State of Florida.[27]

Inter-state tensions around immigration also contribute to immigrant inequities. For instance, "Republican governors of Texas and Arizona have previously sent thousands of migrants on buses to New York, Chicago, and Washington DC…[additionally, groups] were approached in El Paso by people with Florida-linked paperwork, sent to New Mexico, then put on private flights to California."[28] In the most prominent case, the State of Florida used funds from its $12 million migrant relocation initiative to fly South American migrants from Texas to Martha's Vineyard, Massachusetts.[29] These cases highlight the tensions between federal and state-level policy. Although immigration enforcement is technically restricted to the federal government, state-level policies greatly contribute to the immigrant experience.

Management

Administrative barriers also constitute challenges when it comes to accessing equitable services. For example, many immigrants find it difficult to acquire the significant amounts of documentation necessary to demonstrate program eligibility. Moreover, lack of standardization across programs means applicants must file different forms for different services, which complicates rather than expedites the application process.

Even those responsible for collecting applications get confused. HHS found that administrators did not always understand immigration document requirements. The department also found that managers lacked guidance on how to enter data into outdated systems. For instance, many caseworkers were not familiar with naming conventions and did not know how to enter hyphenated last names. This resulted in procedural issues for applicants whose names did not match across documents.[30] This is an example of how cultural competence influences both the management of programs as well as service delivery for immigrants of all legal statuses.

Another consideration in terms of access and process is that immigrants may be fearful of interactions with the government. Even when they are eligible for benefits, some fear that taking advantage of them may put them in the category of being public charges. Or, they feel it necessary to stay "under the radar" rather than risk creating issues for undocumented family members. For all these reasons—administrative burdens, cultural competence, and distrust of government—programs where immigrants are beneficiaries should take heed of the immigrant experience as noted in pathways to action.

Pathways to Action

Given the aforementioned challenges facing immigrants, this section presents pathways to action that have been taken to improve equity. These include one-stop shops for services and information, initiatives that provide voting rights and belongingness, cultural competency training, greater representation of the immigrant experience among government staff, and partnerships with nonprofits for delivering services.

Immigrant Integration Offices

While federal policies set immigration standards, the process of integration occurs "at the local level, primarily through the efforts of families, employers, schools, churches, and communities."[31] Integration here is not defined as a one-way process wherein immigrants abandon their culture to adopt that of their new home. It is a process that occurs within a community when both immigrants and the community combine to acknowledge and accept one another as members of a collective. The goal of effective integration is for immigrants to engage in the life of the community, for them to feel accepted, and for others to see them as belonging.

Interestingly, unlike other countries, the United States does not have a department or office dedicated to immigrant integration. Cities pick up the slack. A 2021 study of U.S. cities with the largest shares of immigrants revealed that 68% had offices dedicated to immigrant affairs either at the city or county level.[32] For example, Aurora, Colorado, Houston, Texas, and San Francisco, California all have offices dedicated to immigrant issues. Houston has its "Office of New Americans" and San Francisco has its "Office of Civic Engagement and Immigrant Affairs." These offices offer citizenship, legal, and economic assistance, as well as integration activities such as translation services and community-building events. And, they usually make clear that they do not report immigration status to federal offices.

More specifically, Houston's "Office of New Americans" offers an immigration rights hotline with information about public safety, education, and health care, and it partners with the United Way to provide emergency information related to childcare, food, and shelter. Offices such as this offer a one-stop shop for information and services for immigrants where they know they are welcome. They can receive a variety of services and do not have to be fearful of government interaction.

Expanded Voting Rights and Public Participation

Limitations on voting are a legal barrier that prevents noncitizen immigrants from full inclusion in American communities. Interestingly, these limitations are relatively new developments. Up until World War I, some states allowed noncitizens to vote in elections. Noncitizen voting in federal elections was only made a crime in 1996.[33] Arguments in support of voting rights stipulate that immigrants bear responsibilities of citizenship, including paying taxes; therefore, they should be permitted to have formal representation of their interests. Furthermore, voting has long been considered an aspect of civic integration, reflecting inclusion as full members of society.[34] Indeed, arguments in favor of noncitizen voting often emphasize the importance of ethical citizenship and civic engagement, defining a citizen as any inhabitant who belongs to a community and has a responsibility to participate in its deliberations.[35]

In recent history, a number of cities have allowed noncitizens to vote in local elections, and proposals for these measures are beginning to resurface. For example, in November 2016, San Francisco began to experiment with noncitizen voting by passing a proposition extending voting rights for San Francisco School Board Elections to noncitizen residents. This extension includes documented as well as undocumented immigrants who are legally recognized guardians of children living in the city.[36,37] Such an expansion of admittedly limited enfranchisement has implications for immigrant inclusion, particularly because schools have long been vessels for integration and assimilation.[37] However, undocumented immigrants were advised that Immigration and Customs Enforcement (ICE) might gain access to registration records, which makes it unlikely that this particular subcategory of immigrants will exercise their new suffrage.

Cultural Competency Training

Cultural competence can be defined as "a set of congruent behaviors, attitudes, and policies that come together in a system, agency, or among professionals and enable that system, agency, or those professionals to work effectively in cross-cultural situations."[38] Cultural competence is demonstrated by measures such as adapting curricula, translating program materials, removing obstacles to accessibility, and training in interpersonal communication. While adapting to the culture of target populations is positively associated with increased program effectiveness, social service providers still report cultural dilemmas.[39] In an examination of the Latino Family Child Care Program, Uttal argues that multiple changes are necessary, beyond the typical language and cultural adaptations.[40] Uttal suggests moving from culturally adapted programming to culturally specific programming, noting:

> In culturally adapted programs, the examples that are used to teach the main lessons are transformed to respect the target culture's practices. For example, exercises that require a lot of writing would be replaced with oral exercises in a program for people with an orally expressive culture . . . . In culturally specific programs, the transformations go beyond adding culturally adapted components . . . [wherein] the design of the program integrates the target group's values and beliefs . . . . For example, in a culture that does not verbally express self-emotions, the expectation for people to talk about themselves is dropped.[41]

Culturally specific competency also includes consideration of the target population's social characteristics when programs are being designed.[42] Such considerations include cultural values, income, education, acculturation, and family systems, The legal context also influences the success of social services, but is often overlooked, even when the predominant target groups are largely comprised of families of immigrants. For instance, Uttal finds that new immigrant populations have specific needs that are unrecognized including wariness over engaging with government, even if they are documented, because they worry about background checks on their family members who may be undocumented. Specifically, among the Latino population that Uttal studied, immigration policy information needed to be added, as well as the ability to use tax identification numbers in lieu of social security numbers for identification to ensure that the social service was accessible. Thus, culturally specific competence is an important contributor to equitable outcomes from service delivery.

Experiential Representative Bureaucracy

Representative bureaucracy theory argues that the public service workforce should, in essence, "look" like the people it serves. Public administrators fill a critical role in reflecting the population. While representative bureaucracy literature has studied gender, race, and ethnicity to a greater extent, to date there is little research on immigrants as a representative group. One major study finds that over an 18-year period, only 7% to 10% of foreign-born individuals were employed by government.[43] The study further finds that, as the number of immigrant ancestors increases, which is a measure of lack of familial connectivity to the United States, the likelihood of government employment also decreases. Further, although they account for the largest immigrant group in the United States, the immigrant experience among Hispanics contributes to a statistically significant decline in the likelihood of government employment.[44] This indicates that the immigrant experience is underrepresented in the American bureaucracy.

These findings are noteworthy, as representative bureaucracy has been linked to a number of differential outcomes. For instance, racial representative bureaucracy can explain youth arrests among minority groups.[45] Further, gender representation in police forces helps to explain the willingness on the part of female victims to report sex crimes,[46] and even policy and budget priorities can be more supportive of minoritized groups when there are higher levels of representation in decision-making positions.[47]

Experiential representative bureaucracy, or representation of those with lived experience similar to the population being served, presents a unique opportunity for improving immigrant service delivery. These employees will be more attuned to the unique needs of the immigrant population and will have ties with those who are impacted by a variety of immigration contexts.

Nonprofit Partnerships for Immigrant Services

Nonprofit organizations serve as important intermediaries between the populations they serve, the community, and government. Because immigrants are often in unique and even precarious situations, they may be hesitant to engage with government directly. For this reason, nonprofit partnerships provide a bridge, assisting with access and improving service quality in the process. In a 2019 study of immigrant-serving nonprofits in Los Angeles, Lee found that noncitizens are especially wary of engaging with government, particularly within the planning space.[48] Learning from a series of interviews, the author suggests partnerships with nonprofits, which provide a safe space to meet and engage with immigrant groups while also assuring cultural competence. Nonprofit providers are better equipped to work with diverse groups, provide tailored services, serve areas where there are gaps in benefit eligibility for immigrants, provide political representation where it may be lacking such as speaking on behalf of immigrants, and provide alternative spaces for engagement. Furthermore, nonprofit collaboration diminishes safety fears for those concerned about deportation.

Summary of Key Points

This chapter has outlined important issues associated with immigrant equity, ranging from warrantless searches to complicated visa policies to exclusionary benefits to barriers to civic engagement. Lack of omnibus immigration reform since the 1980s has resulted in a patchwork of policies. The patchwork contributes to disparities and inequity within the immigrant community. These disparities result in challenges for public administrators tasked with serving immigrant populations. However, opportunities exist to improve equity through targeted integration efforts, expanded voting rights, culturally specific programming, greater bureaucratic representation, and building nonprofit partnerships for delivering services to immigrants.

Discussion Questions

1. Although the United States does not have a central office for immigrant integration, many state and local level governments do. Explore what is available in your city, county, or state. What types of services are provided? What types of services are needed? Should government be responsible for administering these services?

2. Nonprofit organizations provide a number of services to communities. Visit the website of one of the larger nonprofit service providers in your area. Imagine that you are an immigrant

in need of this service. How well does the organization market its services to immigrant groups? Consider eligibility, access, and awareness of the systems in which these services operate.

3. Some states offer driver's licenses to undocumented immigrants (you can see a map of these variations in the additional resource below). What are the pros and cons of offering licenses or state-issued identification cards to the undocumented population?

Additional Resource

To see which states offer driver licenses to undocumented residents visit https://www.ncsl.org/immigration/states-offering-drivers-licenses-to-immigrants

Notes

1. Johnny Diaz, "Greyhound to Stop Allowing Border Patrol Agents on Its Buses Without Warrants," *New York Times,* February 22, 2020, https://www.nytimes.com/2020/02/22/us/greyhound-border-patrol.html
2. Abby Budiman, "Key Findings about U.S. Immigrants," Pew Research Center, August 20, 2020. https://www.pewresearch.org/short-reads/2020/08/20/key-findings-about-u-s-immigrants/
3. Migration Policy Institute (MPI) tabulation of data from U.S. Census Bureau, 2010, 2019, and 2021 American Community Surveys (ACS), and 2000 Decennial Census; data for 1960 to 1990 are from Campbell J. Gibson and Emily Lennon, 'Historical Census Statistics on the Foreign-Born Population of the United States: 1850 to 1990" (Working Paper No. 29, U.S. Census Bureau, Washington, DC, 1999).
4. United States Department of State, "The Immigrant Visa Process," accessed August 2, 2023, https://travel.state.gov/content/travel/en/us-visas/immigrate/the-immigrant-visa-process.html
5. United States Department of State, "Diversity Visa Program, DV 2016-2018: Number of Entries Received during Each Online Registration Period by Country of Chargeability," accessed August 2, 2023, https://travel.state.gov/content/travel/en/us-visas/immigrate/diversity-visa-program-entry/diversity-visa-program-statistics.html
6. Michael D. Shear and Eileen Sullivan, "What Is Asylum and Who Can Seek It? Explaining Trump's New Restrictions," *New York Times* April 17, 2019, https://www.nytimes.com/2019/04/17/us/politics/asylum-facts-seekers-laws.html
7. United States Department of State, "Workload and Adjudication Statistics," July 8, 2019, accessed August 2, 2023 https://www.justice.gov/eoir/workload-and-adjudication-statistics
8. For a full list of humanitarian programs, see https://www.uscis.gov/humanitarian
9. United States Department of Homeland Security, *Annual Flow Report*, August 2018, accessed August 2, 2023, https://www.dhs.gov/sites/default/files/publications/Lawful_Permanent_Residents_2017.pdf
10. For a full list of English Language Exemptions, see: https://www.uscis.gov/us-citizenship/citizenship-through-naturalization/exceptions-accommodations
11. United States Citizenship and Immigration Services, "Naturalization Statistics," accessed August 2, 2023, https://www.uscis.gov/citizenship-resource-center/naturalization-statistics
12. Jeanne Batalova, Mary Hanna, and Christopher Levesque, "Frequently Requested Statistics on Immigrants and Immigration in the United States," migrationpolicy.org, March 17, 2022, https://www.migrationpolicy.org/article/frequently-requested-statistics-immigrants-and-immigration-united-states-2020
13. David M. Greenberg, Sara Fierstein, and Patricia Voltolini, "Supporting the Resilience of America's Immigrant Communities: How Community Organizations Are Responding to Federal Policy Changes," Local Initiatives Support Corporation, January 2019: 7, http://www.lisc.org/media/filer_public/3c/d6/3cd6c801-6931-4e1b-93a7-7a0e825719b4/011419_research_whitepaper_immigration.pdf
14. Mark Hugo Lopez and Karlo Barrios Marcelo, "The Civic Engagement of Immigrant Youth: New Evidence from the 2006 Civic and Political Health of the Nation Survey," *Applied Developmental Science* 12, no. 2 (2008): 66–73.

15. Pew Research Center, "English Proficiency Among U.S. Immigrants, 1980–2017," June 3, 2019, https://www.pewhispanic.org/chart/immigrant-statistical-portrait-english-proficiency-among-u-s-immigrants
16. Krista M. Perreira, Robert Corsnoe, Karina Fortuny, Juan Pedroza, Kjersti Ulvestad, Christina Weiland, Hirokazu Yoshikawa, and Ajay Chaudry, "Barriers to Immigrants' Access to Health and Human Services Programs," Office of the Assistant Secretary for Planning and Evaluation, Office of Human Services Policy, U.S. Department of Health and Human Services, May, 2012, https://aspe.hhs.gov/basic-report/barriers-immigrants-access-health-and-human-services-programs
17. Perreira et al., "Barriers to Immigrants' Access to Health and Human Services Programs."
18. Perreira et al., "Barriers to Immigrants' Access to Health and Human Services Programs."
19. Linda M. Williams, "Beyond Enforcement: Welcomeness, Local Law Enforcement, and Immigrants," *Public Administration Review* 75, no. 3 (2015): 433–442, https://doi.org/10.1111/puar.12335
20. Jynnah Radford and Luis Noe-Bustamante, Luis, "Facts on U.S. Immigrants, 2017," Pew Research Center, June 3, 2019, https://www.pewresearch.org/hispanic/2019/06/03/facts-on-u-s-immigrants-2017-data/
21. Audrey Singer, Roberto Suro, and Jill H. Wilson, "Immigration and Poverty in America's Suburbs," Brookings Institute, August 4, 2011, https://www.brookings.edu/research/immigration-and-poverty-in-americas-suburbs/
22. Gallup, "Immigration," Gallup.com, May 15, 2023, https://news.gallup.com/poll/1660/immigration.aspx
23. *Arizona v. United States*, 567 U.S. 387 (2012).
24. *Jennings et al. v. Rodriguez et al.*, 583 U.S. (2018).
25. *Maslenjak v. United States*, 582 U.S. (2017).
26. *Leocal v. Ashcroft*, 543 U.S. 1 (2004); *Sessions v. Dimaya*, 584 U.S. (2018).
27. "Governor Ron DeSantis Signs Strongest Anti-Illegal Immigration Legislation in the Country to Combat Biden's Border Crisis," Florida Governor Ron DeSantis, accessed July 11, 2023. https://www.flgov.com/2023/05/10/governor-ron-desantis-signs-strongest-anti-illegal-immigration-legislation-in-the-country-to-combat-bidens-border-crisis/
28. Nguyen Truc, and Olga R. Rodriguez, "California Officials: Florida Picked Up Asylum-Seekers on Texas Border and Flew Them to Sacramento," *AP News*, June 6, 2023, https://apnews.com/article/migrants-dropped-off-california-texas-florida-2ea4ea9cc6e976e97358c64bcae164f4
29. Anthony Izaguirre, "DeSantis Signs Immigration Overhaul Ahead of Expected White House Run," *AP News*, May 10, 2023, https://apnews.com/article/florida-desantis-immigration-bill-74d3efde87fe376202ebda74bab123b8
30. Perreira et al., "Barriers to Immigrants' Access to Health and Human Services Programs."
31. Michael Fix, "Immigrant Integration and Comprehensive Immigration Reform: An Overview." In *Securing the Future: U.S. Immigrant Integration Policy, A Reader*, ed. Michael Fix (Washington DC: Migration Policy Institute, 2007): 1.
32. Pamela S. Medina, "The Role of Ethical Citizenship in Advancing Immigrant Integration in the U.S." In *Citizenship and Ethics: From the Neighborhood to the City, Country to the World*, ed. Thomas Bryer and S.S. Jeon (Lanham, MD: Lexington Books, 2021).
33. Voting by Aliens, 18 U.S.C. 611 (1996).
34. Jamin B. Raskin, "Legal Aliens, Local Citizens: The Historical, Constitutional and Theoretical Meanings of Alien Suffrage," *University of Pennsylvania Law Review* 121, no. 4 (1993): 1391–1470.
35. Raskin, "Legal Aliens, Local Citizens."
36. City and County of San Francisco Municipal Elections Code § 128.10 (passed May 22, 2018).
37. Anthony A. Peguero, Jennifer M. Bondy, and Jun Sung Hong, "Social Bonds across Immigrant Generations: Bonding to School and Examining the Relevance of Assimilation," *Youth & Society* 49, no. 6 (2017), https://doi.org/10.1177/0044118X14560335
38. Terry L. Cross, Barbara J. Bazron, Karl W. Dennis, and Mareasa R. Isaacs, "Towards a Culturally Competent System of Care," (Washington, DC: Georgetown University Child Development Center, CASSP Technical Assistance Center): 1, accessed August 2, 2023, https://spu.edu/-/media/academics/school-of-education/Cultural-Diversity/Towards-a-Culturally-Competent-System-of-Care-Abridged.ashx
39. Lynet Uttal, "Organizational Cultural Competency: Shifting Programs for Latino Immigrants from a Client-Centered to a Community-Based Orientation," *American Journal of Community Psychology* 38 (2006): 251–262.
40. Uttal, "Organizational Cultural Competency."
41. Uttal, "Organizational Cultural Competency:" 252.
42. Angela Shartrand, Supporting Latino Families: Lessons from Exemplary Programs, Vol. 2 (Cambridge: Harvard Family Research Project, 1996).
43. Christopher A. Simon and Michael C. Moltz, "Immigrants and Passive Representation in the US Public

Service: 2000–2018," *Administration & Society* 55, no. 3 (2023): 405–427.

44. Simon and Moltz, "Immigrants and Passive Representation in the U.S. Public Service: 2000–2018."
45. William T. Jackson, Milena I. Neshkova, and Kenneth J. Meier, "Justice in Black and Brown: The Impact of Political Control and Representative Bureaucracy on Street Level Outcomes," *Public Administration Review* 83, no. 2 (2023): 333–352.
46. Kenneth J. Meier and Jill Nicholson-Crotty, "Gender, Representative Bureaucracy, and Law Enforcement: The Case of Sexual Assault," *Public Administration Review* 66, no. 6 (2006): 850–860.
47. Sebawit G. Bishu and Alexis R. Kennedy, "Trends and Gaps: A Meta-Review of Representative Bureaucracy," *Review of Public Personnel Administration* 40, no. 4 (2020): 559–588.
48. C. Aujean Lee, "Engaging Non-Citizens in an Age of Uncertainty," *Journal of the American Planning Association*, 85, no. 3 (2019), 271–286, https://doi.org/10.1080/01944363.2019.1616318

8 RACE, ETHNICITY, AND SOCIAL EQUITY IN POLICING

Ty Price Dooley

From the Editors

The first duty of government is to protect its citizens and law enforcement plays a central role. However, the reality for many, especially Black Americans, is anything but safety. Dooley examines racism in U.S. policing, tracing inequities from the nation's founding to the frequent "two steps forward, one step back" impact of laws and politics. Focusing on management of police agencies, the chapter explores police culture, recruitment, training, use of force, and more. Pathways to action include procedural justice training programs, community-oriented policing, implicit bias training, body-worn cameras, and civilian review boards.

Precipitated by societal changes, increasing diversity, and historical racialized disparities in law enforcement, issues of race, ethnicity, and social equity in policing are central to contemporary discourse. This chapter discusses the history and scope of racial and ethnic disparities in policing, analyzes the legal and political dynamics contributing to these inequities, and examines the role of management practices in perpetuating disparities. The central focus is on the experiences of marginalized racial and ethnic groups. Pathways to action are offered, with the aim of achieving a more equitable and just society.

History, Context, and Scope

The relationship between the African American community and law enforcement in the United States forms a labyrinthine tale of realities that are unjust and inequitable. The causes of these inequities are multifaceted and result from systemic biases, individual prejudices, economic disadvantage, and social policy. Stereotyping and implicit bias result in inequalities in stop-and-search practices and use of force incidents.[1] Meanwhile, discriminatory practices in housing, education, and employment have spatially and socially concentrated poverty and crime in certain communities, further aggravating the problem.[2] Research shows that the larger the percentage of African Americans and Hispanics in a community, the greater the likelihood that police will use coercive control strategies in citizen encounters.[3] It is a story as old as the nation itself, an open wound, a profound paradox between the Lockean ideals upon which the U.S. Constitution was founded, and the lived experiences of people of color, particularly African Americans.[4]

The evidence is clear that African Americans face systemic mistreatment. Police are more likely to use force against African Americans than any other racial group.[5] There are significant racial disparities in police-related fatalities in the United States. African Americans, particularly males, face a substantially higher risk of being killed by law enforcement than individuals from other racial or ethnic groups. Even in the absence of justification for deadly force during encounters with police, African Americans are more than twice as likely to be killed.[6] This alarming fact translates to an estimate that about 1 in 1,000 African American males can anticipate a fatal encounter with police—a risk that is 2.5 times greater than that faced by their white male peers.[7] In a review of nearly 100 million traffic stops across the country, researchers found that African American drivers were stopped more frequently than their white counterparts and were less likely to have done something illegal.[8] In fact, the police were almost twice as likely to provide no reason to Black drivers than to their white counterparts as to why they had been stopped.[9] In terms of arrests, African Americans are arrested at significantly higher rates than their white counterparts.[10]

To comprehend the depth of this narrative, we first explore the origins of law enforcement, its evolution, and how the legacy of its practices affects African American communities and their interactions with law enforcement. Racial and ethnic disparities in policing have roots entrenched in structural racism and societal power dynamics.[11] The institution of policing in America began as a mechanism for maintaining racial hierarchy and control, often through brutal means, such as the enforcement of slave laws and later, Jim Crow laws. Historically, law enforcement has played a vital role in maintaining social order.[12] However, this seemingly innocuous function is fraught with implications for communities of color. Prior to the founding, a racial hierarchy was already established in the United States, enshrined in the unjust treatment of non-white populations and the slave labor system, which was restricted to Americans of African descent.[13] Consequently, all 13 colonies deputized Whites to police African Americans, leading to a differential form of justice meted out upon people of color.

Under the Constitution, African Americans were considered property, constituting three-fifths of a person, with few rights, protections, or liberties. This denial of basic human rights and dignity was in stark opposition to the liberal principles of the Constitution and formed a moral paradox that would shape the narrative of law enforcement and its relationship with African Americans. This paradoxical relationship was not isolated to the South; it also prevailed in the North, where police enforced laws that restricted the freedoms of African Americans in almost every facet of life, ranging from voting to owning property.[14]

Post-Civil War dynamics exacerbated the situation. Despite passage of the Thirteenth, Fourteenth, and Fifteenth amendments to the U.S. Constitution, which abolished slavery, extended due process protections, and expanded suffrage to include African Americans, laws in both the North and the South continued to infringe upon the liberties of African Americans. Law enforcement arrested African Americans for minor violations, leading to exorbitant fines, lengthy prison sentences, and virtual re-enslavement on former slave plantations. Law enforcement, essentially, was enforcing racial restrictions intended to discipline those seen as threats to the state. This form of social control, through policing communities of color, stemmed from the deep-seated racial hierarchy in the country, entrenching white supremacy within social systems and institutions.

The evolution of law enforcement, however, was not a linear progression. From volunteer watchmen in the North and slave patrols in the South during the Colonial era, to the formation of a modern police force with an agenda to control disorder, and then the post-Civil War police departments' role in controlling freed slaves, each phase of this evolution has been characterized by its own distinctive form of racial hierarchy enforcement.[15]

A significant turning point came with the Civil Rights era of the 1960s, which brought the issue of police brutality, particularly against African Americans, to the forefront. The Kerner Commission in 1968 identified "white racism" as the main cause of urban riots and highlighted the profound lack of social equity in policing. In response, civil rights activists aimed to ensure that the application of the law, especially the use of force, was fair.[16] This era marked a heightened awareness of racial discrimination and a quest for equal rights. It challenged the status quo and highlighted the need for systemic change in law enforcement practices.

Throughout the 20th century, technological advancements and shifting norms and regulations brought changes in policing. However, these changes often mirrored deep-seated inequities. The Prohibition era, for instance, showcased rampant corruption within police departments, highlighting the impact of norms and regulations on policing practices and demonstrating how social inequity was perpetuated through law enforcement.[17] Prohibition led to disproportionate targeting of African American and immigrant communities, underscoring the role of law enforcement in reinforcing inequities.[18]

The 21st century has witnessed louder calls for police reform, spurred by high-profile incidents of police brutality, primarily against individuals from marginalized communities. Social justice movements like Black Lives Matter shed light on systemic racism in policing, prompting calls to defund or reform the police. Understanding the history of policing is crucial for informing future progress. There is an urgent need for a fair and equitable system that aligns with the constitutional values upon which the United States was founded. To mend the strained relationship between law enforcement and the African American community, the United States must confront the biases that have been, and continue to be, present. Achieving social equity in policing is an ongoing battle, and while strides have been made, the fight for justice continues.[19]

Law

The American legal system wields a profound influence on the racial disparities in law enforcement. Laws and court decisions have either perpetuated or mitigated inequities. This discussion examines the impact of law on policing people of color and the resultant racial disparities, with a focus on significant legislative measures and court rulings.

The Civil Rights Act of 1964 is a milestone in the journey toward racial equity because it outlawed racial discrimination in public domains.[20] However, while the Act intended to address and prevent racial disparities in policing, its effectiveness has been hampered due to inadequate federal oversight and a lack of widespread adherence to its provisions. This inadvertently contributed to perpetuating discriminatory practices in law enforcement.[21]

In the context of policing and racial disparities, the 1968 Supreme Court ruling in *Terry v. Ohio* is significant.[22] This decision permitted police to "stop and frisk" individuals based on "reasonable suspicion," a criterion of a considerably lower threshold than "probable cause." Essentially, this ruling provided law enforcement with greater discretionary power in their encounters with civilians. The broad interpretation of "reasonable suspicion" led to its misuse, disproportionately targeting people of color. This has occurred because the ruling did not detail specific behaviors or actions that would justify stop and frisk under the "reasonable suspicion" standard. Instead, officers' personal interpretation of suspicious behavior is relied on and it is influenced by stereotypes and biases, both conscious and unconscious.[23] Consequently, this decision exacerbated racial disparities in stop-and-search practices and expanded the powers given to law enforcement.[24] Relative to policing, this meant that racial disparities could manifest anywhere (i.e., city streets, vehicles, parks, or private properties) and especially in African American communities that are typically underserved but over-policed.[25]

Legislation implemented during the "War on Drugs" in the 1980s and 1990s had a massive impact on communities of color. These policies resulted in law enforcement disproportionately targeting people of color and resulted in racial disparities in arrest rates, sentencing, and incarceration for drug offenses.[26] The strict punitive measures associated with these policies have had long-term implications for communities of color, particularly African Americans, intensifying the distrust between them and law enforcement. Although these policies have been partially dismantled at the federal level, their legacy continues to influence policing practices and shape perceptions of law enforcement.

The intersection of law and racial disparities in policing illustrates a complex and intricate narrative. On one hand, the legal system has promoted racial equality through laws such as the Civil Rights Act. On the other hand, court rulings and policies have often been interpreted and implemented in a manner that exacerbates disparities. This highlights the importance of legal reform, oversight mechanisms, and law enforcement training and policies to promote equity.

While law is an instrument that can either perpetuate or mitigate disparities, the broader application and enforcement of these laws influence their impact on racial disparities in policing. There is a need for the legal system to consistently scrutinize and reassess its legislation and policies to ensure they are equitable and just and to foster a relationship of trust and cooperation between law enforcement and the communities served.

Politics

The intersection of policing and politics shapes how people of color experience the criminal justice system in the U.S. Public policy, political rhetoric, and societal expectations all contribute to the racial and ethnic disparities seen in policing.[27] These disparities not only highlight systemic injustices but also underline the influence that political ideology exerts on law enforcement practices. Some view this incompatibility as akin to the machinations of a drunken sloth, such is the level of disconnect between ideals and reality.

At the local level, politics shape policing in a number of ways. City councils and mayors influence policing policies and practices through budget allocations, ordinances, and the appointment of police chiefs. Local politics dictate the response to crime, with higher crime areas receiving more policing attention. This exacerbates racial disparities. Community advocacy, protests, and voter preferences also shape policing practices and reform efforts.

State governments also influence policing disparities as they establish state-wide laws and regulations that guide practices. They also control state police departments and highway patrols. State legislatures can implement, amend, or repeal laws impacting policing practices, such as stop and frisk laws, use of force guidelines, and police accountability measures.

At the federal level, politics exerts influence through legislation, federal law enforcement agencies, court rulings, and the Department of Justice. Federal laws and Supreme Court decisions have sweeping effects on policing practices nationwide, as they exacerbate or mitigate disparities. Federal agencies like the Federal Bureau of Investigation (FBI) and Drug Enforcement Administration (DEA) also contribute to law enforcement trends and practices.

Political discourse is powerful. For instance, calls for "law and order," often amplified during political campaigns, may increase aggressive policing, especially in disadvantaged communities.[28] This rhetoric feeds into societal fears and biases and contributes to the over-policing of people of color. It also facilitates the introduction of punitive laws and policies that disproportionately target marginalized communities.

Policies such as the War on Drugs and Three Strikes Laws are examples of how political decisions at both the local and national levels adversely impact marginalized communities. The War on Drugs, initiated in the 1980s, resulted in harsh mandatory minimum sentencing laws for drug offenses. These laws disproportionately affected people of color, leading to their overrepresentation in the prison population. Similarly, Three Strikes Laws, which mandate life sentences for individuals convicted of a third felony, have also disproportionately affected people of color. Moreover, the influence of police unions often impedes reform because policymakers acquiesce to their demands, stymying efforts to introduce changes that would reduce racial disparities.[29] Police unions, through their political influence, have been successful in maintaining the status quo, thus perpetuating racial disparities.

Political decisions can also indirectly impact racial disparities in policing. Policies concerning education, housing, and social services influence the social conditions that contribute to crime and policing disparities. For example, housing policies that perpetuate segregation lead to over-policing in marginalized neighborhoods. Underfunded schools in these neighborhoods contribute to the school-to-prison pipeline, further deepening racial disparities in the criminal justice system. Conversely, public sentiment and political will can drive change. The Black Lives Matter movement has exerted significant political pressure, leading to increased discourse about systemic racism and the need for comprehensive criminal justice reform. As a result, some jurisdictions have reassessed their policing practices, aiming to reduce disparities.

Ultimately, political decisions can significantly impact racial and ethnic disparities in policing. From direct policies that dictate law enforcement practices to indirect decisions influencing social conditions, politics plays an integral role in shaping the racial dynamics of policing. To mitigate these disparities, an objective reassessment of existing policies and the introduction of equitable reforms that uphold the ideals of a just society are needed.

Management

Management practices within law enforcement agencies are significant contributors to the racial and ethnic disparities observed in policing. Disparities are rooted in historical contexts but are also fueled by contemporary practices and cultures within law enforcement agencies.[30] Unpacking these practices provides insight into the institutional mechanisms that perpetuate racial bias in law enforcement and enables policymakers and practitioners to develop more effective strategies for reform.[31]

Policing culture is a factor that influences racial disparities. The warrior-like culture often embraced by police departments fosters an aggressive approach to policing that disproportionately impacts disadvantaged communities.[32] Characterized by an "us versus them" mentality, this culture exacerbates tensions between law enforcement and communities of color, creating a vicious cycle of distrust and antagonism. Therefore, changing the policing culture should be a priority in efforts to address racial disparities.

Police training and recruitment practices are also instrumental in perpetuating disparities. Training programs often fail to address implicit bias, which leads to differential treatment of individuals based on their race. These biases, though often unconscious, influence police officers' perceptions and decision-making, leading to racially skewed outcomes. Therefore, enhancing training that tackles implicit biases should be central to reform initiatives. And, law enforcement agencies often lack representative diversity within their ranks, which further reinforces disparities. Diversity is vital for enhancing cultural understanding and empathy, fostering trust, and promoting fairness. Thus, recruitment strategies should aim at enhancing diversity.

Institutional practices also contribute significantly to racial disparities in policing. These practices include use-of-force policies, lack of de-escalation training, and deficient implicit bias training.[33] Use-of-force policies can allow or even encourage excessive force, particularly against people of color. This leads to tragic outcomes and further erodes public trust in law enforcement. Similarly, the absence of effective de-escalation training in many agencies can increase the likelihood of confrontational and potentially violent encounters with citizens. Such training equips officers with skills to resolve conflicts peacefully, thus minimizing the need for forceful interventions. The lack of implicit bias training exacerbates the impact of unconscious biases in interactions with the public, thus reinforcing racial disparities.

In sum, management practices within law enforcement play a central role in perpetuating disparities in policing. These disparities stem from the warrior-like culture of policing, inadequate training on implicit bias, and a lack of representative diversity within the police force. Reforming these practices is critical in addressing racial disparities, rebuilding trust between police and communities of color, and promoting social equity in public service delivery.

Pathways to Action

The discretionary freedom granted to officers to decide what to do in a given situation is a fundamental aspect of law enforcement. However, it is problematic when it leads to inconsistent or biased practices, particularly those that result in disparities. This is one of the reasons why the United States grapples with the pressing issue of racial and ethnic disparities in policing. Addressing them requires a multifaceted approach given the complexity of these issues. The pathway to reducing disparities involves a range of promising practices including procedural justice training programs, community-oriented policing, implicit bias training coupled with organizational changes, the use of body-worn cameras, and the implementation of civilian review boards.

Procedural Justice Training Programs

Procedural justice training programs have become a focal point in efforts to address racial disparities in law enforcement.[34] This concept emphasizes fairness in the processes that resolve disputes and allocate resources.[35] Procedural justice comprises four principles:

- Voice – the opportunity for individuals to express their viewpoint
- Neutrality – decision-making processes are unbiased and trustworthy
- Respect – individuals are treated with dignity and their rights are respected
- Trustworthiness – authorities are perceived as caring about individuals' welfare and striving to do what's right.[36]

Implementing these principles can significantly improve relationships between law enforcement and communities of color.

Implementing procedural justice training programs requires certain preconditions. First, there must be commitment from leadership because without it, efforts to embed procedural justice into policing culture will falter. Second, law enforcement agencies need resources to develop or adapt training materials, conduct training, and measure the program's impact. Third, incorporating procedural justice training into police culture requires an approach that extends beyond the training room. It involves promoting values that prioritize fair and respectful treatment of all community members, regardless of their race or ethnicity.[37]

Studies show that procedural justice training programs have positive impacts on equity. They promote more positive attitudes toward police, can influence officer behavior, promote willingness to obey the law, and can increase the perceived legitimacy of the police.[38] Additionally, procedural justice training is a vital tool for addressing implicit bias. By promoting impartial decision-making and respect for all individuals, the training counteracts unconscious biases that otherwise influence police interactions with community members.

In sum, procedural justice training programs can be effective in addressing racial disparities in policing. They require leadership support, resources, and an organizational culture that values fairness and respect. When effectively implemented, these programs can foster trust, promote compliance with the law, influence officer behavior, and counteract implicit bias, thereby advancing equity in policing.

Community-Oriented Policing

Community-oriented policing aims to build better relationships between police officers and community members. This, in turn, promotes better perceptions of police and improves quality of life in neighborhoods.[39] Community-oriented policing was created with a focus on building partnerships between community members and police to achieve the goal of safe and sound communities."[40] By focusing on community partnerships, problem-solving, and organizational transformation, community-oriented policing addresses many of the issues that lead to disparities in law enforcement. When effective, it has substantial positive impacts on equity in policing.

Implementing community-oriented policing requires agencies to make changes in their operations, culture, and mindset. It requires a community policing unit that fosters partnerships with community members and stakeholders. Officers should be trained in conflict resolution, de-escalation techniques, and cultural competency to better interact with diverse community members. Organizational structures need to support decentralization, flexibility, and responsiveness to community needs. Successful implementation requires a commitment from police leadership and adequate resources to support the change process. Transparency with the community is also essential to build trust and foster cooperation. To measure the success of the strategy, agencies should establish benchmarks that reflect the goals of community-oriented policing, such as reduced crime rates, improved community satisfaction, and decreased racial disparities in police interactions. By focusing on problem-solving, community-oriented policing addresses the root causes of crime, leading to a reduction in crime rates and less reliance on punitive measures that disproportionately affect communities of color. In addition, community-oriented policing can promote diversity and inclusivity. The focus on community partnership encourages agencies to recruit officers who reflect the communities they serve, which can enhance cultural understanding. Community-oriented policing is promising: it fosters trust, improves police-community relationships, reduces crime rates, and enhances equity. However, success requires significant changes in police practices, organizational structures, and culture. While progress has been made, there is still much to be done to ensure widespread adoption.

Implicit Bias Training

Implicit bias training is another promising approach to addressing racial disparities in policing. This specialized training amplifies awareness of unconscious biases and furnishes tools to offset the effects of biases on behavior and decision-making. The potential for implicit bias training to positively impact equity in policing is a subject of ongoing research. Current evidence presents a promising, yet mixed picture. An examination of various interventions found that only eight out of 17 significantly reduced implicit bias. Even among those interventions that were deemed effective, their impact seemed to wane after 24 hours.[41] Even more notably, there was no observed association between these interventions and changes in explicit bias or behavior.

Diversity training, which is often touted as an essential tool for addressing implicit bias, similarly exhibits inconsistent results. Studies show that these training programs do not consistently affect implicit or explicit bias in the long term.[42] This suggests that while implicit bias training can enhance knowledge and awareness, it does not reliably reduce implicit bias itself. Nevertheless, the efficacy of such training, while varied, requires meticulous planning, execution, and continuous monitoring for successful implementation.[43]

Research underscores that every individual harbors biases, many of which are unconsciously formed and subtly influence our behaviors and decisions. Within the sphere of policing, these implicit biases become a substantial factor contributing to racial disparities, leading to unequal treatment of individuals premised on their race.[44] A pivotal aim of implicit bias training rests on equipping officers with the ability to recognize their personal biases and master strategies to neutralize them. Typically, such training incorporates components of perspective-taking, stereotype replacement, individuation, and counter-stereotypic imaging, all of which aid in reducing biases and fostering more equitable policing practices.[45]

Effective implementation of this type of training requires that the training be customized to the agency environment and incorporate practical exercises reflecting real-world situations that officers are likely to encounter.[46] By tailoring the training to real-world scenarios, it becomes more relevant and applicable, which increases its effectiveness. In addition, leadership buy-in and support are crucial for successful implementation. Leaders must express a clear commitment to the training and its goals and provide the necessary resources for its execution. Furthermore, organizations must have mechanisms to assess the impact of their training programs. This could include surveys to measure changes in attitudes, behaviors, and decision-making following the training, as well as analyses of policing data to evaluate shifts in key metrics such as arrests, stops, and use of force.[47]

In light of these findings, it is clear that while implicit bias training represents a promising approach in the quest to promote racial equity in policing, the results to date are decidedly mixed. Implicit bias training has the potential to be a valuable tool in the fight against racial disparities in policing. By raising awareness of unconscious biases and offering strategies to mitigate them, this form of training may contribute to more equitable practices.

Body-Worn Cameras

Body-worn cameras (BWCs) are increasingly being used in law enforcement agencies around the world as a tool to improve accountability and transparency, and they also offer the potential for addressing racial disparities in policing. The effectiveness of BWCs is contingent on multiple factors, including policy frameworks, officer compliance, and public perceptions. By providing a visual and auditory record of police-citizen interactions, these cameras can help to reduce officers' use of force, provide evidence for investigations of police misconduct, and increase transparency and accountability.[48] Moreover, BWCs can potentially reduce racial disparities by holding officers accountable for their actions. Research has shown that the presence of BWCs influences officer behavior and decision-making, potentially leading to more equitable policing outcomes This technology also provides a factual account of police-citizen encounters, reducing reliance on subjective narratives.

The effectiveness of BWCs in addressing racial disparities depends significantly on how they are used. Law enforcement agencies must establish clear policies governing the use of BWCs, including when to record, how to store and review footage, and how to protect individuals' privacy.[49] These policies should be communicated to both officers and the public.

Training is a crucial component of successful BWC implementation. Officers need to understand how to operate the cameras and be familiar with policies surrounding their use and the legal and ethical implications. Furthermore, agencies must ensure that officers comply with these policies to maximize the benefits of BWCs. The impacts of BWCs on equity are multifaceted. While they have the potential to reduce racial disparities in policing, their effectiveness depends on multiple factors, including departmental policies, officer compliance, and community engagement. Importantly, BWCs alone cannot address the systemic issues contributing to racial disparities; they must be part of a broader strategy encompassing policy reform, training, and organizational change.

BWCs offer a promising tool for improving transparency and accountability in law enforcement and reducing racial disparities. However, their successful implementation requires planning, training, and policy development. Future research should continue to investigate the impacts of BWCs on equity in policing, exploring how they can best be used to promote fair and just law enforcement practices.

Civilian Review Boards

Civilian Review Boards (CRBs) have emerged as a crucial tool in addressing racial disparities. These oversight bodies, typically composed of community members, play a vital role in increasing police accountability, promoting transparency, and fostering a sense of justice. However, their effectiveness varies depending on the scope of their powers, their composition, and the level of community support they receive. Supporters of citizen review argue that traditional internal review procedures, which have historically been used to handle citizen complaints regarding officer misconduct, are inadequate when it comes to being impartial and punishing guilty officers. By contrast, if complaints are addressed by an independent review board, citizens are likely to feel more comfortable stepping forward and reporting incidents.

For public service agencies to implement effective CRBs, prerequisites are necessary. First, political will and public support are paramount because CRBs often face opposition from law enforcement agencies and police unions, making political backing crucial.[50] Second, CRBs should be granted sufficient authority to conduct independent investigations, to make disciplinary recommendations, and to ensure that their recommendations are acted upon. Last, the composition of CRBs matters. To be credible, CRBs should reflect the diversity of the community they serve. Examples of CRBs that contain the elements detailed here include the Detroit and San Francisco CRBs. Both of these have the subpoena, discipline, and policy review authority relative to policing in their jurisdictions.[51]

Despite their potential benefits, the effectiveness of CRBs in addressing racial disparities is contingent on their authority, independence, and community support. When well implemented, CRBs can significantly contribute to enhancing social equity in policing yet they are not a panacea. They must be part of a broader suite of reforms aimed at transforming policing culture, improving training, and enhancing diversity within law enforcement. Civilian Review Boards can play a significant role in fostering police accountability and in enhancing social equity. However, for these bodies to be effective, they need political support, sufficient authority, independence, and a diverse composition that reflects the community they serve.

Summary of Key Points

This chapter examined the historical context, causes, and impacts of racial and ethnic disparities in policing. It also analyzed the role of the legal system, political decisions, and management practices in perpetuating disparities. Finally, it identified several promising practices for addressing these issues, including procedural justice training, community-oriented policing, strategies for addressing implicit bias, body-worn cameras, and civilian review boards.

Discussion Questions

1. How do historical context and systemic biases contribute to racial and ethnic disparities in policing?
2. How do political decisions and debates shape these disparities?
3. What role does the management of law enforcement agencies play in perpetuating disparities, and how can it contribute to addressing them?
4. What are the strengths and weaknesses of the promising practices discussed in this chapter? What barriers might impede their implementation and how might these be overcome?
5. How can we ensure that the promising practices identified are widely adopted and effectively implemented?
6. What additional measures can be taken to promote social equity in policing?

Additional Resources

To learn more, visit the following websites:

1. Center for Policing Equity: https://policingequity.org/
2. Economics Research on Racial Disparities in Policing: https://econofact.org/economic-research-on-racial-disparities-in-policing
3. National Association of Criminal Defense Attorneys on Race and Policing: https://www.nacdl.org/Content/Race-and-Policing
4. Public Policy Institute of California: https://www.ppic.org/publication/racial-disparities-in-law-enforcement-stops/
5. Center for Police Research and Policy: https://www.theiacp.org/research

Notes

1. Dominic Bearfield, Nicole Humphrey, Shannon Portillo, and Norma Riccucci, "Dismantling Institutional and Structural Racism: Implementation Strategies Across the United States," *Journal of Social Equity and Public Administration* 1, no. 1 (2023): 75–92.
2. Douglas S. Massey and Nancy A. Denton, American *Apartheid: Segregation and the Making of the Underclass* (Cambridge: Harvard University Press, 1993).
3. Brad W. Smith and Malcolm D. Holmes, "Police Use of Excessive Force in Minority Communities: A Test of the Minority Threat, Place, and Community Accountability Hypotheses," *Social Problems* 61, no. 1 (2014): 83–104.
4. Ty Price Dooley, "The Undelivered Dream: Policing, Administrative Rules and Social Equity," *Administrative Theory & Praxis* (2021): 1–12.
5. Margaret Bull Kovera, "Racial Disparities in the Criminal Justice System: Prevalence, Causes, and a Search for Solutions," *Journal of Social Issues* 75, no. 4 (2019): 1139–1164.
6. Jeffrey Fagan and Alexis D. Campbell, "Race and Reasonableness in Police Killings," *Boston University Law Review* 100 (2020): 951, https://www.bu.edu/bulawreview/files/2020/05/07-FAGAN-CAMPBELL.pdf
7. Frank Edwards, Hedwig Lee, and Michael Esposito, "Risk of Being Killed by Police Use of Force in the

United States by Age, Race–Ethnicity, and Sex," *Proceedings of the National Academy of Sciences* 116, no. 34 (2019): 16793–16798.

8. Emma Pierson, Camelia Simoiu, Jan Overgoor, Sam Corbett-Davies, Daniel Jenson, Amy Shoemaker, Vignesh Ramachandran et al, "A Large-Scale Analysis of Racial Disparities in Police Stops Across the United States," *Nature Human Behaviour* 4, no. 7 (2020): 736–745.
9. Lynn Langton and Matthew R. Durose, Police Behavior During Traffic and Street Stops, 2011 (Washington, DC: US Department of Justice, Office of Justice Programs, Bureau of Justice Statistics, 2013).
10. Andrea M. Headley and James E. Wright. "Is Representation Enough? Racial Disparities in Levels of Force and Arrests by Police." *Public Administration Review* 80, no. 6 (2020): 1051–1062.
11. Michelle Alexander, T*he New Jim Crow: Mass Incarceration in the Age of Colorblindness* (New York: The New Press, 2020).
12. Geoffrey P. Alpert, and William C. Smith, "How Reasonable Is the Reasonable Man: Police and Excessive Force," *Journal of Criminal Law and Criminology* 85, no. 2 (1994): 481.
13. Gary Potter, "The History of Policing in the United States," *EKU School of Justice Studies*, June 25, 2013, accessed July 27, 2023, https://ekuonline.eku.edu/blog/police-studies/the-history-of-policing-in-the-united-states-part-1/
14. Alexander, *The New Jim Crow*; Kevin F. Steinmetz, Brian P. Schaefer, and Howard Henderson, "Wicked Overseers: American Policing and Colonialism," *Sociology of Race and Ethnicity* 3, no. 1 (2017): 68–81.
15. Sally E. Hadden, *Slave Patrols: Law and Violence in Virginia and the Carolinas* (Cambridge: Harvard University Press, 2003).
16. Jonathan Simon, Bradford Ben, Jauregui Beatrice, Loader Ian, and Steinberg Jonny, "Policing after Civil Rights: The Legacy of Police Opposition to the Civil Rights Movement for Contemporary American Policing." In *The SAGE Handbook of Global Policing*, eds. Ben Bradford, Beatrice Jauregui, Ian Loader, and Jonny Steinberg (London: Sage, 2016): 373–388.
17. Potter, "The History of Policing in the United States."
18. Brittany Arsiniega, Teresa Crosby, Spencer Richardson, and Kylie Berube, "Race and Prohibition Movements," *Tennessee Journal of Race, Gender, & Social Justice,* Vol. 11, no. 2 (2021): 16–75.
19. RaJade M. Berry-James, Brandi Blessett, Rachel Emas, Sean McCandless, Ashley E. Nickels, Kristen Norman-Major, and Parisa Vinzant, "Stepping Up to the Plate: Making Social Equity a Priority in Public Administration's Troubled Times," *Journal of Public Affairs Education* 27, no. 1 (2021): 5–15.
20. Civil Rights Act, Public Law No. 88-352, 78 Stat. 241, 246, and 252, (1964).
21. Elizabeth Hinton, LaShae Henderson, and Cindy Reed, "An Unjust Burden: The Disparate Treatment of Black Americans in the Criminal Justice System," *Vera Institute of Justice* 1, no. 1 (2018): 1–20, https://www.vera.org/publications/for-the-record-unjust-burden
22. *Terry v. Ohio*, 392 U.S. 1 (1968).
23. L. Song Richardson, and Phillip Goff, "Implicit Racial Bias in Public Defender Triage," *Yale Law Journal* 122 (2013): 13–24, accessed July 27, 2023, https://papers.ssrn.com/sol3/papers.cfm?abstract_id=2259079#
24. David Harris, "The Stories, the Statistics, and the Law: Why Driving While Black Matters," *Minnesota Law Review*, (1999): 265–326, https://scholarship.law.umn.edu/cgi/viewcontent.cgi?article=2132&context=mlr
25. Jeffrey Fagan and Garth Davies, "Street Stops and Broken Windows: Terry, Race, and Disorder in New York City," *Fordham Urban Law Journal* 28, no. 2 (2000): 457–504.
26. Jamie Fellner, "Race, Drugs, and Law Enforcement in the United States," *Stanford Law & Policy Review* 20 (2009): 257, https://law.stanford.edu/publications/race-drugs-law-enforcement-united-states/
27. James Forman Jr., *Locking Up Our Own: Crime and Punishment in Black America* (New York: Farrar, Straus and Giroux, 2017).
28. Elizabeth Hinton and DeAnza Cook, "The Mass Criminalization of Black Americans: A Historical Overview," *Annual Review of Criminology* 4 (2021): 261–286.
29. Samuel Walker, "Institutionalizing Police Accountability Reforms: The Problem of Making Police Reforms Endure," *Saint Louis University Public Law Review* 32, no. 1 (2012): 57–92.
30. Vicky M. Wilkins and Brian N. Williams, "Black or Blue: Racial Profiling and Representative Bureaucracy," *Public Administration Review* 68, no. 4 (2008): 654–664.
31. Charles R. Epp, Steven Maynard-Moody, and D. P. Haider-Markel, *Pulled Over: How Police Stops Define Race and Citizenship* (Chicago: The University of Chicago Press, 2014).
32. Kyle McLean, Scott E. Wolfe, Jeff Rojek, Geoffrey P. Alpert, and Michael R. Smith, "Police Officers as Warriors or Guardians: Empirical Reality or Intriguing Rhetoric?," *Justice Quarterly* 37, no. 6 (2020): 1096–1118.
33. Kimberly Barsamian Kahn and Karin D. Martin,

"Policing and Race: Disparate Treatment, Perceptions, and Policy Responses," *Social Issues and Policy Review* 10, no. 1 (2016): 82–121.

34. Emily Owens, David Weisburd, Karen L. Amendola, and Geoffrey P. Alpert, "Can You Build A Better Cop? Experimental Evidence on Supervision, Training, and Policing in the Community," *Criminology & Public Policy* 17, no. 1 (2018): 41–87.
35. Tom R. Tyler, "Policing in Black and White: Ethnic Group Differences in Trust and Confidence in the Police," *Police Quarterly* 8, no. 3 (2005): 322–342.
36. Emma Antrobus, Ian Thompson, and Barak Ariel, "Procedural Justice Training for Police Recruits: Results of a Randomized Controlled Trial," *Journal of Experimental Criminology* 15, no. 1 (2019): 29–53.
37. William Terrill, Eugene A. Paoline III, and Peter K. Manning, "Police Culture and Coercion," *Criminology* 41, no. 4 (2003): 1003–1034.
38. Antrobus et al., "Procedural Justice Training for Police Recruits."
39. Charlotte Gill, David Weisburd, Cody W. Telep, Zoe Vitter, and Trevor Bennett, "Community-Oriented Policing to Reduce Crime, Disorder and Fear and Increase Satisfaction and Legitimacy Among Citizens: A Systematic Review," *Campbell Systematic Reviews* 13, no. 1 (2017): 1–30.
40. Cheon Geun Choi and Sang Ok Choi, "Collaborative Partnerships and Crime in Disorganized Communities," *Public Administration Review* 72, no. 2 (2012): 228–238.
41. Calvin K. Lai, Maddalena Marini, Steven A. Lehr, Carlo Cerruti, Jiyun-Elizabeth L. Shin, Jennifer A. Joy-Gaba, Arnold K. Ho et al. "Reducing Implicit Racial Preferences: I. A Comparative Investigation of 17 Interventions." *Journal of Experimental Psychology* 143, no. 4 (2014): 1765. Calvin K. Lai, Allison L. Skinner, Erin Cooley, Sohad Murrar, Markus Brauer, Thierry Devos, Jimmy Calanchini et al., "Reducing Implicit Racial Preferences: II. Intervention Effectiveness across Time." *Journal of Experimental Psychology: General* 145, no. 8 (2016): 1001.
42. Ivuoma N. Onyeador, Sa-kiera TJ Hudson, and Neil A. Lewis Jr., "Moving Beyond Implicit Bias Training: Policy Insights for Increasing Organizational Diversity," *Policy Insights from the Behavioral and Brain Sciences* 8, no. 1 (2021): 19–26.
43. Justin Nix and Scott E. Wolfe, "Sensitivity to the Ferguson Effect: The Role of Managerial Organizational Justice," *Journal of Criminal Justice* 47 (2016): 12–20.
44. Justin Nix, Bradley A. Campbell, Edward H. Byers, and Geoffrey P. Alpert, "A Bird's Eye View of Civilians Killed by Police in 2015: Further Evidence of Implicit Bias," *Criminology & Public Policy* 16, no. 1 (2017): 309–340.
45. Lai et al., "Reducing Implicit Racial Preferences: I. A Comparative Investigation of 17 Interventions."
46. Cynthia Lum and Christopher S. Koper, "Evidence-Based Policing." In *Critical Issues in Policing: Contemporary Readings* (7th ed.), eds. R. Dunham and G. Alpert (Longrove: Waveland Press, 2015): 260–274, accessed July 27, 2023, https://cebcp.org/wp-content/evidence-based-policing/EvidenceBasedPolicingDefined.pdf
47. Lorie A. Fridell, *Producing Bias-Free Policing: A Science-Based Approach* (New York: Springer, 2017).
48. Barak Ariel, Alex Sutherland, Darren Henstock, Josh Young, Paul Drover, Jayne Sykes, Simon Megicks, and Ryan Henderson, "Wearing Body Cameras Increases Assaults against Officers and Does Not Reduce Police Use of Force: Results from a Global Multi-Site Experiment," *European Journal of Criminology* 13, no. 6 (2016): 744–755; Barak Ariel, William A. Farrar, and Alex Sutherland, "The Effect of Police Body-Worn Cameras on Use of Force and Citizens' Complaints against the Police: A Randomized Controlled Trial," *Journal of Quantitative Criminology* 31, no. 3 (2015): 509–535.
49. Lum and Koper, "Evidence-Based Policing;" Cynthia Lum, Megan Stoltz, Christopher S. Koper, and J. Amber Scherer, "Research on Body-Worn Cameras: What We Know, What We Need to Know," *Criminology & Public Policy* 18, no. 1 (2019): 93–118.
50. Barry Friedman and Maria Ponomarenko, "Democratic Policing," *New York University Law Review* 90, no. 6 (2015): 1827.
51. Udi Ofer, "Getting It Right: Building Effective Civilian Review Boards to Oversee Police," *Seton Hall Law Review* 46, no. 4 (2016): 1033–1062, accessed July 27, 2023, https://scholarship.shu.edu/cgi/viewcontent.cgi?article=1572&context=shlr

9 MATERNAL MORTALITY AND SEVERE MATERNAL MORBIDITY AMONG BLACK WOMEN

Simone Martin-Howard

From the Editors

Health care is essential for a safe, productive life and few areas touch on the importance of equitable health care as does maternal mortality and morbidity. Martin-Howard examines how maternal health issues impact Black women in particular, using social determinants to parse equity issues relating to access to health care, differential outcomes based on socioeconomic status and educational attainment, and inadequate housing. She notes promising strategies, including addressing systemic and structural racism within health care, expanding access to care, delivering high-quality care, requiring cultural competency for those delivering health care, offering mental health and substance abuse care, and funding community organizations working to improve maternal care.

The United States is in a maternal health crisis. Women in the United States have the highest rate of maternal mortality among high-income countries and Black women, in particular, are three times more likely to die from problems related to pregnancy than White women.[1] Also alarming, rates of severe maternal morbidity (SMM), which is comprised of unforeseen and deadly complications that arise during pregnancy and after delivery, are also increasing.[2] Social determinants of health (SDoH), which comprise the structural and individual elements that affect health outcomes, serve as the conceptual foundation to grasp maternal mortality and SMM. First, this chapter defines these two terms and provides statistics on these issues. Then a breakdown is presented that shows its impact on Black women. Systemic and structural racism is discussed and examples are provided on how this country's sordid past is now displayed via the mistreatment of Black women in health care.[3]

Next, to elucidate the impact of SDoH on maternal mortality and SMM, this chapter discusses problems of access to quality health care; effects of low socioeconomic status and educational attainment; and inadequate housing. This is followed by a discussion of maternal mental health challenges.

Pathways to action are then illustrated through six recommendations for federal, state, and local governments to consider: 1) address systemic and structural racism, mistreatment, and bias within health care; 2) provide women with access to free or affordable primary care; 3) deliver high-quality obstetric care through a diverse perinatal workforce; 4) require cultural competency training of all health care providers; 5) offer affordable mental health care and substance abuse services for women; and 6) fund community-based organizations focused on improving maternal health outcomes. The chapter's key points are then summarized; followed by discussion questions; and links to additional resources.

Social Equity Issues

The U.S. health care system is fraught with inequities. For example, maternal health is one of the most important indicators of the overall health of a nation; how women are treated during childbirth can affect the health and well-being of the entire family.[4] However, the most developed country in the world has become one of the most dangerous places to give birth, with mothers in the United States (particularly Black women) dying at an alarming rate during labor and/or delivery. Compared to their White counterparts, Black women face inequities linked to systemic and structural racism as well as SdoH. Social determinants include both structural and individual elements. Structural determinants include economic and social policies that affect an individual's income, working and housing conditions, and educational attainment. Individual elements include health behaviors such as diet and exercise, tobacco use, and alcohol use.

Health equity, defined as "the absence of unfair and avoidable or remediable differences in health among population groups defined socially, economically, demographically, or geographically"[5] is becoming a pressing public health issue nationally. Examples of SDoH covered in this chapter focus on the structural determinants and include lack of access to quality health care, socioeconomic status and educational attainment, and inadequate housing, all of which lead to health disparities and inequities. These disparities and inequities have an early and profound impact on health status across the life course of individuals.[6]

Health inequities are health differences that are socially produced, systematic across the population, and unfair.[7] The key feature of the SDoH theoretical framework is its emphasis on social position as the main determinant of inequity.[8] Social position is defined by relations of ownership or control over productive resources and is captured through social markers such as ethnicity/race, income, gender, and education.[9] The weight and relevance of social position are influenced by the socioeconomic and political context, which includes governmental policies, cultural values, and the macroeconomic condition of a country.[10] The impact of these structural factors on health equity is mediated by behaviors and living conditions and is manifested in housing and access to health services.[11]

Maternal Mortality

The World Health Organization defines maternal mortality rate (MMR) as deaths that take place during pregnancy or within 42 days following delivery.[12] The MMR in the United States was 24 deaths per 100,000 live births in 2020. This rate surpasses that of other high-income countries by more than three-fold.[13] In 2021, the U.S. rate increased to 32.9 maternal deaths per 100,000 live births,[14] almost doubling the rate from 2019 at 17.4 per 100,000 live births.[15] Seventy-five percent of all maternal deaths are due to complications from severe bleeding or infections after childbirth, high blood pressure during pregnancy (preeclampsia and eclampsia), delivery complications, and unsafe abortions.[16]

Severe Maternal Morbidity

Widely discussed along with maternal mortality is severe maternal morbidity (SMM), which is also increasing in the United States.[17] In fact, SMM is 50–100 times more common than maternal mortality.[18] While there is no single definition of SMM, it is thought of as a near miss for maternal mortality because if risk factors are not remedied immediately, a sequence of conditions and complications follow that lead to maternal death.[19] Maternal morbidity and SMM are the principal measures used to tackle maternal health inequities.[20] Individuals who undergo SMM are at risk for maternal mortality in the short term or long term. SMM affects 50,000 to 60,000 women overall each year in the United States[21] This number is alarming and includes numerous conditions that may occur during pregnancy, during childbirth, and in the postpartum period: cardiac arrest, heart failure, aneurysm, eclampsia, sepsis, and acute renal failure, to name a few.[22]

Maternal Mortality and Severe Maternal Morbidity for Black Women in the United States

While maternal mortality and SMM are significant concerns for all women, they are especially of concern for Black women. The U.S. maternal death rate for Black women is especially high. It is more than double the average rate and nearly three times higher than the rate for White women.[23] To be specific, in 2021 it was 69.9 per 100,000, which is 2.6 times higher than the rate for White women.[24] Differences in SMM among races and ethnicities are comparable to the disparity in the MMR between Blacks and Whites. Black women had a case-fatality rate approximately three times higher than White women for five pregnancy conditions—pre-eclampsia, eclampsia, abruptio placentae, placenta previa, and postpartum hemorrhage.[25] From 2016–2017, non-Hispanic Black mothers were more than twice as likely as non-Hispanic White mothers to experience SMM at 226 per 10,000 births vs. 105 per 10,000 births.

SMM occurs at higher rates among those with lower socioeconomic status and who lack health insurance.[26] It is well-known that Black women have been neglected in medical settings for centuries and this history is a critical factor in explaining maternal health inequities.[27] The history of slavery, racism, and discrimination continues to impact maternal health outcomes today. During slavery, Black women were often used as breeders for slave owners and were subjected to cruel and atrocious treatment, including forced pregnancies, lack of prenatal care, and high rates of maternal and infant mortality.

In the early 20th century, advances in medical technology and increased access to health care led to improvements in maternal health outcomes for all women. And in the 1960s and 1970s, the civil rights movement and feminist movement brought attention to issues of health care access and racial and gender discrimination in health care. In response, the federal government passed several laws aimed at improving health care access and reducing disparities in maternal health outcomes, including the Civil Rights Act of 1964 and the Pregnancy Discrimination Act of 1978. Regardless, Black women continue to experience higher rates of maternal mortality and SMM, often due to systemic and structural racism within the health care system. This reality materializes in the form of neglect, mistreatment, limited access to quality health care, low socioeconomic status, low educational attainment, and inadequate housing.[28]

Systemic and Structural Racism: The Mistreatment of Black Women in Health Care

Racial disparities that Black women face in the United States are partly a result of systemic and structural racism that shape the inequities seen today in educational attainment, access to health care, and maternal comorbidities.[29] Child-bearing women of different races, ethnicities, and sociodemographic factors report different levels of disrespectful care or mistreatment in hospitals. A disproportionate percentage of Black women report poor treatment when their opinions of proper care for their newborns differ from those of their caregivers.[30]

Mistreatment, in the form of neglect and abuse, results in skepticism of the health care system and subsequent avoidance of prenatal care.[31] This is a problem because almost a fifth of all women report mistreatment from their health care providers, including being ignored, violations of physical privacy, threats to withhold treatment, or being given unwanted treatment. Worse, women of color who had preexisting health conditions or were low-income reported higher rates of mistreatment than their healthier, more affluent counterparts.[32] Many studies document adverse encounters during hospital births in high-income countries, including the United States.[33] The fact is that the ill-treatment of women during labor and delivery is an indicator of a health care system that lacks quality and accountability.[34]

Limited or Lack of Access to Quality Health Care

In addition to mistreatment, the limited quality of services received and access to quality health care is another type of inequity faced by pregnant Black mothers in the United States Hospital quality is responsible for some of the disparities that women face when accessing prenatal care, services received during labor and delivery, and postpartum treatment. Hospitals that provide services to a significant percentage of people of color or to individuals of lower socioeconomic status may have an inferior quality of care compared to hospitals located in more affluent communities that serve a higher percentage of white patients.[35] This may be due to structural, organizational, and/or clinical factors as well as differential patterns of care, or implicit bias.[36] A New York City study, for example, found that hospitals with the highest rates of SMM are the same hospitals that have low-performance levels and high mortality rates.[37] These hospitals are often underresourced and are in densely populated minority neighborhoods. White counterparts are more likely to visit a high-performing, low-mortality rate hospital than their African American counterparts. Another element of quality care involves cultural competence. More African Americans in the health care workforce will improve cultural competence.[38]

Residential segregation and hospital location also factor into quality health care. Hospitals in neighborhoods that have a high density of African Americans are more at risk than hospitals in white neighborhoods.[39] This is noteworthy because receiving timely health care is critical for women who experience SMM. Hospital closures mean that women in distress must travel farther to receive care, thus increasing their risk.[40] It is important that hospitals they visit are equipped to handle cases of SMM; many hospitals in African American neighborhoods are not.

Hospitals in low-income areas lack the resources, skilled staff, and array of services to handle cases of SMM.[41] One study researched Black–White differences by analyzing the extent to which SMM is connected to poor-quality health care sites.[42] Findings revealed that Black women with postpartum problems usually deliver their babies in a concentrated portion of health care sites that operated at a lower level. Moreover, the study compared the health care sites according to cost of their services and concluded that Black women, in most cases, delivered at the same price level as White women.[43] SMM and maternal mortality are largely preventable and improving the quality of health care to reduce racial and ethnic inequities is important.[44]

Low Socioeconomic Status and Educational Attainment

Low socioeconomic status and educational attainment, the second and third SDoH, are linked to poor maternal health outcomes. Areas with a high density of African Americans often face high levels of poverty and lower levels of educational attainment.[45] These are also the neighborhoods that face the largest percentage of SMM.[46] Higher levels of education correlate with access to better health care, health insurance, and a better understanding of one's overall health. Moreover, a mother's education is instrumental in reducing and remedying adverse health outcomes.[47] The link between maternal educational attainment, literacy, and preventive health behaviors is associated with using health care facilities for labor and delivery and effectively reduces maternal morbidity.[48] Women who lack education and who are also at higher risk for poor maternal outcomes face a rate of death five times higher than what would otherwise be expected.[49]

Inadequate Housing

Housing and neighborhood conditions are another SDoH,[50] and inadequate housing is closely linked to poor health outcomes. In fact, housing is a frequently used indicator of health in the United States and abroad.[51] Infectious and chronic diseases, as well as maternal and reproductive health, are often linked to inadequate housing.[52] Inadequacy comes in the form of overcrowding, unsafe water, pest infestation, lack of heating, and/or exposure to mold, lead, and asbestos.[53] A byproduct of living in poverty, substandard housing, or housing instability is associated with chronic illnesses like hypertension, asthma, or diabetes, all of which are comorbidities that increase the risk of complications during and after pregnancy.

Individuals of color and low-income populations are disproportionately at risk for exposure to substandard housing. For example, African Americans are 1.7 times more likely to occupy homes that are in need of repair, and low-income individuals are 2.2 times as likely as others. The high expenses associated with housing create a significant financial strain on low-income households, compelling them to make choices between electricity, food, and other essentials to meet their housing obligations.[54] Low-income individuals who struggle to pay their rent, mortgage, or utility bills are less prone to possess a regular source of health care, which is detrimental to the expecting mother.[55] Disparities are further pronounced across racial lines where low-income neighborhoods comprised of greater percentages of minority groups encounter more environmental hazards.[56]

Maternal Mental Health Challenges

While not a main focus of this chapter, it is important to highlight maternal mental health as yet another challenge that women face before, during, and after pregnancy. Mental wellness is a significant factor during pregnancy and the likelihood of women delivering preterm and low-birth-weight infants has been linked to anxiety, depression, and stress.[57] Crime, quality of housing, and trash in the streets are risk factors in predominately African American neighborhoods and these living conditions lead to stress, which increases the risk of maternal morbidity.[53] In sum, housing insecurity has a detrimental impact on maternal mental health and physical health as well as the health of the unborn child.

Living in poverty adds multiple stressors to the soon-to-be mother. Compared to expectant women with more stable living arrangements, constant relocation is associated with anxiety disorders for pregnant mothers. Furthermore, eviction is associated with depression and increased stress.[59] Stress negatively impacts the health of expectant mothers and aggravates preexisting conditions that can worsen or increase the risk of SMM in African American women.[60]

This discussion has summarized the health effects that result from systemic and structural racism, limited access to quality health care, low socioeconomic status and educational attainment, inadequate housing, and maternal mental health challenges. The discussion turns now to pathways to action that will improve maternal health outcomes.

Pathways to Action

Interventions are called for that will address the disparities in SMM and maternal mortality rates for Black women in the United States This chapter has already discussed the social determinants of health (SDoH)—access to quality health care, socioeconomic status, educational attainment, and housing conditions—and how these factors negatively impact maternal health outcomes for women of color. Combating mental health challenges in vulnerable communities is also integral for improving maternal health outcomes, as are systemic factors, such as mistreatment and bias in health care delivery. By adopting a multidisciplinary and multisectoral approach that addresses factors at community and individual levels, it is possible to improve health outcomes.

As street-level bureaucrats, health care workers can use their discretion to ensure that vulnerable populations are able to access quality health care and do not come face-to-face with mistreatment and bias.[61] Nurses, midwives, and primary care physicians are in direct contact with citizens and have decision-making power as well as substantial autonomy.[62]

Address Systemic and Structural Racism, Mistreatment, and Bias

Beyond street-level bureaucrats, policy changes are necessary at the societal level to address systemic issues such as income inequality and racial discrimination.[63] Toward this end, the Biden administration took action in June 2022 when it proposed the "Blueprint for Addressing the Maternal Health Crisis". Through a "whole-of-government" approach, the federal government made it clear that this country has to address decades of systemic and structural racism. The blueprint states "this maternal health crisis is particularly devastating for Black women, Native women, and women in rural communities who all experience maternal mortality and morbidity at significantly higher rates than their white and urban counterparts."[64] One of the blueprint's actions is to expand social services by creating partnerships between the Departments of Housing and Urban Development, Agriculture, and Health and Human Services. This initiative acknowledges that health care is only one part of what makes for a healthy pregnancy.

Programs for housing, food, childcare, and income assistance all have a role to play. Administrators within the agencies have a large role to play in implementing programs and deciding who receives vital services and who is left out. Just as the blueprint acknowledges, improving health care cannot be accomplished by one agency working alone. Multi-department collaboration is necessary to minimize the racial gap in the health care system.

Beyond direct health care providers and government agencies, professional organizations also play an important role in reducing maternal health inequities. The Race, Ethnicity, and Culture in Health (REACH) committee, for example, aims to reduce health disparities between different racial, ethnic, and cultural groups through advocacy, education, and service.[65] Organizations such as REACH could play a more proactive role in developing programs that will improve access to health care and education. Such programs should be able to identify and analyze racial segregation, housing instability, and low educational attainment and illuminate how these phenomena influence maternal health. By addressing systemic issues, Black women can receive equitable care and achieve better maternal health outcomes.

Provide Women with Access to Free or Affordable Primary Care

Under the SDoH, this chapter has discussed factors that adversely affect maternal health outcomes for Black women. These include access to quality health care, socioeconomic status, educational attainment, and housing conditions. With regard to access and socioeconomic inequities, roughly 10 million women lack health insurance. This shortcoming may be attributed to cost in terms of high co-payments and deductibles.[66] Uninsured women have inadequate access to care, get a lower standard of care, and have poorer health outcomes. Moreover, they receive fewer Pap tests, blood pressure checks (which can detect preeclampsia), and mammograms.[67] Even with insurance coverage, limitations on the types of maternity services exist. For instance, Medicaid coverage related to pregnancy only lasts 60 days after a mother delivers her child. Medicaid coverage should be extended to at least one year and cover preventive services for all women. As *de facto* gatekeepers, this is another example of policymakers' ability to use their discretion to improve access for all women of reproductive age.

Even when insured, women often endure high out-of-pocket payments when receiving maternity care services due to exorbitant copays and deductibles.[68] Approximately one-quarter of child-bearing American women spend at least $2,000 or more annually in out-of-pocket medical costs, which dissuades many from seeking care in the first place. In fact, a survey of women of reproductive age found that half of women of reproductive age in the United States reported skipping or delaying needed care due to the costs.[69] To reduce maternal deaths and SMM, U.S. policymakers must guarantee free or affordable primary care to all women.[70]

The high costs of health care prove extremely difficult for women of color. Fortunately, the Affordable Care Act (ACA) expanded access to affordable coverage through a combination of Medicaid expansions, private insurance reforms, and tax credits and it put an end to cost-sharing for preventive services. As of 2014, Medicaid expansion under the ACA covered almost all adults with incomes below 138% of the poverty line and the rate of those uninsured dropped historically.[71] Passage of the ACA brought positive gains for Black, low-income, pregnant women, and mothers. Undeniably, Medicaid expansion has been exceptionally valuable for Black mothers and pregnant women by mandating coverage for contraception and forbidding discrimination for those with pre-existing conditions.[72]

Despite benefits of the ACA, American women still pay elevated out-of-pocket costs for services outside of preventive care and can face high out-of-pocket costs for other care.[73] Additionally, a coverage gap exists in eleven states that elected not to adopt the ACA Medicaid expansion for adults who are not eligible for Medicaid coverage or subsidies in the health care marketplace.[74] Furthermore, a disproportionate number of Black women have been left vulnerable when Medicaid ends after 60 days postpartum.

In June 2022, the Biden administration proposed to extend Medicaid coverage for mothers to one year postpartum under the Blueprint for Addressing the Maternal Health Crisis.[75] This act will address the hardships that women of lower socioeconomic status face after receiving prenatal, perinatal, and postpartum services. Additionally, through the "No Surprises Act," which was enacted on January 1, 2022, women are now protected from unexpected medical bills that may occur during pregnancy, postpartum care, and/or delivery.

Another boost came on May 19, 2023, when the U.S. Department of Health and Human Services (HHS) announced an award of more than $65 million to address the maternal health crisis. Monies go to 35 health centers funded by the Health Resources and Services Administration (HRSA) to implement innovations designed to reduce maternal health inequities. The initiative helps individuals and families who are uninsured or enrolled in Medicaid; living in rural or underserved areas; struggling to afford their health insurance copays; experiencing homelessness; residing in public housing; and/or otherwise having difficulty finding a doctor or paying for the cost of care.[76]

Deliver High-Quality Obstetric Care through a Diverse Perinatal Workforce

As previously mentioned, U.S. hospitals located in majority-minority communities have many challenges. Fewer of their patients are insured so they provide more uncompensated care, which affects their financial viability. Patients often arrive sicker than at hospitals in advantaged communities and, thus, their mortality rates are higher. It is difficult to tease out whether care is of inferior quality or whether patients' illnesses have poorer prognoses when they arrive at the hospital. Regardless, their image suffers and confidence in their services is eroded. Poorly funded hospitals are at risk of closure and this makes recruiting and retaining staff difficult. Neither do they have the sophisticated equipment that better-funded hospitals have and this makes it difficult to properly handle cases of SMM.[77]

The United States is unique in its delivery of perinatal services when compared to peer nations. In the United States 98% of births occur in hospital settings[78] and almost 91% of hospital births are physician attended. Only 8.7% of births are attended by midwives.[79] Most high-income countries provide higher rates of midwifery care and a smaller percentage of hospital births.[80] Midwifery is skilled, knowledgeable care for childbearing women, newborn infants, and families across the continuum from pre-pregnancy, pregnancy, birth, postpartum, and the early weeks of life and is successful in reducing maternal and newborn mortality.[81] However, in the United States, doula, and midwifery services, as well as non-hospital births, are not covered under Medicaid so these services have to be paid out-of-pocket,[82] making them unaffordable for those of lower income. The research is clear, however, that midwifery and doula care offer substantial benefits. They reduce medical interventions during labor and delivery, promote patient satisfaction, and most important, reduce maternal and neonatal morbidity and death.[83]

Midwives and Doulas

Evidence is clear that adding midwifery services to conventional maternal health care reduces SMM and mortality.[84] Midwifery offers more racial diversity in the perinatal workforce, and this improves access and quality of care for Black women,[85] which leads to two policy recommendations: 1) increasing the number of states where midwives can operate freely and sovereignly without being governed by physicians, and 2) investing in programs that diversify the racial and ethnic composition of the perinatal workforce across all types of training.[86]

Fortunately, federal funding in 2023 included the provision of bilingual doula services.[87] And, through the Health Resources and Services Administration (HRSA) Maternal Health Workforce Programs, newly certified nurse-midwives and community-based doulas are being trained and incentivized to practice in underserved and rural health care systems.[88] These pathways to action are steps that embrace the need for culturally competent health care providers who are trained to recognize and respond to complications during childbirth. Health care providers who work in underserved areas are usually dealing with resource scarcity. In such contexts, discretion is of utmost importance as providers need to determine how best to allocate the resources available amid unanticipated demands. An example is reducing unnecessary cesarean sections and improving communication between providers and the women they serve.[89]

Require Cultural Competency for Health Care Providers

Another strategy to improve maternal health care for Black women is the requirement of comprehensive and culturally sensitive prenatal care. Cultural competence is an important factor in maternal health but the U.S. perinatal workforce is predominantly White. This does not mirror the racial and ethnic makeup of the country.[90] According to Rayburn and colleagues, only 14% of the birthing workforce identify as Black. Of these, 6.3% are certified nurse midwives (CNMs), and 11% are OB/GYNs.[91]

Cultural competency champions insist that health care providers be well acquainted with the customs, beliefs, and values of different racial and ethnic groups. The goal is that familiarity will decrease inequities. Cultural sensitivity is also key to ensuring that Black women feel comfortable seeking care and trusting those who provide it.[92] The Biden administration amplifies this imperative in its Blueprint, saying "more providers will be trained on implicit biases as well as culturally and linguistically appropriate care, so that more women are listened to, respected, and empowered as a decision-makers in their own care."[93]

Offer Affordable Mental Health Care and Substance Abuse Services for Women

There is a link between housing insecurity and maternal mental health.[94] Estimates are that 11% to 21% of pregnant women experience perinatal mood and anxiety disorders and these are related to negative outcomes.[95] American women also reportedly avoid seeking mental health care due to cost.[96] Additionally, the association between mental health and substance abuse is well-established. Substance use, which ranges in incidence depending on the specific drug, includes smoking cigarettes, alcohol consumption, and illicit drugs. These factors require practical interventions when it comes to expectant women.

Verbal screening for substance abuse has shown success because patients are receptive to being asked about it.[97] It would be advantageous for policymakers to support funding for consultation hotlines and telehealth. Another recommendation is to extend the ACA requirement to cover mental health care.[98] Thankfully, as part of the White House Blueprint, HHS is intent on providing "culturally aware mental and behavioral health care for pregnant women and their families."[99] In fact, the Blueprint calls behavioral health services integral to maternal health outcomes. The Health Resources and Services Administration is aware that "pregnancy and a new baby can bring a range of emotions where many new moms feel overwhelmed, sad, anxious, or exhausted at different times during their pregnancy or after the baby is born."[100] As a result, a confidential hotline for pregnant and new mothers is now available 24 hours a day, 7 days a week, and is free. Services are provided in English and Spanish (as well as interpreter services in 60 different languages) and expecting or new mothers can call or text culturally sensitive professional counselors and receive real-time support and information.[101]

Another initiative is the Screening and Treatment for Maternal Depression and Related Behavioral Disorders Program (MDRBD). The program has four goals:

1) improving the mental health and well-being of pregnant and postpartum women, and in turn, the social and emotional development of their infants;
2) increasing health care providers' identification of maternal mental health conditions;
3) using evidence-based and culturally appropriate practices to provide treatment and referral;
4) improving access to affordable, community-based treatment and recovery support services, locally or via telehealth, especially in rural and medically underserved areas.[102]

The program provides instruction for OB/GYNs, CNMs, and additional maternal care providers and partners with community-based organizations to ensure that addiction services and people trained in substance use disorder during pregnancy are more available.[103]

Fund Community-Based Organizations Focused on Improving Maternal Health Outcomes

Interventions to improve an individual's socioeconomic status and educational attainment work well when they involve partnerships with community-based organizations (CBOs). Initiatives can improve access to affordable housing, transportation, and community resources such as food banks and job training programs. Those employed at CBOs may use outreach and communication strategies to ensure that Black mothers know of these community resources. While federal and state initiatives play an important role in improving maternal health outcomes, public health programs through CBOs may have a greater effect because they provide a bottom-up approach for empowering impoverished communities and changing maternal behaviors.

CBOs are well-suited for supporting expectant women and new mothers because they are fully involved with the communities they serve.[104] Especially for low-income mothers, CBOs can mitigate the social determinants of health through providing access to food, affordable housing, doula and midwifery care, and more.[105] Unfortunately, a lot of CBOs could have a greater impact if they received more funding.[106] Therefore, a final recommendation is that government allocate funding for CBOs, particularly Black-led CBOs, that provide much needed maternal health care services for women and families in underserved communities.

Summary of Key Points

Addressing the issues of severe maternal morbidity and maternal mortality among Black women requires a multifaceted approach that considers the social determinants of health and the systemic factors that contribute to racial and ethnic disparities in maternal health outcomes. Efforts to address these disparities require attention to a complex array of factors, including bias and mistreatment within the health care system, the provision of free or low-cost primary care, first-rate obstetric care, cultural competency training, mental health and substance abuse services, and funding for CBOs whose mission is to reduce maternal death and severe morbidity.

The Biden administration's Blueprint for Addressing the Maternal Health Crisis, put forth in 2022, is the most recent significant initiative to improve maternal health. The announcement by the U.S. Department of Health and Human Services in 2023 demonstrates this country's commitment to addressing the maternal health crisis and suggests that pathways are opening that focus on innovative, comprehensive approaches to improving maternal health.

Discussion Questions

1. What other approaches can the federal government propose that were not mentioned in the Blueprint for Addressing the Maternal Health Crisis? (Consider, for example, the migrant and refugee population; incarcerated women; female veterans; extensions of maternity leave, and more.)
2. As stated, the United States has the highest maternal mortality rate of all high-income countries. Why has maternal health not been higher on the public health agenda in the United States?
3. What reproductive health policies from other high-income countries should the United States copy to improve maternal health outcomes?

Additional Resources

1. FACT SHEET: President Biden's and Vice President Harris's Maternal Health Blueprint Delivers for Women, Mothers, and Families, available at https://www.whitehouse.gov/briefing-room/statements-releases/2022/06/24/fact-sheet-president-bidens-maternal-health-blueprint-delivers-for-women-mothers-and-families/
2. HHS Announces Over $65 Million to Address the Maternal Health Crisis and Invest in New Approaches to Care. See report at https://www.hhs.gov/about/news/2023/05/19/hhs-announces-over-65-million-address-maternal-health-crisis-invest-new-approaches-care.html

Notes

1. Eugene R. Declercq, Carol Sakala, Maureen P. Corry, Sandra Applebaum, and Ariel Herrlich, "Major Survey Findings of Listening to Mothers SM III: New Mothers Speak Out: Report of National Surveys of Women's Childbearing Experiences Conducted October–December 2012 and January–April 2013," *Journal of Perinatal Education* 23, no. 1 (2014): 17–24.
2. Jodie Katon, Daniel A. Enquobahrie, Kate Jacobsen, and Laurie Zephyrin, "Policies for Reducing Maternal Morbidity and Mortality and Enhancing Equity in Maternal Health: A Review of the Evidence," The Commonwealth Fund, November 16, 2021, https://www.commonwealthfund.org/publications/fund-reports/2021/nov/policies-reducing-maternal-morbidity-mortality-enhancing-equity#28
3. Maeve E. Wallace, Pauline Mendola, Danping Liu, and Katherine L Grantz, "Joint Effects of Structural Racism and Income Inequality on Small-for-Gestational-Age Birth," *American Journal of Public Health* 105, no. 8 (2015): 1681–1688.
4. Saraswathi Vedam, Kathrin Stoll, Tanya Khemet Taiwo, Nicholas Rubashkin, Melissa Cheyney, Nan Strauss, Monica McLemore, et al., "The Giving Voice to Mothers Study: Inequity and Mistreatment during Pregnancy and Childbirth in the United States," *Reproductive Health* 16, no. 1 (2019): 77–77.
5. World Health Organization, "Equity Team" definition. Health and Human Rights and Equity Working Group Draft Glossary, Unpublished, 2005 (Geneva: World Health Organization, 2005).
6. Michael R. Fraser, "Bringing It All Together: Effective Maternal and Child Health Practice as a Means to Improve Public Health," *Maternal and Child Health Journal* 17, no. 5 (2013): 767–775.
7. Margaret Whitehead and Goran Dahlgren, *Concepts and Principles for Tackling Social Inequities in Health: Levelling up Part 1* (Copenhagen: World Health Organization, 2007).
8. Mats Målqvist, Dinh Thi Phuong Hoa, and Sarah Thomsen, "Causes and Determinants of Inequity in Maternal and Child Health in Vietnam," *BMC Public Health* 12, no. 1 (2012): 641–641.
9. Målqvist et al., "Causes and Determinants of Inequity in Maternal and Child Health in Vietnam."
10. Målqvist et al., "Causes and Determinants of Inequity in Maternal and Child Health in Vietnam."
11. Orielle Solar and Alec Irwin, *A Conceptual Framework for Action on the Social Determinants of Health* (Geneva: WHO Document Production Services, 2010), https://doi.org/10.13016/17cr-aqb9; Juha Mikkonen and Dennis Raphael, Social Determinants of Health: The Canadian Facts (Toronto: York University, School of Health Policy and Management, 2010), accessed August 14, 2023, https://thecanadianfacts.org/the_canadian_facts.pdf
12. World Health Organization, "Maternal Mortality," World Health Organization, February 22, 2023, accessed August 14, 2023, https://www.who.int/news-room/fact-sheets/detail/maternal-mortality; World Health Organization, "ICD-11 for Mortality and Morbidity Statistics" World Health Organization, accessed August 14, 2023, https://icd.who.int/browse11/l-m/en#/http%3a%2f%2fid.who.int%2ficd%2fentity%2f1151689960
13. Munira Z. Gunja, Evan D. Gumas, and Reginald D. Williams, "The U.S. Maternal Mortality Crisis Continues to Worsen: An International Comparison," The Commonwealth Fund, December 1, 2022, https://www.commonwealthfund.org/blog/2022/us-maternal-mortality-crisis-continues-worsen-international-comparison
14. Selena Simmons-Duffin and Carmel Wroth, "Maternal Deaths in the U.S. Spiked in 2021, CDC

Reports," NPR, March 16, 2023, https://www.npr.org/sections/health-shots/2023/03/16/1163786037/maternal-deaths-in-the-u-s-spiked-in-2021-cdc-reports

15. Laura Santhanam, "U.S. Maternal Mortality Spiked During the Worst Days of COVID, New Data Shows," PBS News Hour, March 16, 2023, https://www.pbs.org/newshour/health/u-s-maternal-mortality-spiked-during-the-worst-days-of-covid-new-data-shows
16. World Health Organization, "Maternal Mortality."
17. William M. Callaghan, Andreea A. Creanga, and Elena V. Kuklina, "Severe Maternal Morbidity Among Delivery and Postpartum Hospitalizations in the United States," *Obstetrics & Gynecology*, 120, no. 5 (2012): 1029–1036.
18. João Paulo Souza, José Guilherme Cecatti, Mary Angela Parpinelli, Maria Helena de Sousa, and Suzanne Jacob Serruya, "Systematic Review of Near Miss Maternal Morbidity," *Cadernos de Saúde Pública* 22, no. 2 (2006): 255–264.
19. Sarah K. Kilpatrick, Jeffrey L. Ecker, and William M. Callaghan, "Severe Maternal Morbidity: Screening and Review," *American Journal of Obstetrics and Gynecology* 215, no. 3 (2016): B17–B22.
20. Eugene Declercq and Laurie C. Zephyrin, "Severe Maternal Morbidity in the United States: A Primer," The Commonwealth Fund, October 28, 2021, https://www.commonwealthfund.org/publications/issue-briefs/2021/oct/severe-maternal-morbidity-united-states-primer
21. Declercq and Zephyrin, "Severe Maternal Morbidity in the United States: A Primer."
22. Declercq and Zephyrin, "Severe Maternal Morbidity in the United States: A Primer."
23. Gunja et al., "U.S. Maternal Mortality Crisis Continues to Worsen: An International Comparison."
24. Simmons-Duffin and Wroth, "Maternal Deaths in the U.S. Spiked in 2021, CDC Reports."
25. Myra J. Tucker, Cynthia J. Berg, William M. Callaghan, and Jason Hsia, "The Black-White Disparity in Pregnancy-Related Mortality From 5 Conditions: Differences in Prevalence and Case-Fatality Rates," *American Journal of Public Health* 97, no. 2 (2007): 247–251.
26. Declercq and Zephyrin, "Severe Maternal Morbidity in the United States: A Primer."
27. Stephanie Arteaga, Erin Hubbard, Jennet Arcara, Alli Cuentos, Marna Armstead, Andrea Jackson, Anu Manchikanti Gomez, and Cassondra Marshall, "'They're Gonna Be There to Advocate for Me So I'm Not by Myself': A Qualitative Analysis of Black Women's Motivations for Seeking and Experiences with Community Doula Care," *Women and Birth: Journal of the Australian College of Midwives* 36, no. 3 (2023): 257–263.
28. Timothy Abuya, Charity Ndwiga, Julie Ritter, Lucy Kanya, Ben Bellows, Nancy Binkin, and Charlotte E. Warren, "The Effect of a Multi-Component Intervention on Disrespect and Abuse During Childbirth in Kenya," *BMC Pregnancy and Childbirth* 15, no. 1 (2015): 224–224, https://doi.org/10.1186/s12884-015-0645-6; Todd E. Elder, John H. Goddeeris, and Steven J. Haider, "Racial and Ethnic Infant Mortality Gaps and the Role of Socio-Economic Status," *Labour Economics* 43 (2016): 42–54; Daphne N. McRae, Patricia A. Janssen, Saraswathi Vedam, Maureen Mayhew, Deborah Mpofu, Ulrich Teucher, and Nazeem Muhajarine, "Reduced Prevalence of Small-for-Gestational-Age and Preterm Birth for Women of Low Socioeconomic Position: a Population-Based Cohort Study Comparing Antenatal Midwifery and Physician Models of Care," *BMJ Open* 8, no. 10 (2018): e022220–e022220.
29. Eileen Wang, Kimberly B. Glazer, Elizabeth A. Howell, and Teresa Janevic, "Social Determinants of Pregnancy-Related Mortality and Morbidity in the United States: A Systematic Review," *Obstetrics & Gynecology* 135, no. 4 (2020), 896–915; Eileen Wang, Kimberly B. Glazer, Shoshanna Sofaer, Amy Balbierz, and Elizabeth A. Howell, "Racial and Ethnic Disparities in Severe Maternal Morbidity: A Qualitative Study of Women's Experiences of Peripartum Care," *Women's Health Issues* 31, no. 1 (2021): 75–81.
30. Declerq et al., "Major Survey Findings of Listening to Mothers SM III."
31. Meghan A. Bohren, Erin C. Hunter, Heather M. Munthe-Kaas, João Paulo Souza, Joshua P Vogel, and A. Metin Gülmezoglu, "Facilitators and Barriers to Facility-Based Delivery in Low- and Middle-Income Countries: A Qualitative Evidence Synthesis," *Reproductive Health* 11, no. 1 (2014): 71.
32. Vedam et al., "The Giving Voice to Mothers Study: Inequity and Mistreatment during Pregnancy and Childbirth in the United States."
33. Sarah R. Baker, Precilla Y.L. Choi, Carol A. Henshaw, and Joanne Tree, "'I Felt as though I'd Been in Jail': Women's Experiences of Maternity Care during Labour, Delivery and the Immediate Postpartum," *Feminism & Psychology* 15, no. 3 (2005): 315–342; Cheryl Tatano Beck, "A Secondary Analysis of Mistreatment of Women During Childbirth in Health Care Facil-

ities," *Journal of Obstetric, Gynecologic, and Neonatal Nursing* 47, no. 1 (2018): 94–104; Claudia Ravaldi, Elena Skoko, Alessandra Battisti, Michela Cericco, and Alfredo Vannacci, "Abuse and Disrespect in Childbirth Assistance in Italy: A Community-Based Survey," *European Journal of Obstetrics & Gynecology and Reproductive Biology* 224 (2018): 208–209.

34. Lynn P. Freedman, and Margaret E. Kruk, "Disrespect and Abuse of Women in Childbirth: Challenging the Global Quality and Accountability Agendas," *The Lancet* (British Edition) 384, no. 9948 (2014): e42–e44.
35. Elizabeth A. Howell, and Jennifer Zeitlin, "Improving Hospital Quality to Reduce Disparities in Severe Maternal Morbidity and Mortality," *Seminars in Perinatology* 41, no. 5 (2017): 266–272.
36. Howell and Zeitlin, "Improving Hospital Quality to Reduce Disparities in Severe Maternal Morbidity and Mortality."
37. Elizabeth A. Howell, Natalia Egorova, Amy Balbierz, Jennifer Zeitlin, and Paul L. Hebert, "Black-White Differences in Severe Maternal Morbidity and Site of Care," *American Journal of Obstetrics and Gynecology* 214, no. 1 (2016): 122.e1–122.e7.
38. Howell et al., "Black-White Differences in Severe Maternal Morbidity and Site of Care."
39. Michelle Ko, Jack Needleman, Kathryn Pitkin Derose, Miriam J. Laugesen, and Ninez A. Ponce, "Residential Segregation and the Survival of U.S. Urban Public Hospitals," *Medical Care Research and Review* 71, no. 3 (2014): 243–260.
40. Ko et al., "Residential Segregation and the Survival of U.S. Urban Public Hospitals."
41. Ko et al., "Residential Segregation and the Survival of U.S. Urban Public Hospitals."
42. Howell et al., "Black-White Differences in Severe Maternal Morbidity and Site of Care."
43. Howell et al., "Black-White Differences in Severe Maternal Morbidity and Site of Care."
44. Paula Braveman, "What Are Health Disparities and Health Equity? We Need to Be Clear," *Public Health Reports* 129, no. 1 suppl 2 (2014): 5–8.
45. James Krieger, and Donna L Higgins, "Housing and Health: Time Again for Public Health Action," *American Journal of Public Health* 92, no. 5 (2002): 758–768.
46. Howell et al., "Black-White Differences in Severe Maternal Morbidity and Site of Care."
47. Barbara S. Mensch, Erica K. Chuang, Andrea J. Melnikas, and Stephanie R. Psaki, "Evidence for Causal Links between Education and Maternal and Child Health: Systematic Review," *Tropical Medicine & International Health* 24, no. 5 (2019): 504–522.
48. Oona M.R. Campbell, and Wendy J Graham, "Strategies for Reducing Maternal Mortality: Getting on with What Works," *The Lancet* (British edition) 368, no. 9543 (2006): 1284–1299.
49. Ö. Tunçalp, J.P. Souza, M.J. Hindin, C.A. Santos, T.H. Oliveira, J.P. Vogel, G. Togoobaatar, D.Q. Ha, L. Say, and A.M. Gülmezoglu, "Education and Severe Maternal Outcomes in Developing Countries: A Multicountry Cross-Sectional Survey," *BJOG: An International Journal of Obstetrics and Gynecology* 121, no. s1(2014): 57–65.
50. Lauren Taylor, "Housing and Health: An Overview of the Literature," *Health Affairs Health Policy Brief* 10, no. 10.1377 (2018), https://doi.org/10.1377/hpb20180313.396577
51. Kriger and Higgins, "Housing and Health: Time Again for Public Health Action."
52. Carolyn B. Swope and Diana Hernández, "Housing as a Determinant of Health Equity: A Conceptual Model," *Social Science & Medicine* 243 (2019): 112571–112571.
53. Kriger and Higgins, "Housing and Health: Time Again for Public Health Action."
54. Kriger and Higgins, "Housing and Health: Time Again for Public Health Action."
55. Swope and Hernández, "Housing as a Determinant of Health Equity: A Conceptual Model."
56. Rachel Morello-Frosch, Miriam Zuk, Michael Jerrett, Bhavna Shamasunder, and Amy D Kyle, "Understanding the Cumulative Impacts of Inequalities in Environmental Health: Implications For Policy," *Health Affairs* 30, no. 5 (2011): 879–887.
57. Kathryn M. Leifheit, Gabriel L. Schwartz, Craig E. Pollack, Kathryn J. Edin, Maureen M. Black, Jacky M. Jennings, and Keri N. Althoff, "Severe Housing Insecurity during Pregnancy: Association with Adverse Birth and Infant Outcomes," *International Journal of Environmental Research and Public Health* 17, no. 22 (2020): 1–12.
58. Marie Lynn Miranda, Pamela Maxson, and Sharon Edwards, "Environmental Contributions to Disparities in Pregnancy Outcomes," *Epidemiologic Reviews* 31, no. 1 (2009): 67–83.
59. Leifheit et al., "Severe Housing Insecurity during Pregnancy: Association with Adverse Birth and Infant Outcomes."
60. Paula Braveman, Kristen Marchi, Susan Egerter, Soowon Kim, Marilyn Metzler, Tonya Stancil, and Moreen Libet, "Poverty, Near-Poverty, and Hardship

Around the Time of Pregnancy," *Maternal and Child Health Journal* 14, no. 1 (2010): 20–35.

61. Michael Lipsky, *Street-Level Bureaucracy: Dilemmas of the Individual in Public Services* (30th Anniversary Expanded ed.) (New York: Russell Sage Foundation, 2010).
62. Sergio Cárdenas and Edgar E. Ramírez de la Cruz, "Controlling Administrative Discretion Promotes Social Equity? Evidence from a Natural Experiment," *Public Administration Review* 77, no. 1 (2017): 80–89.
63. Cárdenas and Ramírez de la Cruz, "Controlling Administrative Discretion Promotes Social Equity? Evidence from a Natural Experiment," 2.
64. The White House, *FACT SHEET:* President Biden's and Vice President Harris's Maternal Health Blueprint Delivers for Women, Mothers, and Families, June 24, 2022, https://www.whitehouse.gov/briefing-room/statements-releases/2022/06/24/fact-sheet-president-bidens-maternal-health-blueprint-delivers-for-women-mothers-and-families/
65. American Medical Student Association, "Race, Ethnicity, and Culture in Health," American Medical Student Association, accessed August 14, 2023, https://www.amsa.org/action-committee/race-ethnicity-and-culture-in-health/#:~:text=The%20Race%2C%20Ethnicity%2C%20and%20Culture%20in%20Health%20(REACH),advocacy%2C%20education%2C%20and%20service
66. Robin Rudowitz, Patrick Drake, Jennifer Tolbert, and Anthony Damico, "How Many Uninsured Are in the Coverage Gap and How Many Could Be Eligible If All States Adopted the Medicaid Expansion?" The Kaiser Family Foundation, March 31, 2023, https://www.kff.org/medicaid/issue-brief/how-many-uninsured-are-in-the-coverage-gap-and-how-many-could-be-eligible-if-all-states-adopted-the-medicaid-expansion/
67. Rachel Garfield, Kendal Orgera, and Anthony Damico, "The Uninsured and the ACA: A Primer—Key Facts about Health Insurance and the Uninsured amidst Changes to the Affordable Care Act," The Commonwealth Fund, January 25, 2019, https://www.kff.org/uninsured/report/the-uninsured-and-the-aca-a-primer-key-facts-about-health-insurance-and-the-uninsured-amidst-changes-to-the-affordable-care-act/; Rudowitz et al., "How Many Uninsured Are in the Coverage Gap and How Many Could Be Eligible If All States Adopted the Medicaid Expansion?"
68. Gunja et al., "U.S. Maternal Mortality Crisis Continues to Worsen: An International Comparison"; Rudowitz et al., "How Many Uninsured Are in the Coverage Gap and How Many Could Be Eligible If All States Adopted the Medicaid Expansion?"
69. Gunja et al., "U.S. Maternal Mortality Crisis Continues to Worsen: An International Comparison."
70. Gunja et al., "U.S. Maternal Mortality Crisis Continues to Worsen: An International Comparison."
71. Garfield et al., "The Uninsured and the ACA: A Primer—Key Facts about Health Insurance and the Uninsured amidst Changes to the Affordable Care Act."
72. Erica L. Eliason, "Adoption of Medicaid Expansion Is Associated with Lower Maternal Mortality," *Women's Health Issues* 30, no. 3 (2020): 147–152.
73. Gunja et al., "U.S. Maternal Mortality Crisis Continues to Worsen: An International Comparison."
74. Rudowitz et al., "How Many Uninsured Are in the Coverage Gap and How Many Could Be Eligible If All States Adopted the Medicaid Expansion?"
75. The White House, "FACT SHEET: President Biden's and Vice President Harris's Maternal Health Blueprint Delivers for Women, Mothers, and Families."
76. U.S. Department of Health and Human Services, "HHS Announces Over $65 Million to Address the Maternal Health Crisis and Invest in New Approaches to Care," May 19, 2023, https://www.hhs.gov/about/news/2023/05/19/hhs-announces-over-65-million-address-maternal-health-crisis-invest-new-approaches-care.html
77. Howell et al., "Black-White Differences in Severe Maternal Morbidity and Site of Care"; Howell and Zeitlin, "Improving Hospital Quality to Reduce Disparities in Severe Maternal Morbidity and Mortality"; Ko et al., "Residential Segregation and the Survival of U.S. Urban Public Hospitals."
78. The National Academies Press, Birth Settings in America: Outcomes, Quality, Access, and Choice (Washington, DC: The National Academies Press, 2020).
79. Katon et al., "Policies for Reducing Maternal Morbidity and Mortality and Enhancing Equity in Maternal Health: A Review of the Evidence."
80. Aaron B. Caughey and Melissa Cheyney, "Home and Birth Center Birth in the United States Time for Greater Collaboration Across Models of Care," *Obstetrics & Gynecology* 133, no. 5 (2019): 1033–1050.
81. World Health Organization, "Midwifery Education and Care," World Health Organization, accessed August 14, 2023, https://www.who.int/teams/maternal-newborn-child-adolescent-health-and-ageing/

maternal-health/midwifery/maternal-health-83-percent-midwifery-care; see also World Health Organization, "ICD-11 for Mortality and Morbidity Statistics," accessed August 14, 2023, https://icd.who.int/browse11/l-m/en#/http%3a%2f%2fid.who.int%2ficd%2fentity%2f1151689960; World Health Organization, "Maternal Mortality," February 22, 2023, accessed August 14, 2023, https://www.who.int/news-room/fact-sheets/detail/maternal-mortality; World Health Organization, "Equity Team" definition. Health and Human Rights and Equity Working Group Draft Glossary, Unpublished 2005 (Geneva: World Health Organization, 2005).

82. Katon et al., "Policies for Reducing Maternal Morbidity and Mortality and Enhancing Equity in Maternal Health: A Review of the Evidence."
83. Meghan A. Bohren, G. Justus Hofmeyr, Carol Sakala, Rieko K Fukuzawa, and Anna Cuthbert, "Continuous Support for Women During Childbirth," *Cochrane Database of Systematic Reviews* 7, no. 7 (2017): CD003766–CD003766, https://doi.org/10.1002/14651858.CD003766.pub6; Mary-Powel Thomas, Gabriela Ammann, Ellen Brazier, Philip Noyes, and Aletha Maybank, "Doula Services within a Healthy Start Program: Increasing Access for an Underserved Population," *Maternal and Child Health Journal* 21, no. Suppl 1 (2017): 59–64; Kenneth J. Gruber, Susan H. Cupito, and Christina F. Dobson. "Impact of Doulas on Healthy Birth Outcomes," *The Journal of Perinatal Education* 22, no. 1 (2013): 49–58.
84. Mary J. Renfrew, Alison McFadden, Maria Helena Bastos, James Cambell, Andres Amos Cannon, Ngai Fen Cheung, Deborah Rachel Audebert Delage Silva, et al., "Midwifery and Quality Care: Findings from a New Evidence-Informed Framework for Maternal and Newborn Care," *The Lancet* 384 (2014): 1129–45.
85. Health Resources and Services Administration, "Supporting Diversity in the Health Professions," May 2016, accessed August 14, 2023, https://www.hrsa.gov/sites/default/files/hrsa/advisory-committees/graduate-medical-edu/publications/may-2016.pdf
86. Zoë Julian, Diana Robles, Sara Whetstone, Jamila B. Perritt, Andrea V. Jackson, Rachel R. Hardeman, and Karen A. Scott, "Community-Informed Models of Perinatal and Reproductive Health Services Provision: A Justice-Centered Paradigm Toward Equity among Black Birthing Communities," *Seminars in Perinatology* 44, no. 5 (2020): 151267–151267.
87. U.S. Department of Health and Human Services, "HHS Announces Over $65 Million to Address the Maternal Health Crisis and Invest in New Approaches to Care."
88. U.S. Department of Health and Human Services, "HHS Announces Over $65 Million to Address the Maternal Health Crisis and Invest in New Approaches to Care."
89. Elizabeth A. Howell, "Reducing Disparities in Severe Maternal Morbidity and Mortality," *Clinical Obstetrics and Gynecology* 61, no. 2 (2018): 387–399.
90. Katon et al., "Policies for Reducing Maternal Morbidity and Mortality and Enhancing Equity in Maternal Health: A Review of the Evidence."
91. William F. Rayburn, Imam M. Xierali, Laura Castillo-Page, and Marc Nive, "Racial and Ethnic Differences between Obstetrician–Gynecologists and Other Adult Medical Specialists," *Obstetrics & Gynecology* 127, no. 1 (2016): 148–152.
92. Allison S. Bryant, Ayaba Worjoloh, Aaron B. Caughey, and A. Eugene Washington, "Racial/Ethnic Disparities in Obstetric Outcomes and Care: Prevalence and Determinants," *American Journal of Obstetrics and Gynecology* 202, no. 4 (2010): 335–343.
93. The White House, FACT SHEET: President Biden's and Vice President Harris's Maternal Health Blueprint Delivers for Women, Mothers, and Families.
94. Leifheit et al., "Severe Housing Insecurity during Pregnancy: Association with Adverse Birth and Infant Outcomes"; Braveman et al., "Poverty, Near-Poverty, and Hardship Around the Time of Pregnancy"; Miranda et al., "Environmental Contributions to Disparities in Pregnancy Outcomes."
95. Susan Kendig, John P. Keats, M. Camille Hoffman, Lisa B. Kay, Emily S. Miller, Tiffany A. Moore Simas, Ariela Frieder, et al., "Consensus Bundle on Maternal Mental Health: Perinatal Depression and Anxiety," *Journal of Midwifery & Women's Health* 62, no. 2 (2017): 232–239.
96. Gunja et al., "U.S. Maternal Mortality Crisis Continues to Worsen: An International Comparison."
97. Signy M. Toquinto, Nancy F. Berglas, Monica R. McLemore, Ana Delgado, and Sarah C.M. Roberts, "Pregnant Women's Acceptability of Alcohol, Tobacco, and Drug Use Screening and Willingness to Disclose Use in Prenatal Care," *Women's Health Issues* 30, no. 5 (2020): 345–352.
98. Gunja et al., "U.S. Maternal Mortality Crisis Continues to Worsen: An International Comparison."
99. U.S. Department of Health and Human Services, "HHS Announces Over $65 Million to Address the Maternal Health Crisis and Invest in New Approaches to Care."

100. Health Resources and Services Administration, "National Maternal Mental Health Hotline," accessed August 14, 2023, https://mchb.hrsa.gov/national-maternal-mental-health-hotline
101. Health Resources and Services Administration, "National Maternal Mental Health Hotline."
102. Health Resources and Services Administration, "Screening and Treatment for Maternal Depression and Related Behavioral Disorders Program (MDRBD)," accessed August 14, 2023, https://mchb.hrsa.gov/programs-impact/screening-treatment-maternal-depression-related-behavioral-disorders-program-mdrbd
103. The White House, FACT SHEET: President Biden's and Vice President Harris's Maternal Health Blueprint Delivers for Women, Mothers, and Families.
104. Julian et al., "Community-Informed Models of Perinatal and Reproductive Health Services Provision: A Justice-Centered Paradigm Toward Equity among Black Birthing Communities."
105. Kristina Wint, Thistle I. Elias, Gabriella Mendez, Dara D. Mendez, and Tiffany L. Gary-Webb, "Experiences of Community Doulas Working with Low-Income, African American Mothers," *Health Equity* 3, no. 1 (2019): 109–116.
106. Karen A. Scott, Stephanie Bray, and Monica R McLemore, "First, Do No Harm: Why Philanthropy Needs to Re-Examine Its Role in Reproductive Equity and Racial Justice," *Health Equity* 4, no. 1 (2020): 17–22.

10 EQUITY IN HOUSING

Megan E. Hatch

From the Editors

Few issues affect someone's quality of life to the degree that housing does. Market forces lead to profoundly different outcomes in terms of access to housing, quality of housing, processes for finding housing, or outcomes related to lack of housing. Hatch details four broad dimensions: home ownership, unsubsidized renting and evictions, subsidized renting, and homelessness. She suggests reshaping politics and power to allow marginalized populations a voice to influence policy debates; using administrative discretion to enhance equity; expanding access to credit and voucher programs; proactive monitoring of mortgage practices; and changing how care protocols address homelessness.

Housing in the United States is not a right. Rather, it is a commodity, something to be bought and sold. This leads to reliance on the market, where private actors sell, rent, and purchase housing. But markets are not equitable. Even in cases where government steps in to address market failures, such as under-provision of housing or transactions that negatively impact other parties, there is a policy preference for market mechanisms such as vouchers and public/private partnerships. While the 1968 Fair Housing Act and its amendments made many blatantly discriminatory practices illegal, discrimination and disparate impact by race/ethnicity, gender, and familial status, among other protected classes, still occurs. Housing providers' profit motivation further prevents some people from obtaining affordable, safe, and healthy housing.

Despite housing being a private market, public administrators play a key role in upholding and rectifying social inequities. The purpose of this chapter is to explain ways public administrators engage in housing policies and practices that are detrimental to social equity and to suggest how they could enhance equity instead. Housing policy is wide-ranging and public administrators are not directly involved in all its aspects. This chapter focuses only on issues in the public domain and I examine one policy area per tenure status. (In housing lingo, tenure refers to the financial arrangement and ownership structure under which a person has the right to live in an apartment or house.) The tenure statuses discussed here are access to mortgages, evictions of unsubsidized renters, the Housing Choice Voucher (HCV) program for subsidized renters, and Continuums of Care (CoC) programs for people experiencing homelessness.

I begin by discussing the legal, policy, and political context of housing in the United States. Then I outline the four market-related areas of housing where public administrators influence social equity. Next, I suggest ways to improve housing equity and I conclude with a summary.

Housing: A History of Social Inequity

Starting with the displacement of Indigenous people before the country's founding, denizens in the United States have been limited, particularly by their race/ethnicity and socioeconomic status, in where they can live. Public policies exacerbate(d) segregation while a lack of affordable housing continues to make housing in preferred neighborhoods unavailable to many.

Legal and Policy Context

The U.S. Constitution does not mention housing. Unlike countries such as France, there is no federally protected right to housing in the United States. States do not grant a broad right to shelter either, apart from Massachusetts, which guarantees a right to shelter to families but not individuals. Not requiring everyone to have housing has led to the commodification of housing and market-based housing solutions, which allows for market failures such as discrimination and exclusion.

Many federal laws govern housing. One of the most important is Title VIII of the Civil Rights Act of 1968, otherwise known as the Fair Housing Act. The Act and its subsequent amendments prohibit discrimination based on protected class—race, color, national origin, religion, sex, familial status, and disability—and thus provide baseline legal protections for equity in housing rentals and purchases.

Much of housing policy is left to states or local governments. This decentralization leads to significant variation in landlord-tenant laws as well as building and zoning codes. Some states allow cities extensive discretion, while others preempt their cities from enacting policies that might increase affordable housing. This variety allows for tailoring policy to local contexts, but it also leads to interjurisdictional inequities. Subnational governments are also responsible for implementing federal policies. Therefore, administrators have a significant role, often with substantial discretion, in ensuring housing equity within their jurisdictions.

Political Context

In the United States, the housing ideal is a single-family detached, owner-occupied home. The largest wealth generator in the country is homeownership. Therefore, protecting property values is a top priority for homeowners and policymakers. A long-held belief is that people racialized as non-white and those with low incomes will decrease property values. This belief accounts for inequitable practices and policies benefiting white homeowners to the detriment of other groups.[1] Examples include slum clearance, redlining (the practice of not providing mortgages or mortgage insurance in neighborhoods marked as unsuitable), demolition, and a lack of political will to invest in neighborhoods with large non-white populations.[2]

This is not to say that policy change is impossible. For example, grassroots organizations in race/class-subjugated communities have been able to pass right-to-counsel legislation to the benefit of tenants facing eviction.[3] Later I discuss other ways denizens, administrators, and policymakers can work toward more equitable housing policies.

Contemporary Issues in Housing Equity

Housing policy is extensive, making it impossible to discuss all policies in a single chapter. Instead, I focus on one social equity-related issue, policy, or program for each of the four most common housing experiences: owning one's home, renting one's home without a subsidy, renting one's home with a subsidy, and experiencing homelessness.

Homeowners: Access to Mortgages

One of the clearest examples of discrimination in housing is the practice of redlining. It began with the Federal Housing Administration (FHA)'s underwriting manual and neighborhood evaluation maps. Until the Fair Housing Act outlawed the practice, it meant banks would not invest in "redlined" neighborhoods, usually defined by their racial/ethnic composition,

However, that legislation did not end discriminatory practices. Norms of the real estate industry—that racial segregation is necessary to ensure high property values—dominate real estate lending, leading to what Keeanga-Yamahtta Taylor calls *predatory exclusion.*[4] Under it, groups previously excluded from the mortgage market are given mortgages, but under less favorable terms. For example, Black and Latinx homeowners were more likely than white homeowners to have a subprime mortgage, and therefore were disproportionately negatively impacted during the foreclosure crisis.

It is also difficult for families with low incomes, or who want to live in neighborhoods with low property values, to purchase homes with a mortgage. Many banks will not provide mortgages under $70,000, so only 27.5% of homes sold for less than $70,000 have a mortgage compared to 79.3% of homes selling for between $70,000 and $150,000.[5] If a family does not have access to capital to buy without a mortgage, they are shut out of the greatest wealth generator. There are geographic equity concerns with this as well, as lower-value homes are more likely to be in the South or industrial Midwest.

To address these inequities in the mortgage market, a series of federal laws aimed to reduce barriers. The 1975 Home Mortgage Disclosure Act (HMDA) requires financial institutions to collect and disclose loan-level mortgage data, which enables identification of discriminatory or exclusionary loan practices. The Consumer Financial Protection Bureau (CFPB) now administers HMDA. Related to HMDA is the 1974 Equal Credit Opportunity Act (ECOA), which makes it illegal for banks to discriminate against protected classes in mortgages. The Department of Justice (DOJ) administers the ECOA and has been involved in several high-profile investigations of banks for ECOA violations. These two laws complement the 1977 Community Reinvestment Act (CRA), which requires banking regulators to encourage mortgage lenders to provide mortgages to low- and moderate-income neighborhoods.

Public administrators, through their work in organizations such as the CFPB, DOJ, and other regulators, play a vital role in ensuring that mortgage lenders adhere to the Fair Housing Act, HMDA, ECOA, CRA, and related legislation. Without oversight, mortgage lenders would have free reign to maximize profits, which could involve discrimination in credit access or terms. Implementation and monitoring, therefore, are essential for ensuring equity in mortgage access.

Unsubsidized Rental Housing: Evictions

Annually, landlords file around 3.6 million eviction cases; this means almost 7% of renting families receive an eviction filing.[6] The incidence of evictions is not spread equally across all socio-demographic groups, geographies, or landlord types. Black women with children are more likely to be evicted, as are renters with low incomes.[7] Evictions are more likely in some neighborhoods than others and large-scale landlords file for eviction more often than small-scale landlords.[8] Adding to inequities in who gets evicted is the significant state and local variation in landlord-tenant policies and assistance programs available to renters who face eviction.

The rules that result from Court proceedings significantly impact the eviction experience and outcomes for landlords and tenants. People who are in eviction court more often, such as landlords and their lawyers, are more likely to know the formal and informal rules that benefit them as compared to those with less familiarity, such as renters.[9] One way to solve this information asymmetry is by ensuring renters have access to a lawyer. Most landlords have a lawyer, but only about 10% of tenants do. This is starting to change with the right-to-counsel movement. New York City was the first place in the United States to pass such a policy, but it has expanded to Cleveland, San Francisco, and Philadelphia, among others. Early evaluations of these programs indicate they are reducing the number of eviction filings that turn into court-ordered eviction judgments. Despite their salutary effects, right-to-counsel advocates struggle to find lawyers and pay for services. Administrators can be instrumental in raising awareness of the availability of legal services and in helping renters who face eviction to understand their rights.

Another major anti-eviction policy in some jurisdictions is rental assistance. While these programs have existed in some cities for years, they proliferated during the COVID-19 pandemic. For example, the 2021 Consolidated Appropriations Act and the 2021 American Rescue Plan Act provided almost $47 billion in emergency rental assistance. Despite the largesse, there was significant variation in how quickly and for what purposes states spent this money, with subnational governments and their administrators having significant discretion over fund allocation. One of the biggest challenges for administrators was a lack of capacity to develop programs and review and process applications.[10] Some of the most effective efforts were where legal groups were able to partner with administrators to ensure the timely provision of funds.[11] However, one-time infusions of money for rental assistance, while useful, are insufficient to address the eviction crisis; rather, sustained funding is needed.

Perhaps the most expansive COVID-era policy aimed at renters was eviction moratoria. There were two primary federal eviction moratoria: the Coronavirus Aid, Relief, and Economic Security (CARES) Act moratorium on federally subsidized properties and the more expansive Centers for Disease Control (CDC) moratorium. The latter is notable because it was a federal agency, that is, administrators, who initiated this far-reaching moratorium. Local jurisdictions had a lot of discretion in how they implemented and interpreted the moratoria with some judges defying them because they felt the moratoria went against their responsibility to protect property rights.[12] In sum, 43 states and the District of Columbia had some form of eviction moratorium, which varied by policy justification, eviction stage targeted, duration, who issued the moratoria, and eligible renters.[13] The moratoria were effective in reducing evictions.

Subsidized Rental Housing: The Housing Choice Voucher Program

Over 35% of households in the United States rent their homes, with over 40% of renters spending more than 30% of their income on housing.[14] Historically, renters with low incomes were eligible for public housing, but during urban renewal, many cities demolished public housing as symbols of blight. This benefited white households but not Black and Hispanic households.[15] In many cities, despite promises to the contrary, sufficient replacement housing was not built.

Today, housing vouchers are more common than public housing as a means of providing subsidized affordable housing. The Housing Choice Voucher (HCV) program (established in Section 8 of the 1974 Housing and Community Development Act) provides a market-based solution to housing unaffordability by giving recipients a voucher. Recipients pay up to a third of their income on rent and the voucher covers the rest, up to a geographically specified amount called the fair market rent. The federal government provides funds to local Public Housing Agencies (PHAs) for the program. The HCV program is colloquially called Section 8; however, this is now considered a racial slur because of the racialized history of public housing, which equated housing assistance recipients with being Black. In 2022, 70% of HCV recipients were non-white, with 48% reporting being Black, 77% were female-headed households, and 25% had a family member with a disability.[16]

The reality of the HCV program is that, because it is not an entitlement program where everyone who meets eligibility requirements receives a voucher, many jurisdictions have long or closed waiting lists. Even if a family receives a voucher, they must find a landlord who will accept it within a specified period. This is challenging because of the source of income discrimination, whereby landlords refuse to rent to a prospective tenant because of their source of income, in this case, an HCV. Source of income discrimination is illegal in 21 states and many counties and cities, although three states preempt their local governments from outlawing source of income discrimination.[17] Landlords may not want to rent to voucher holders for many reasons, including racist tropes about voucher recipients, the burden of working with a PHA and its inspection process, or unfamiliarity with the program. In general, voucher holders are more appealing in some markets than others. For example, landlords may be less likely to accept vouchers in high-income neighborhoods, but in high-poverty neighborhoods they prefer HCV recipients to unsubsidized tenants because of the guaranteed rent from the PHA or because they can charge higher rents than they would to unsubsidized renters.[18] Because of source of income discrimination and the limited time to find a unit that accepts a voucher, the HCV program does not lead to large migrations to higher income areas, especially for non-white recipients.[19]

The HCV program is designed so local administrators working in PHAs have significant discretion over how the program works. PHAs use their discretion to ration vouchers through eligibility criteria, lotteries, waitlists, voucher requirements, administrative processes, and institutional barriers.[20] One example of this discretion arises in deciding who gets a voucher. Administrators often see voucher prioritization (moving people to the top of the list based on characteristics such as having children, experiencing homelessness, etc.) as an additional administrative burden.[21] Still, some PHAs still engage in prioritization. Often, it is not need that determines who gets a voucher, but rather being an existing resident of the community, receiving an organizational referral, or already being a PHA tenant.

Administrators also have discretion to monitor and punish HCV recipients and potential recipients. They assess who will be successful in the housing market and use those assessments to cream recipients, providing vouchers according to likelihood of success. This creates inequities as the most vulnerable renters—those who need the most services—are less likely to receive a voucher because of concerns that they will not be able to utilize their voucher and stay in their new unit. It is important to remember that housing agencies govern not only those fortunate enough to gain access to rental assistance, but the countless families left lingering on waitlists or denied access to benefits altogether.[22] Because the HCV program is not an entitlement, administrators' decisions have social equity implications. Some have the opportunity to live in an affordable home while others are left to face the rental market on their own.

People Experiencing Homelessness: Continuums of Care

According to the January 2022 Point-in-Time count, there were 582,462 people experiencing homelessness in the United States,[23] of which 28% were families with children.[24] There are stark racial disparities in who experiences homelessness: for every 10,000 people of each race, 121 Native Hawaiian or Pacific Islanders, 48 Black people, and 11 white people are homeless. In 2022, 1% of people experiencing homelessness were transgender or gender nonbinary.[25]

Laws affecting people experiencing homelessness generally fall into one of two philosophies: criminalization or assistance. Laws criminalizing homelessness, such as prohibiting sleeping and camping in public, have increased over time. These laws perpetuate homelessness and increase social inequities, leading many advocates to call for their dissolution.

The second philosophy focuses on assisting people experiencing homelessness. Here I focus on the central federal legislation. The 1987 Stewart B. McKinney Homeless Assistance Act (later renamed the McKinney-Vento Act) established and provided funding for a variety of programs to assist people experiencing homelessness. The 2009 Homeless Emergency Assistance and Rapid Transition to Housing Act (HEARTH Act) consolidated homeless assistance programs into the Continuums of Care (CoC) program, codifying existing CoC procedures that had been around since the McKinney-Vento Act. The CoC Program Interim Rule, first written in 2012 and updated in 2017, is the regulatory implementation of the program.[26] It provides for community-wide planning and strategic use of resources to address homelessness, improve coordination with existing programs, improve data collection and performance measurement, and allow each community to tailor its programs to fit its context.

The HEARTH Act dictates how McKinney-Vento Act money is allocated to CoCs. While the U.S. Department of Housing and Urban Development (HUD) sets general requirements for CoCs, there is wide variation in size and structure. A 2014 survey found about 40% of CoCs were nonprofit or collaboratively led, 34% were government-led, and 28% were independent nonprofits.[27] When CoCs are truly collaborative, they give providers a meaningful voice in planning and are more effective at reducing homelessness.[28] However, not all CoCs coordinate services and planning, other than the minimum required by HUD.

Three major inter-related challenges of the CoC system are lack of capacity, lack of support to innovate, and equity. CoCs identify obtaining HUD funding as their top priority.[29] Yet, even with HUD funding, there are service gaps or differences between services needed and services available. Service gaps mean CoCs and their members must decide who gets access to scarce resources. Some CoCs "don't even try" to provide services in their most far-flung areas.[30] Likewise, a survey revealed that each CoC is aware of at least one group—such as the chronically homeless, youth, or ex-offenders—who are difficult to serve and therefore remain underserved.[31] Conversely, when there is funding for specific groups, such as veterans, CoCs provide more resources. With limited resources, CoCs engage in creaming, providing services to groups that are easier to reach and serve, thus increasing the social inequities of those not served.

Moving Toward More Equitable Housing

It is possible for housing to be more equitable. Over time, policies have made incremental steps toward equity, yet there is still much to be done to improve procedural fairness, access, quality, and outcomes. While there is not broad agreement on the best way to achieve equitable housing, there are promising solutions. This section discusses some of the ways public administrators can enhance housing equity, first generally, and then specifically, for each tenure type. While far from comprehensive, these recommendations offer ideas for initial interventions.

Philosophical Reframing of Housing and Associated Politics

Housing equity will not be achieved without addressing politics and power. Politics favor those with power—generally white homeowners whose priority is to protect their wealth by maintaining property values. Dismantling housing inequities based on race/ethnicity, income, and tenure status requires rejecting the "ideal home" as a single-family detached owner-occupied house in a racially homogeneous (white) neighborhood. Letting go of this vision necessitates decoupling housing from wealth. The paradigm of housing as wealth is at odds with the goal of access to affordable housing.

Those with power benefit from the existing housing policy environment; therefore, the only way to achieve this philosophical reorientation is by changing power dynamics and politics. Currently, homeowners vote at higher rates than renters—58.1% vs. 36.5%.[32] Homeowners regularly harness their political and civic energy toward exclusionary ends,[33] which decreases housing equity. If renters and people experiencing homelessness vote at rates equal to or exceeding homeowners, policymakers would be more likely to address their policy concerns.

In addition to voting and political efficacy, power also comes from social constructions of groups as being deserving (or not). Groups seen as "the other" and therefore not deserving, such as single mothers or families with LGBTQ+ parents and children, do not receive the benefits of housing policy. This, in turn, reinforces negative images, thus further reducing their political power.[34] To break this cycle, negative identities must be challenged.

Housing is a collective, rather than individual, problem. Coalition building can change politics and challenge inequities, particularly for race-class subjugated communities. For instance, groups have won victories that increased housing equity. A coalition of community groups came together in the mid-1970s to sue Mount Laurel, New Jersey, for zoning laws that eliminated affordable housing, thus excluding people of color and those with low incomes. The New Jersey Supreme Court ruling in favor of the coalition became known as the Mount Laurel Doctrine. It required all municipalities within the state to provide their fair share of affordable housing. More recently, coalitions of elites and grassroots groups got the right-to-counsel passed in New York City and San Francisco.[35] Unified by the housing crisis and the waning of COVID-era protections, tenant groups mobilized to elect pro-tenant city officials who passed new renter protections in Los Angeles and the right-to-counsel in Kansas City.[36] These coalitions consist of groups crossing race/ethnicity, socioeconomic status, and tenure-type lines.

Housing markets suffer market failure. When failure happens, discrimination and exclusion follow. If housing policy remains focused on market-based solutions, it will continue to be inequitable, which is why some advocates call for a decommodification of housing. These ideas are part of the housing justice movement. The Urban Institute defines housing justice as "Ensuring everyone has affordable housing that promotes health, well-being, and upward mobility by confronting historical and ongoing harms and disparities caused by structural racism and other systems of oppression."[37] Perhaps the best way to achieve housing justice is by ensuring a right to housing. If everyone has a right to a place to live, housing becomes a public good, under the purview of government rather than the market.

Policy Management and Discretion

Administrators play a key role in housing equity and one of their most important tools is discretion. In evaluating whether to cite a mortgage lender for discrimination, in determining how to distribute rental or homelessness assistance, or in forecasting who will benefit from an HCV, administrators punish or aid individuals and groups. Both too little and too much discretion can be problematic. With too much discretion, administrators may select HCV recipients in ways that benefit some groups more than others. When they have too little discretion, they cannot respond to the unique needs of people experiencing homelessness. The key, then, is for programs to allow for sufficient levels of discretion that expert administrators can exercise to address social equity explicitly.

While discretion is important, so is overcoming resource scarcity. A right to housing would require sufficient financial, human resource, and administrative resources to provide housing to everyone, fundamentally changing the housing landscape. Assuming such resources exist, a policy solution prioritizing equality would provide everyone with the same housing. In contrast, equitable implementation would require attention to procedural fairness, access, quality, and outcomes for different social groups.

Administrators could enhance procedural fairness by ensuring representation from all groups in the decision-making process. For example, CoC planning and financing should involve substantive, not just symbolic, representation by those experiencing homelessness. Policymakers can enhance access to new housing programs by shifting the administrative burdens of applying for these programs from participants to those with sufficient resources to absorb these new responsibilities, such as administrators. Instead of requiring voucher recipients to endure a lengthy process of proving their eligibility for a housing voucher, PHA authorities could collaborate with social service agencies to identify and reach out to eligible families.

To ensure quality and outcome equity, administrators will need to monitor program implementation with an awareness of differences between groups. While the CFPB and DOJ already have watchdog duties surrounding mortgages and access to housing credit, they are dependent on information from lenders and information gained from complaints filed by those who feel they were not treated appropriately. A better way would be for these agencies to have sufficient clout to monitor and enforce anti-discrimination policies proactively through their own investigations. This would pave the way for greater equity with regard to quality. It would ensure there is no difference in lending to those of different races with similar incomes.

Outcome equity is perhaps the most difficult form of equity to achieve because it asks: Do all groups have housing that meets their needs while taking into consideration the racialized and discriminatory history of housing policy and its consequences? Many housing policies have unintended consequences. For example, if a tenant requests a housing inspection and the landlord fixes the violations, the landlord may then raise the rent on the renovated unit, forcing the original tenant to move to a more affordable home.[38] In this case, the tenant does not experience outcome equity. Ensuring procedural fairness, access, quality, and outcome equity will not be easy, but there are ways, both small and large, immediately and on a longer time horizon, to increase housing equity for homeowners, renters, and people experiencing homelessness.

Tenure-Specific Recommendations to Enhance Social Equity

While there are universal policies and practices that will help all people, regardless of their housing tenure (homeowner, renter, experiencing homelessness), tenure-specific policies are also necessary to ensure social equity. While blatant discrimination in access to credit and mortgages has been illegal for decades, this does not mean it does not exist. Two practices would improve equity: expanded access to credit and proactive monitoring of mortgage practices.

Lending institutions make decisions about mortgages based on complex calculations including factors such as credit scores and mortgage amounts. People with low credit scores have difficulty getting a mortgage or receive worse mortgage terms than people with higher credit scores. Yet, credit scores are racially biased.[39] Reducing the reliance on credit scores would expand credit access to previously marginalized individuals. Furthermore, banks are reluctant to provide low-value mortgages. This makes it nearly impossible for people with low incomes to secure a mortgage, thus greatly limiting their ability to purchase a home.

To address the need for mortgages under $70,000, HUD [40] recommends a reduction in mortgage origination and service costs as well as incentives to make these loans profitable for mortgage providers. At the same time, regulatory agencies need to take a more proactive role in ensuring equity in mortgage practices, including loan terms, amounts, and locations. To these ends, the Federal Reserve, Federal Deposit Insurance Corporation, and Office of the Comptroller of the Currency proposed rulemaking changes to the CRA in 2022. These proposed changes include CRA assessment of online and mobile banking, a metrics-based approach to lending evaluations, and clarification of eligible CRA activities in underserved communities. Such periodic administrative reviews and updates are important for ensuring that housing-related policies and regulations continue to achieve their objectives and serve communities equitably.

The variation in state and local landlord-tenant and eviction policies provides innovative examples of how to improve rental housing equity by reducing evictions. Renters must know their rights and be able to defend them. Federal law requires landlords to provide prospective tenants with a notification of the potential for lead paint in buildings built before 1978. A similar requirement mandates that landlords provide information about what tenants must do if their landlord files an eviction against them and what their rights are in terms of health and safety.

Right-to-counsel is one of the best ways to ensure renters have an advocate to protect their rights and to counterbalance the power of landlords and their lawyers. These programs are not cheap, however. So, if the goal is to increase housing equity, pro bono lawyers could be assigned to those groups most disadvantaged in eviction court proceedings. For example, the City of Cleveland's right-to-counsel only covers tenants with incomes at or below the federal poverty line and with at least one child in the household.

An upstream approach to preventing evictions would be rental assistance programs to keep renters from getting behind on their rent. COVID-era assistance programs demonstrate rental assistance is an effective policy tool,[41] but if left to local governments, such programs will likely lead to vastly different programs with varying effects on reducing housing equity. State or federal assistance programs would create more uniformity across jurisdictions.

Although entitlement programs are rarely politically feasible, they offer greater prospects for equity. They can be designed to maximize equity by focusing, like right-to-counsel, on groups most vulnerable to eviction. While policy can establish basic program requirements, administrators will still need substantial discretion to balance costs, serve the most renters possible, and aid the neediest applicants.

There are several equity enhancing options for subsidized renters. As a best case scenario, the HCV program should be made an entitlement with universal vouchers. Such an expansion would require significant financial investment and would require advocates to build coalitions that change the political climate to make this politically feasible. An intermediate solution would be to ensure equitable HCV prioritization. "First come, first served" is not equitable for any public program because those with the greatest need are the ones who face the largest barriers to applying. Therefore, PHAs need to make prioritization decisions according to transparent and need-based criteria. While there may be a temptation to allow algorithms to determine priority, this technology is not neutral; it is often biased against individuals racialized as non-white and those with low incomes.[42] While technology may be helpful in increasing equal treatment, it cannot replace the discretion of trained professionals.

Regardless of which approach to vouchers is taken, the HCV program only works if recipients can find landlords to rent to them. To ensure this, there needs to be a federal anti-discrimination policy regarding the source of income. This could be done as a stand-alone policy or by making source of income a protected class under the Fair Housing Act. Anti-discrimination laws regarding source of income would increase voucher acceptance rates and assist renters in moving to preferred neighborhoods.[43] The advantage of a federal policy over the existing patchwork of state and local source of income laws and preemptions is this: A federal law would ensure all HCV recipients are treated the same across jurisdictions. Once such a federal policy exists, of course, it will need to be enforced to ensure such discrimination does not continue.

Many recommendations for subsidized and unsubsidized rental housing are part of The White House Blueprint for a Renters Bill of Rights. This Biden administration document argues for five principles to create equity for renters: safe, quality, accessible, and affordable housing; clear and fair leases; education, enforcement, and enhancement of renter rights; the right to organize; and eviction prevention, diversion, and relief. The blueprint is a statement of policy guidelines. It remains to be seen how, and to what degree, the principles will be put into practice.

In addition to the Renters Bill of Rights for those in housing, those who are experiencing homelessness need equitable solutions related to housing affordability, education, criminal justice, health care, and more. Related to the CoC program, several interrelated changes have the potential to increase social equity. First, CoCs need to focus on their mission of serving people experiencing homelessness, rather than on seeking funding. CoCs with this mission-focused orientation are more likely to be high-performing.[44] HUD funding offers the possibility of incentivizing a mission orientation. Currently, only 10% of the grant can be used for project administration, but additional funding for infrastructure would improve collaborative planning. CoCs are more likely to develop programs for underserved groups if there is funding attached, so HUD has an opportunity to enhance equity by providing needed dollars. For these programs to be successful, members of underrepresented groups need to have meaningful representation in planning. Such involvement can lead to greater client trust and satisfaction.[45]

Summary of Key Points

Housing policy in the United States is dominated by the ideal of single-family owner-occupied homes and keeping property values high as a source of wealth building for those who are politically advantaged. Many policies are market-based, which comes with the inequities of all markets, including discrimination and exclusion. Whether a person is a homeowner, unsubsidized renter, subsidized renter, or a person experiencing homelessness, some social groups are advantaged while others are not. It is also important to note inequities between these tenure types because of the privileged status of homeownership. Furthermore, there are many policies related to public management that affect all tenure types, such as zoning and land use policies.

Despite the market-based approach to housing in the United States, policymakers and administrators frequently intervene in housing. It is crucial to ensure these interventions enhance equity, rather than entrench and institutionalize discrimination and inequity, as has happened in past policies of racialized dispossession and exclusion.[46] The existence of anti-discrimination policies is insufficient, as evidenced by the social inequities that still exist despite the more than 40-year-old Fair Housing Act.

Expanding access to mortgages, anti-eviction policies, a redesigned HCV program, and better funded, mission-driven CoCs, have the potential to increase housing equity. But, inequities will remain if there is no right to housing. As Chester Hartman argues: "because housing is so central to one's life, it merits attaining the status of a right."[47] Only when housing is a right will policymakers and administrators design housing policies to assist all individuals, groups, and tenure statuses. Seeing housing as a right involves a fundamental shift in political philosophy and power, but coalition building and advocacy can guide the way.

Discussion Questions

1. From the housing bubble and foreclosure crisis, to devastating hurricanes, to COVID-19 and the eviction cliff, disasters threaten housing for millions. How can administrators ensure equitable responses to these events for people with all housing tenure types?

2. Housing policy is political, with each administration having its own philosophy as to what HUD should do. What is the role of administrators? How can they ensure a continuum of equitable policymaking and implementation across administrations?

3. What do you think is the most important housing equity concern in your community? What is being done, if anything, to address it?

4. How likely do you think it is that there will be a right to housing in the United States in the next decade? What actions would need to be taken, and by whom, for this to happen?

Additional Resources

1. White House Blueprint for a Renters Bill of Rights https://www.whitehouse.gov/wp-content/uploads/2023/01/White-House-Blueprint-for-a-Renters-Bill-of-Rights.pdf
2. U.S. Department of Housing and Urban Development Office of Fair Housing and Equal Opportunity (FHEO) at https://www.hud.gov/program_offices/fair_housing_equal_opp

Notes

1. Keeanga-Yamahtta Taylor, *Race for Profit: How Banks and the Real Estate Industry Undermined Black Homeownership* (Chapel Hill, NC: University of North Carolina Press, 2019).
2. Jason Hackworth, *Manufacturing Decline: How Racism and the Conservative Movement Crush the American Rust Belt* (New York: Columbia University Press, 2019).
3. Jamila Michener, "Power from the Margins: Grassroots Mobilization and Urban Expansions of Civil Legal Rights," *Urban Affairs Review* 56, no. 5 (2020): 1390–1422.
4. Taylor, *Race for Profit.*
5. Alanna McCargo et al., "Small-Dollar Mortgages for Single-Family Residential Properties" (Washington, DC: The Urban Institute, 2018), https://www.urban.org/research/publication/small-dollar-mortgages-single-family-residential-properties
6. Ashley Gromis et al., "Estimating Eviction Prevalence across the United States," *Proceedings of the National Academy of Sciences* 119, no. 21 (2022): e2116169119, https://doi.org/10.1073/pnas.2116169119
7. Peter Hepburn, Renee Louis, and Matthew Desmond, "Racial and Gender Disparities among Evicted Americans," *Sociological Science* 7 (2020): 649–662. Chester Hartman and David Robinson, "Evictions: The Hidden Housing Problem," *Housing Policy Debate* 14, no. 4 (2003): 461–501.
8. Henry Gomory, "The Social and Institutional Contexts Underlying Landlords' Eviction Practices," *Social Forces* 100, no. 4 (2022): 1774–1805; Kyle Nelson et al., "Spatial Concentration and Spillover: Eviction Dynamics in Neighborhoods of Los Angeles, California, 2005–2015," *Housing Policy Debate* 31, no. 3–5 (January 8, 2021): 670–695.
9. Isaiah Fleming-Klink, Brian J. McCabe, and Eva Rosen, "Navigating an Overburdened Courtroom: How Inconsistent Rules, Shadow Procedures, and Social Capital Disadvantage Tenants in Eviction Court," *City & Community* 22, no. 3 (2023): 220–245.
10. Vincent J. Reina et al., "COVID-19 Emergency Rental Assistance: Analysis of a National Survey of Programs," 2021, https://nlihc.org/sites/default/files/HIP_NLIHC_Furman_Brief_FINAL.pdf
11. John Walsh, "Distributing Emergency Rental and Mortgage Assistance to Vulnerable Households during the COVID-19 Pandemic: A Housing Innovation Program-Case Study," Research to Action Lab (Washington, DC: The Urban Institute, 2023), https://www.urban.org/research/publication/distributing-emergency-rental-and-mortgage-assistance-vulnerable-households
12. Kathryn A. Sabbeth, "Eviction Courts," *University of St. Thomas Law Journal* 18, no. 2 (2022): 359–404.
13. Emily A. Benfer et al., "Covid-19 Housing Policy: State and Federal Eviction Moratoria and Supportive Measures in the United States during the Pandemic," *Housing Policy Debate* 33, no. 6 (2023): 1390–1414.
14. Joint Center for Housing Studies of Harvard University, "America's Rental Housing 2020" (Cambridge, MA: Harvard University, 2020).
15. Milena Almagro, Eric Chyn, and Bryan A. Stuart, "Urban Renewal and Inequality: Evidence from Chicago's Public Housing Demolitions," Working Paper, Working Paper Series (National Bureau of Economic Research, January 2023), https://doi.org/10.3386/w30838
16. US Department of Housing and Urban Development, "Picture of Subsidized Households," 2022, https://www.huduser.gov/portal/datasets/assthsg.html
17. Poverty & Race Research Action Council, "Appendix B: State, Local, and Federal Laws barring Source-of-Income Discrimination" (Washington, DC: Poverty & Race Research Action Council, March 2023), https://prrac.org/pdf/AppendixB.pdf
18. Matthew Desmond and Kristin L. Perkins, "Are Landlords Overcharging Housing Voucher Holders?" *City & Community* 15, no. 2 (June 1, 2016): 137–162.
19. Victoria Basolo and Mai Thi Nguyen, "Does Mobility Matter? The Neighborhood Conditions of Housing Voucher Holders by Race and Ethnicity," *Housing Policy Debate* 16, no. 3–4 (January 1, 2005): 297–324.

20. Kathleen M. Moore, "Lists and Lotteries: Rationing in the Housing Choice Voucher Program," *Housing Policy Debate* 26, no. 3 (May 3, 2016): 474–487.
21. Brian J. McCabe, "Ready to Rent: Administrative Decisions and Poverty Governance in the Housing Choice Voucher Program," *American Sociological Review* 88, no. 1 (2023): 86–113.
22. McCabe, 87.
23. Following Jennifer Safstrom and Joseph Mead "Developing Inclusive Language Competency in Clinical Teaching," *Clinical Law Review* 29, no. 2 (2023): 349–404. I use the term "people experiencing homelessness" because it is person-focused language rather than condition-focused and to emphasize that homelessness is temporary, which opens the possibility of intervention.
24. National Alliance to End Homelessness, "State of Homelessness: 2023 Edition," National Alliance to End Homelessness, 2023, https://endhomelessness.org/homelessness-in-america/homelessness-statistics/state-of-homelessness/
25. Tanya de Sousa et al., "The 2002 Annual Homelessness Assessment Report (AHAR) to Congress. Part 1: Point-in-Time Estimates of Homelessness" (Washington, DC: The U.S. Department of Housing and Urban Development Office of Community Planning and Development, December 2022), https://www.huduser.gov/portal/sites/default/files/pdf/2022-AHAR-Part-1.pdf
26. U.S. Department of Housing and Urban Development, "Continuum of Care (CoC) Program Eligibility Requirements," HUD Exchange, n.d., para. 1, https://www.hudexchange.info/programs/coc/coc-program-eligibility-requirements
27. Meghan Jarpe, Jennifer E. Mosley, and Bikki Tran Smith, "Understanding the Collaborative Planning Process in Homeless Services: Networking, Advocacy, and Local Government Support May Reduce Service Gaps," *Journal of Public Health Management and Practice: JPHMP* 25, no. 3 (2019): 262–269.
28. Jennifer E Mosley and Sunggeun Park, "Service Providers' Influence in Collaborative Governance Networks: Effectiveness in Reducing Chronic Homelessness," *Journal of Public Administration Research and Theory* 32, no. 1 (2022): 130–149.
29. Jennifer E Mosley, "Cross-Sector Collaboration to Improve Homeless Services: Addressing Capacity, Innovation, and Equity Challenges," *The ANNALS of the American Academy of Political and Social Science* 693, no. 1 (2021): 246–263.
30. Mosley, "Cross-Sector Collaboration to Improve Homeless Services," 257.
31. Martha R. Burt et al., "Evaluation of Continuums of Care for Homeless People: Final Report," U.S. Department of Housing and Urban Development (Washington, DC: The Urban Institute, 2002), https://webarchive.urban.org/publications/310553.html
32. U.S. Census Bureau, "2022 Voting and Registration Data Now Available," Census.gov, May 2, 2023, https://www.census.gov/newsroom/press-releases/2023/2022-voting-registration.html
33. Chloe Thurston, "How Should We Govern Housing Markets in a Moral Political Economy?" *Daedalus* 152, no. 1 (2023): 194–197.
34. Maren Trochmann, "Identities, Intersectionality, and Otherness: The Social Constructions of Deservedness in American Housing Policy," *Administrative Theory & Praxis* 43, no. 1 (2021): 1–20.
35. Michener, "Power from the Margins."
36. Nicholas Slayton, "How Los Angeles Tenants Beat the Landlords—for Now," The American Prospect, February 17, 2023, https://prospect.org/api/content/3cdbd2d0-ae38-11ed-a6db-12b3f1b64877/. LINC, "Right to Legal Counsel for KC Tenants Facing Eviction Begins June 1," Local Investment Commission, May 31, 2022, https://kclinc.org/news/2022/5/31/right-to-legal-counsel-for-tenants-in-kc-begins-june-1
37. Bill Pitkin, Katharine Elder, and Danielle DeRuiter-Williams, "Building a Housing Justice Framework, Second Edition," Metropolitan Housing and Communities Policy Center (Washington, DC: Urban Institute, 2023), 9, https://www.urban.org/sites/default/files/2023-02/Building%20a%20Housing%20Justice%20Framework%202nd%20edition.pdf
38. Robin Bartram, *Stacked Decks: Building Inspectors and Reproduction of Urban Inequality* (Chicago, IL: University of Chicago Press, 2022).
39. National Consumer Law Center, "Past Imperfect: How Credit Scores and Other Analytics 'Bake in' and Perpetuate Past Discrimination," Racial Justice & Equal Economic Opportunity Project (Washington, DC: National Consumer Law Center, May 2016), https://www.nclc.org/resources/past-imperfect-how-credit-scores-and-other-analyticsbake-in-and-perpetuate-past-discrimination/
40. U.S. Department of Housing and Urban Development, "Financing Lower-Priced Homes: Small Mortgage Loans," October 2022, https://www.huduser.gov/portal/publications/Financing-Lower-Priced-Homes-Small-Mortgage-Loans.html
41. Reina and Lee, "Covid-19 and Emergency Rental Assistance."

42. Ruha Benjamin, *Race after Technology: Abolitionist Tools for the New Jim Code* (Medford, MA: Polity Press, 2019).
43. J. Rosie Tighe, Megan E. Hatch, and Joseph Mead, "Source of Income Discrimination and Fair Housing Policy," *Journal of Planning Literature* 32, no. 1 (2017): 3–15.
44. Mosley, "Cross-Sector Collaboration to Improve Homeless Services."
45. Jurgen Willems, Marc Jegers, and Lewis Faulk, "Organizational Effectiveness Reputation in the Nonprofit Sector," *Public Performance & Management Review* 39, no. 2 (April 2016): 454–475.
46. Kathryn Howell and Benjamin Teresa, "'The Map of Race Is the Map of Richmond': Eviction and the Enduring Regimes of Racialized Dispossession and Political Demobilization," *Journal of Race, Ethnicity and the City* 3, no. 2 (2022): 182–203.
47. Chester Hartman, "The Case for a Right to Housing," *Housing Policy Debate* 9, no. 2 (1998): 223–246.

11 HOW TRANSIT MATTERS FOR SOCIAL EQUITY

Samantha June Larson and Lynnsey Erickson

From the Editors

Transportation makes it possible for people to get to jobs, to school, to health care, to leisure activities, and to be better connected to the community. Despite these positives, the history, laws, politics, and management of transit are marked by racism, sexism, and classism. This results in inequities for women, Black people, Indigenous people, and people of color. To demonstrate promising solutions, the authors describe how transit bus access was improved in Oshkosh, Wisconsin. And they examine transit in the post-COVID world. Because convenient transit plays an outsized role in quality of life, the authors encourage public administrators to take creative approaches to identify inequities and avoid mistakes of the past.

Transportation has always deeply mattered to us, the authors. As a Millennial raised on a farm in rural North Dakota, coauthor Sam Larson was a product of white European immigration, colonization, and settlement. She grew up in an isolated area defined by rugged individualism. Her family lived on a gravel road 17 miles from the small town where she graduated high school. Starting in kindergarten, a yellow school bus picked her up around 7:30 am and delivered her just before the bell rang at 8:30 am. She spent two hours a day on that bus, sleepy-eyed in the mornings, fighting hunger in the afternoons, and working to stay warm in the winter since the heater rarely worked. As her older sister and brothers got their driver's licenses, they sometimes gave Sam a ride to school. Later, she stayed with her grandmother in town and walked to class. Sam got her driver's license and a car of her own at 14 years old. It was the ultimate goal. A car promised freedom, connection, and possibility.

For more than a century, American policy and culture have promoted *car-dependent* lifestyles like the one Sam knew. As she went off to college and then started her first job, Sam drove everywhere for the next 10 years, never once considering public transit. That all changed when she began graduate school and was given a bus pass by her university. Sam could ride for free (or at least that's how she thought of it, even though the services were covered at a reduced rate through her student fees). Having a "free" ride made the difference for Sam.

In the 2010s, she became a faithful rail commuter while earning her PhD at the University of Colorado Denver. The Regional Transportation District (RTD) opened a new line in the fall when she started classes. Her ride downtown was an excellent way to be environmentally friendly, avoid parking fees, and catch up on reading for class. Sam was most inspired by reading scholars like Camilla Stivers and Susan Gooden, who called on students like her to advance equity in public service delivery.

Spending hours each week on the rail, her gaze soon turned to neighborhoods outside her window. One house was impossible to miss. For months, a large white sheet was draped across the side. The words "RTD Ruined My House" were written six feet tall, in red spray paint. Sam stared at that sign and could not stop wondering, "how could public transit possibly *ruin* someone's home?" She sat there in her position of privilege, only seeing the rail as a positive thing. That homemade protest sign inspired her to explore the question of how public transit impacts equity.

Coauthor Lynnsey Erickson grew up in a small city in northeast Wisconsin with a population of 7,000 in the 2000s. Growing up in a family that teetered between lower and middle income depending on employment stability and access, transportation had always been a deciding factor between opportunity and isolation. Public transit and ride-sharing services did not exist in her hometown. While the school district served the city and surrounding rural communities, most students living within city limits did not have access to bus service provided by the district even though a new high school was built on the outskirts of the city. Without family in the area to rely on when a car inevitably broke down, the family often had to miss work or juggle early mornings with one car trying to get to manufacturing jobs outside of the city while also getting to school.

Once Lynnsey got to college at the University of Wisconsin Madison in 2010, the opportunities afforded by public transit were both thrilling and overwhelming. Students could receive a yearly bus pass paid for by university fees, but having the confidence and knowledge of how to ride the bus was a barrier. "How do I read the bus schedule? What if I get on the wrong bus? What's the yellow cord for?" Lynnsey eventually overcame the uncertainty of riding the bus with the help of friendly bus drivers. And being able to access transit meant access to opportunity. Public transit allowed students to reach more affordable or specialized health care options when care was not accessible on campus. Internship and job opportunities expanded with more reliable transportation. Green spaces, like the arboretum, and more welcoming community spaces were within reach because of public transit. Accessible transit service meant the difference between staying isolated within the campus area or being able to get to know a new city and all it had to offer.

In the pages that follow, we incorporate our lived experiences and reveal what we have uncovered as scholars and practitioners in the transit equity space. We begin by discussing the key dimensions of public transit and mobility-related inequities that have developed since the 1800s. Highlights include the history of racial segregation, related legal actions, policy changes, and transit-induced gentrification. Then we provide two pathways for fostering transit access for historically disadvantaged groups. First, an in-depth case of a "zero-fare" bus pilot program for K–12 students in Oshkosh, WI is provided. Coauthor Lynnsey Erickson, a practitioner and policymaker in this urban area of about 80,000 people, provides a firsthand account of the history, challenges, and progress that has come from this promising initiative.

Second, we present promising ideas for reimagining public transit in a post-COVID-19 world. Between 2000–2014, transit use grew more than travel by car.[1] However, ridership plummeted in 2020 due to the pandemic, increased remote work, and online shopping. It still has not recovered in most places.[2] American car culture is also changing. Gen Z (born in the late 1990s and early 2000s) and Millennials (born in the early 1980s and 1990s) have far different preferences from previous generations. For instance, in 2021, 68% of 19-year-olds had their driver's license, compared to 90% in 1983.[3] These trends are essential for public administrators to consider when designing transit infrastructure for the future.

Equity Issues and the Paradox of Access to Public Transit

To understand their root causes, persistent inequities must be mapped over time. The discussion begins in the 1800s and traces the development of public transit infrastructure and the inequities that accompanied it over time. Throughout American history, transit agencies have been "bound by the rule of law,"[4] in David Rosenbloom's words, to follow federal policies and Supreme Court decisions. Although they were designed to enhance mobility, these policies and decisions have often hindered progress.

History and Legal Underpinnings

Massive public transit infrastructure projects transformed America into what we know it today, revolutionizing how people moved to, from, and throughout the new nation. In the 1830s, the first horse-drawn streetcar system was introduced in New York City. Richmond, Virginia became the first to develop an electric system in 1888. Between 1880 and 1929, urban growth increased faster than ever before, made possible by expanding transit systems.

Influxes were partly fueled by millions of people fleeing oppression. European immigrants from places like Germany, Italy, and Ireland escaped persecution and sought the hope of better opportunities across the United States. After fighting for women's right to vote for 60 years, the 1910s were a turning point partially attributed to a campaign tour across the Western states aboard the "Suffrage Special" train. Around 1910, the Great Migration of an estimated 6 million African Americans from the rural South to the North, Midwest, and western cities also began. Soaring skyscrapers, grander factories, and new economic prospects lured millions to take a chance on city life. None of it would have been possible without a national rail transportation network, city streetcars, and suburban railroads.

Despite these advancements, inequitable access to transit was also widespread from the very beginning. Streetcars were segregated in the North and South. The pivotal Supreme Court case of *Plessy v. Ferguson,* 163 U.S. 537 (1896) cemented transit segregation into place. In 1896, Homer Plessy, a man of mixed race, was arrested for sitting in the "white" car on the East Louisiana Railroad. The Court ruled that it was constitutional to provide separate railcar accommodations for white and black passengers if both cars were of *equal* quality. The ruling set separate but equal spaces for different races in public facilities as policy, leading to the federal case that established Jim Crow laws and statutes that legally sanction segregated public restrooms, schools, housing, and transit.

Many state and local governments reinforced racial separation. For instance, between 1901–1906, the State of Virginia passed a series of anti-black transit laws. As the *St. Luke Herald* reported: "The very dangerous power placed in the hands of hot headed and domineering young white men . . . will certainly provoke trouble, when they order Negroes to this seat or that, to move from seat to seat at their sweet will."[5] Several southern cities followed suit, including New Orleans (LA), Memphis (TN), and Savannah (GA), inciting protests for decades.

During the Progressive Era (1890s–1920s), streetcar ridership began to fall as automobiles became more affordable. Transit was further set back due to the financial strictures caused by the Great Depression (1929 to the late 1930s). Cities like Chicago struggled to maintain infrastructure and began eliminating rail lines.[6] Thus, while streetcars provided 100% of urban transit in 1914, just 4% of commuters relied on the rails by 1937. "Nonessential" personal travel briefly fell by an astounding 32% during U.S. involvement in World War II (1941–1945). However, that quickly changed with further societal shifts and economic growth after the war.

New suburban housing developments triggered white flight. Railways were replaced by widening roads, enabling cars filled with mostly white middle-class men to drive from the suburbs to inner cities.

The automotive takeover created a need for more sophisticated roadways. The Federal-Aid Highway Act of 1956 funded an interstate highway system from coast to coast. It was the largest American public works project in American history at that time. Many of the interstate systems were built in, over, and through low-income communities of color. For instance, *Ghosts along the Freeway* details the experience of thriving black communities who were displaced in Oakland, CA and the Rondo neighborhood in St. Paul, MN. As Mohl reflects: "Not many blacks lived in Minnesota, but the highway builders found out where they lived and built an expressway through their neighborhood."[7]

As car ownership skyrocketed, buses replaced streetcars and urban railways, expanding services even further into suburbia.[8] Although technology advanced, segregation remained. Many black communities depended on city buses. As Rosa Parks recalled the experience that led to her arrest in Montgomery, AL in 1955: "More than seventy-five, between eighty-five and I think ninety, percent of the patronage of buses were black people, because more white people could own and drive their own cars than blacks."[9] Groups like the Women's Political Council had been organizing to end segregation for nearly a decade, and Parks' arrest was the tipping point. It sparked the Montgomery bus boycott coordinated by Martin Luther King Jr. and the Montgomery Improvement Association (MIA). Approximately 40,000 black riders, who made up most of Montgomery's ridership, boycotted for 13 months until the Supreme Court ruled segregation on public buses was unconstitutional in *Browder v. Gayle* (1956).[10]

Early successes in transit desegregation fueled the larger Civil Rights Movement of the 1960s. The Civil Rights Act of 1964 outlawed discrimination within voting, education, and employment. Segregation of public accommodations was ruled unconstitutional, and federal agencies were charged with instituting practices to reduce disparities. Title VI of the Civil Rights Act of 1964 required state and local government agencies to show that low-income communities of color would not be disproportionately impacted by new transit projects to qualify for federal funding. It was a major turning point.

Politics

Although progress was being made to desegregate, political problems with growing residential racial segregation were rising. From an economic standpoint, outsourcing businesses and the closure of downtown factories made employment less available in city centers, where most communities of color lived. Many job opportunities followed suburban development to places with retail businesses, shopping malls, and work like childcare in white, middle-class homes. Therefore, planning and economic development policies resulted in BIPOC workers living farther and farther from where they could earn a paycheck.[11]

In the 1960s, *spatial mismatch theory* began to explain the phenomenon of low-income communities of color living in neighborhoods far from work opportunities. In cities like Detroit and Chicago, black residents who relied on the train faced more challenging transit routes, longer rides, and inconvenient schedules. Since then, many scholars have found evidence of spatial mismatch and strategies to curb it through revised transit policies. Access to transit—which includes affordable fares, commute times that match work schedules (including shift work, evenings, and weekends), and ease of information about job openings that are accessible by public transit—have contributed to spatial mismatch for decades.[12]

As transit infrastructure increased, so did residential racial and economic segregation.[13] This matters because segregated neighborhoods have a direct impact on residents' quality of life. In fact, health disparities in racially segregated neighborhoods have been attributed to inequitable access to education and employment. Furthermore, adults aged 30 and older who live in concentrated poverty areas in the 30 largest cities have an elevated mortality risk, even after controlling for income.

In the 1990s, the U.S. Department of Housing and Urban Development (HUD) conducted a randomized social experiment called the *Moving to Opportunity* program. They examined what happened when residents moved from higher to lower-poverty neighborhoods. Findings showed improvements in long-term physical health, mental health, and well-being. The study's conclusion is obvious: Where people live correlates with economic and social well-being over their entire life. Transit policies play a role in this. They have the capacity to maintain inequities or to mitigate them. For instance, when bus routes and rail lines are developed in higher-income communities to provide more convenient access but equivalent routes are not implemented in poorer communities, inequity is perpetuated. When commute times to social service agencies are shorter for those living in white neighborhoods than for those living in predominantly Hispanic and black communities, inequity persists. And when individuals must purchase their own vehicles to access the best education, employment opportunities, and health care, inequity is maintained.

At the start of the 21st century, interest in sustainable development inspired a political shift aimed at addressing some of these issues. Transit became a policy tool to reduce carbon emissions, improve economic development, and enhance quality of life. In 1998, the U.S. Congress passed the Transportation Equity Act for the 21st Century. The law presented multiple goals, such as enhancing economic vitality, environmental protection, public safety, connectivity, historical preservation, efficiency, and accessibility. Across the political spectrum, Transit-Oriented Development (TOD)—characterized by dense, walkable, mixed-use neighborhoods built around rail systems—became a popular strategy to achieve such targets.[14]

This movement diffused into state and local legislatures. For example, California passed the Sustainable Communities and Climate Protection Act of 2008, which charged metropolitan planning organizations (MPOs) to reduce greenhouse gas emissions by increasing transportation. The Great Recession (December 2007– June 2009) also boosted transit usage. It forced many people, hard-hit by the economic downturn, to take the bus or rail for the first time. New passengers realized the benefits of transit and continued riding it, even after the recovery.[15] Policymakers in cities like Portland and Atlanta also expanded public transportation to better serve low-income and communities of color.

But equitable transit development remains elusive, even as access grows. Just as road systems were tailored to suburban white, middle-class Americans with cars in the 1950s, new public transit developments have catered to their modern contemporaries, leading to gentrification. "Redeveloping" low-income neighborhoods through infrastructure projects has led to housing cost increases, which has forced residents out of their homes and led to an influx of more affluent, predominantly white residents.[16] Although Title VI of the Civil Rights Act of 1964 requires public transit agencies to show projects will not disproportionately impact low-income residents and communities of color in order to receive federal funding, the lack of longitudinal reporting requirements allows for transit-inducing gentrification. While transit development and access may help in the short term, it can quickly price residents out of their communities and lead to displacement, just as the interstate highway system did.

Policy Implementation and Management

Administrators can advance transit equity, along with social mobility, in many ways. As Wellman notes: "Few public administrators wield as much power over the life chances and outcomes of poor populations as transit administrators; their selections between policy alternatives determine which jobs transit dependents can access and when, how much they must pay for transit, how long they must spend en route to destinations, and which locations will be inaccessible except by foot."[17] The four social equity measures—access, quality, procedural fairness, and outcomes—are all areas in which transit agencies have the ability to advance equity in their communities.

Access pertains to the distribution of services across groups. It concerns who benefits from policies and programs. Access to transit is a building block of a better life for many. Engaging riders who depend on transit is an effective way to expand access. Riders can provide valuable perspectives in the planning and administration of public transit services. For example, the Birmingham Transit Citizens Advisory Board plays an important role in ensuring that people who rely on public transit are part of the decision-making process through the "Riders Voices Matter" community input program.

Access also plays a prominent role in mitigating disasters, such as when designated hurricane evacuation routes are designated. Conversely, it can exacerbate disasters, such as Hurricane Katrina in 2005.[18] While no level of government provided the proper services to poor, black residents after the levees broke, mobility constraints played a major role before Katrina hit land. Many who did not evacuate from New Orleans were low-income, elderly, African American caregivers who did not own a car. The evacuation order only considered residents who could leave on their own in a vehicle. Furthermore, local governments still had not considered socially vulnerable groups in their emergency operations plans four years post-Katrina.[19] Inequitable access is another reason disparities persist in disaster-related contexts. As climate change continues to inundate coastal areas and produce more extreme weather, evacuation procedures must ensure that residents who are transit dependent can get out of harm's way. Disaster planning, adaptation, and mitigation efforts are crucial. New Orleans is now leading such resiliency efforts to ensure they can survive the next Katrina by improving flood protection systems, green infrastructure, and the transportation system.

Quality considers the degree to which existing services are consistently provided and to whom. The quality of transportation relies on more than just public transit itself. Transit administrators in Orlando highlight strong public-private partnerships as the key to a high-quality rider experience. Their business community supports a robust transit system that can affordably provide convenient access to and from work. Partnerships with health care administrators have also examined how transit affects and can improve health outcomes.

Furthermore, the quality of transit experiences is often better for men, who are less likely to have safety concerns. Women are at greater risk of assault on public transit.[20] Transit stations and surrounding areas, such as parking lots, must have good lighting. In addition, alternative design strategies, security technology, policing, and education and outreach can enhance transit riders' perceptions of safety and discourage crime.[21]

Procedural fairness examines problems unique to groups in terms of rights, treatment, and how eligibility is determined for policies and programs. One of the first steps to improve managerial approaches to fairness is to normalize discussions about inequity. For example, to advance such dialogue, Minneapolis-St. Paul's Metro Transit launched the Everyday Equity program. In two years, it held 58 employee engagement events that facilitated numerous conversations about race and social equity in the transit system. The program built a network of leaders through training and professional development activities and communicated equity-related stories across the agency. Moreover, it reinforced and coordinated human resource efforts, such as employer-sponsored childcare. These actions demonstrate that as equity embeds itself in organizational processes, more socially equitable practices that go beyond one service, like public transit, can emerge throughout communities.[22]

Outcome measures assess disparities between groups based on historically disadvantaged traits such as race, income, gender identity, sexual orientation, immigration status, socioeconomic status, and more. Federal reporting requirements attempt to ensure that local and state transportation agencies do not create disproportionate neighborhood outcomes in accordance with Title VI of the Civil Rights Act of 1964. Yet, cities' diminishing fiscal health puts pressure on planners to serve business and tourism interests over residents. For example, the Chicago Loop has prioritized access to major destinations such as Millennium Park, Michigan Avenue shopping, and the Chicago Bulls United Center, while pushing low-income housing out of the city center.[23] Similar effects have been documented in Overton,

Florida, an African American neighborhood near downtown Miami that instituted housing and transit policies that served businesses and white residents.[24]

Community changes and displacements occur over time, as if inexorable. For instance, gentrification as we know it today began in the 1970s. Businesses relocated to neighborhoods with better bus and rail access. They are willing to pay a higher dollar for buildings that were not attractive to developers in the past. This causes property values to rise and as new businesses and transit access increases, developers follow suit and invest in housing supply at a higher value. Thus, as property values rise, low-income residents can no longer afford to rent or pay property taxes. They are forced to leave.

Public transit has many positive outcomes, such as decreasing traffic congestion and improving air quality. Improvements for transit-dependent riders can enhance the experience for all. And better experiences lead to higher rates of use, which ultimately produces a more efficient system for the entire urban area. Yet, while responding to transit needs by increasing access, the expansion of public transit, particularly rail systems, has also perpetuated residential racial and income segregation and displacement of low-income communities of color. One of today's most pressing challenges in major cities is to increase mobility while forestalling gentrification. However, these tensions can be mitigated through thoughtful, evidence-based, strategic actions, as next described.

Pathways to Action

This section presents two actions that advance transit equity. The first is a case of community stakeholders working to improve transit access in the small urban area of Oshkosh, WI. The case spans nearly 15 years, providing important insight into how long and incremental the process of collective action and policy change can be. The case offers an example of a process and a program that works. In the second half of this section, we highlight societal shifts that have dramatically impacted transportation since 2020. On this basis, we note promising, evidence-based remedies to improve transit equity.

Zero Fare for Students: The Case of Improving Transit Access in Oshkosh, WI

Transit funding and policy are complex and nuanced, which makes it difficult for the community and for transit riders to engage in advocacy for policy changes. This is a story of how multiple policy decisions and urgency collided to threaten the existence of public transit systems in northeast Wisconsin and how the organizing and relationship-building that happened ultimately created an opportunity to improve student access to transit.

Threat to Transit Systems in Small Urban Areas

In 2018, coauthor Lynnsey Erickson became involved in advocacy for zero-fare transit for students in Oshkosh, Wisconsin. At that time, she was working as a community health strategist for a local public health department focusing on systems and policy change to improve community health. ESTHER, an interfaith social justice nonprofit based in the Fox Valley region of Wisconsin, has been advocating on this issue since 2015 and had completed a study in 2017 assessing transportation access for middle and high school students in Oshkosh.

Before explaining zero-fare transit for students, we first step back a few years to show how small transit systems, like GO Transit in Oshkosh, have survived. In 2010, Oshkosh was one of Wisconsin's 18 urbanized areas with a population of 50,000 or more and in 2010, the Oshkosh metropolitan planning area had a population of 79,543.[25] Also in the northeast Wisconsin region was the Appleton urbanized area, which included the City of Neenah to the north of Oshkosh, with a population of 216,154, and the Green Bay urbanized area with a population of 206,520 in 2010.

Federal funding rules at the time only permitted federal funds to be used for transit operating expenses in urbanized areas with populations below 200,000. Urbanized areas with populations above 200,000 could only use federal aid for capital expenses such as transit infrastructure and the purchase of vehicles. Because the Appleton and Green Bay areas surpassed the population threshold of 200,000 with the 2010 Census, both transit systems were facing the loss of flexibility in using the $1.5 million of federal dollars each system received.

In addition to the federal funding rule restriction, after the 2010 Census, the Census Bureau issued the "Proposed Urban Area Criteria for the 2010 Census" and considered a process of agglomeration, or grouping cities together into larger metropolitan areas for purposes of statistics gathered by the U.S. Census Bureau. This process proposed merging the City of Oshkosh's urbanized area with Appleton's.[26] Appleton was already facing the potential restriction in how their federal transit aid could be used and merging Oshkosh with Appleton would now put Oshkosh's transit system in jeopardy, both from a funding perspective and from losing routes because of having to consolidate into a larger system.

At the same time, Wisconsin state budget cuts were threatening transit systems. In 2011, Governor Scott Walker proposed a 10% cut to public transit in the state budget, while demand for services and operating expenses had been increasing around the state. In his 2013–2015 state budget, the governor also proposed moving funding for the state's mass transit operating assistance program from the segregated transportation fund to the general fund. This fund, in turn, would be impacted by reductions in appropriations and would require transit to compete with all other needs in the general fund, such as education, Medicaid, shared revenue, corrections, and other programs. This move would allow for more room in the transportation fund for Governor Walker's priority of strengthening Wisconsin's major highway infrastructure.

In Wisconsin, the state transportation fund is the largest source of funding for transportation. This fund combines revenues from gas taxes, vehicle registration, driver's license fees, and other fees collected by the Department of Transportation. Funds are pooled and the legislature makes budgetary decisions for all transportation modes without regard to the respective amounts collected from transportation taxes and fees.[27] Transportation advocates argued that public transit is a form of transportation and should remain in the transportation fund. They also argued that local communities would not benefit from increased highway spending.

This was also at a time when the newly elected Governor Walker was pursuing aggressive policies aimed at shrinking the public sector and signed a bill that ended collective bargaining for most public union employees at state and local levels.[28] Proposing to remove transit from the larger transportation fund was a strategic move to force competition with all other needs addressed by the state budget. The state was prioritizing highways and meeting the needs of suburban car owners over those who relied on transit within cities. In other words, the historically inequitable policies of the 1950s (described earlier) were being repeated once again.

Millions of extra dollars were being put into the state's transportation fund to speed up highway expansion projects. One of those projects was the Zoo Interchange in Milwaukee which has been under reconstruction since 2014 and was intended to rebuild the western Milwaukee County crossroads of I-94, I-894, and U.S. Highway 45. In 2012, the American Civil Liberties Union (ACLU) of Wisconsin and Midwest Environmental Advocates sued the state and federal transportation departments on behalf of Milwaukee Innercity Congregations Allied for Hope (MICAH) and the Black Health Coalition of Wisconsin. The lawsuit alleged that the Walker administration was not adequately addressing the needs of mass transit riders by favoring a highway project that largely benefited the predominantly white Milwaukee suburbs.

In addition, there was concern that the Zoo Interchange project was being built with the capacity to expand to eight lanes, bringing more traffic and air pollution.[29] Ultimately, the Walker administration agreed to pay $13 million in a settlement to extend buses from Milwaukee to suburban counties so Milwaukee residents would have transportation to the suburbs.[30] Yet, the Interchange project and tension between suburbs and the inner city continued, highlighting how funding and transportation policies prioritize access for white suburban residents.

With these potentially devastating impacts on public transit—the potential merging of urbanized areas, restricted funding for populations over 200,000, and state budget cuts—community organizers and advocates met with transit systems and elected representatives to find solutions. Much of the challenge in organizing around public transit is being able to distill complex policy and funding language into the language of the real transit rider. For ESTHER in the Fox Valley, this meant building trust and relationships with people impacted by transit access so they could share their stories directly with decision-makers in Madison and Washington, DC. Luckily, two members of Congress representing northeast Wisconsin sat on the House Transportation and Infrastructure Committee, Representatives Reid Ribble and Tom Petri. After many meetings with transit riders and organizers, both offices realized the severe impact of potentially losing two transit systems in their districts because of the proposed merging of urbanized areas and inflexible funding for areas with populations over 200,000.[31]

Both Congressmembers pushed House leadership to include a solution within the massive federal transportation bill, Moving Ahead for Progress in the 21st Century (MAP-21), which continued Federal Transit Administration programs through fiscal year 2014.[32] As part of MAP-21, transit systems with less than 75 buses running during the busiest part of the day could use up to 75% of federal aid for operating expenses. Transit systems that run between 76 to 100 buses at peak hour could use up to 50% of federal funding for operations. At the time, Valley Transit ran 20 buses at peak hour. Part of the solution that was offered in MAP-21 was increased flexibility for mid- and small-sized transit systems.

This case shows how three major threats to public transit in northeast Wisconsin paved the way for community organizers, transit riders, elected officials, and public administrators to build relationships and understand the need for public transit across the region. Their collaboration enabled municipal leaders to see the ability and value of community organizers raising an issue and supporting solutions, in this case for student access to transit.

K–12 Student Transportation in Oshkosh, WI

In 2016, there were 9,915 students enrolled in the Oshkosh Area School District (OASD). Of those, 2,955 students were enrolled at the two high schools, and 2,023 students were enrolled in the five middle schools.[33] About 44% of students within the district qualified for free (household income at or below 130% of the federal poverty level) and reduced lunch programs (household income 130%–185%of the federal poverty level).[34] Almost 19% of families with children under 18 years old in Oshkosh were below the poverty level in 2016 with 92% of those families having at least one person in the household identifying as a race other than White.[35]

Many readers may remember getting picked up by a yellow school bus to get to and from school while growing up, as coauthor Larson described. But for most families in Oshkosh, that was not their experience. In Wisconsin, state law requires school districts to provide transportation to students who live more than two miles from their school or who have to navigate an unusually hazardous route, such as no sidewalks, busy railroad crossings, or heavy traffic.[36] State law also exempts school districts from providing transportation through the "city option" if the school district is within a city and public transit can provide transportation.[37] There are exceptions for students who have special needs or require special accommodations. For most students in the City of Oshkosh living within the city limits or less than two miles from their school, they did not qualify for any district-supported transportation.

In 2017, ESTHER conducted a study of the transportation habits and needs at Oshkosh's middle and high schools.[38] All schools reported concerns about transportation, including truancy that resulted from lack of access to transportation, lack of evening and late-night transit service for students in extra-curricular activities or jobs, and stigma and stress for students needing to ask for bus passes. Although the district allocated some funding for school social workers to provide free bus passes, staff reported not having enough passes and not being allowed to disperse them until a serious attendance problem surfaced. In 2017, GO Transit's fare for adult riders was $1 per ride, with a monthly pass costing $25. Fares eventually increased in 2019 to $1.50 per ride and $35 for a monthly pass. For many students and families, paying $3 a day or $15 a week to get to school placed too much of a burden on already tight budgets.

ESTHER also surveyed 705 students and found that in 2017, 4% of them reported riding public transit to and from school and 18% reported riding GO Transit in the past 12 months. When asked why they did not ride public transit, reasons included having access to other transportation, not knowing how to ride the bus, fear of riding the bus, and cost. A third of students reported worries about how to afford transportation, and over half of daily transit riders reported worrying about affordable transportation. ESTHER also found that other community organizations outside of OASD, including the county, the Boys and Girls Club, and the public library, were spending almost $20,000 each year to distribute free bus passes to students.

Historically, there were many neighborhood schools or smaller schools spread throughout Oshkosh. Many students were able to walk or bike to school during warmer months, but transportation became a more serious issue during colder months or for students in the two high schools that had a wider attendance area. After a $107 million referendum was approved in 2020, the school district began implementing a long-range facilities plan to consolidate 20 schools into 14, causing a more urgent need to help students having to travel farther to and from school.[39]

At the time, several other Wisconsin transit systems, school districts, and educational institutions had revenue agreements to allow students to ride public transit for free. To the north, the Appleton Area School District and Valley Transit had an agreement to allow public and parochial middle and high school students to ride free during the school year with a valid student ID, costing the district $40,000 in 2017. The city of Sheboygan, a community with a population of 48,346 in 2017, paid $90,000 for free rides for students throughout the year, but required middle and high school students to obtain and show a bus pass in order to board the bus.

Organizers and advocates for reducing the burden on students set priorities to frame the issue. The message was that families should not have to pay to get children to school; the shared value was that it should not be a child's burden to pay to get to school. However, the question for decision-makers was who would pay for it.

Finally, in February 2020, the City of Oshkosh, OASD, and a private funder unanimously approved and funded a two-year pilot program to provide rides to public and private K–12 students free of charge year-round. The revenue agreement included that the three entities would evenly split the costs, totaling $90,000 a year. At the Common Council meeting, nearly a dozen students, school social workers, and nonprofit leaders spoke in favor of the program. When one council member commented after a student testified, "Regardless of what happens tonight, we're going to make sure you get a bus pass for the rest of the year," the student responded, "I would like to make sure that all my friends, who weren't able to come because they had to ride the bus, also get bus passes."[40] The advocacy and storytelling that occurred leading up to this decision highlight the gap that sometimes exists, especially within transportation policy, between those impacted by decisions and those making decisions.

Since being implemented in July 2020 and extended to a three-year pilot due to the COVID-19 pandemic, student ridership on GO Transit has grown substantially. When classes began in September 2020, 2,428 rides were given in September alone, despite OASD switching to virtual learning later in the month because of the pandemic. For all of 2020, 7,688 total rides were given, rising to 86,979 student rides in 2021 and 142,814 rides in 2022. Despite COVID-19, GO Transit became an effective popular means of transportation for students in Oshkosh.

Nearing the end of the three-year pilot, the Winnebago County Health Department, in partnership with coauthor Sam Larson and the University of Wisconsin Oshkosh Whitburn Center for Governance and Policy Research, evaluated the qualitative impacts of the program. Along with a team of community stakeholders and GO Transit administrators, the study found educational, health, and financial benefits. The most positive impact was the financial benefit, with 30% of students indicating the program highly impacted their access to work, internships, job interviews, job fairs, volunteering, or college campus visits.[41] Students and families/caretakers reported a high impact on school attendance and participation in school activities. From a health perspective, one of the greatest impacts of the program was the ability for students to partake in social activities, such as hanging out with friends and family or going to community events, enhancing social well-being and reducing isolation.

During the pilot program, three main challenges have been raised relating to bus hours, bus pass requirements, and safety concerns. Currently, GO Transit buses operate Monday through Saturday beginning at 6:15 am and ending between 6:15 and 6:45 pm. For students and other transit riders, these limited hours can be a barrier, especially for those who work second or third shift jobs or have commitments later in the evening. In January 2023, GO Transit instituted a new pass requirement for middle and high school students to address problem behavior as ridership increased. For students without access to a smartphone, this new requirement posed a barrier because they had to get a paper pass from their schools. Although some students and families/caretakers described concerns with the high number of riders, others noted safety as a positive outcome with transit being safer than walking.

Overall, zero-fares for students in Oshkosh have proven to have a positive impact on access to transit and have produced positive outcomes for student well-being and involvement in the community. Although working out the details of funding and handling the substantial increase in riders were challenges, the zero-fare program improved how decision-makers in Oshkosh think about transportation access. The program continues through another five-year agreement passed by OASD and the Oshkosh Common Council in July 2023.

Public transit is one piece in an entire system of transportation needed within a community, and one subset of the population not having access to it creates ripple effects. From a broader perspective, this case also shows how community organizers, people impacted, and public administrators can work together to improve a system. Had community organizers not been involved as far back as 2011 when they advocated for transit systems, against budget cuts, and for more flexible funding, zero-fare transit for students would not have had the support and thoughtful discussions that led up to 2020. Strong relationships, trust, and a shared understanding of the importance of public transit allowed for collective action.

Public Transit and Shared Mobility in a Post-COVID World

While the zero-fare case offers one example of increased bus ridership after 2020, most public transit systems have suffered significant losses since COVID-19. Several factors contribute to the downward spiral. At first, shutdowns, shelter-in-place orders, and social distancing led to a 73% drop in transit use across all forms of transit in major metropolitan areas, and 90% fewer rides taken on rail alone.[42] Ridership has still not recovered due to increased remote work, telehealth services, online education, and online shopping and delivery.

Looking through an equity lens, ridership reductions have impacted socioeconomic groups differently.

For instance, major metropolitan areas with a higher median household income, a percentage with a Bachelor's degree or more, a high employment rate, and a larger Asian population experienced greater losses in ridership. However, areas with a higher percentage of the population living in poverty, and a larger Hispanic population, had fewer reductions.[43] Again, the reasons for such disparities are vast. For instance, people in poverty are more likely to work in the service industry and are also less likely to have work-from-home employment options.

Due to these societal, technological, and economic shifts, it is time to reimagine public transit policy and planning. One of the most important strategies involves focusing on shared mobility, "the shared use of a vehicle, bicycle, or other mode that enables users to have short-term access to transportation modes on an 'as-needed' basis."[44] Sharing of a vehicle or other mobility device includes services such as car-sharing, scooter sharing, and bike-shares as well as on-demand ride-hailing services.

For instance, ride-hailing companies such as Lyft and Uber have become prominent public-private partners with local governments. A number of municipalities choose to contract with ride-hailing services rather than fund city buses. Washington, DC has subsidized late-night rides, especially for residents who work after normal operating hours. Contracting reduces costs in the beginning and provides greater access and flexibility for riders. However, as demands increase with convenient, discounted fares, costs to supply services will rise.[45] The opposite is generally true when transit is provided by city buses: when more people ride, costs go down. This is the problematic side of contracting for individualized services.

Microtransit is another form of passenger ride-sharing that has gained in popularity. The services vary but often include more flexible rides and routes in smaller shuttle vehicles that utilize smartphone technology. Via is a microtransit company that has partnered with large and small municipalities, from rural Gainesville, Georgia to Sacramento, California—to increase access, convenience, and comfort. Via provides tools for transit professionals, such as a microtransit + fixed route builder that allows users to explore what their system could look like if they maintained a popular rail or bus route, and then added on-demand microtransit to the mix.[46]

The $550 billion Bipartisan Infrastructure Law (BIL), signed in 2021, has also set goals that are important to consider when seeking funding opportunities to improve transit equity. Some of those highlighted by the U.S. Department of Transportation include:

- The "Justice40" Initiative with the goal of delivering at least 40% of the benefits of investments in climate and clean energy to underserved and disadvantaged communities
- $1.5 billion for Rebuilding American Infrastructure with Sustainability and Equity Grants
- Disadvantaged Business Enterprise and Workforce Development Programs, which provide $32 million for disadvantaged individuals and businesses
- $578 million to the Tribal Transportation Program, providing transportation and roads that provide access to tribal land or are associated with a tribal government, while contributing to economic development, self-determination, and employment
- Rural Opportunities to Use Transportation for Economic Success (ROUTES), a grant program to improve analysis of projects from rural areas, tribes, and historically disadvantaged communities
- $350 million to upgrade legacy rail fixed guideway systems for people with disabilities[47]

Over the next several years, the federal BIL will provide a tremendous opportunity to design more equitable transit systems at every level.

Summary of Key Points

At the beginning of this chapter, we shared a story of how Sam observed transit-related inequities on her daily light rail commute in Denver, Colorado. Then we reviewed the history of challenges and opportunities associated with public transportation policies, programs, and practices in the United States. From Homer Plessy on the train to Rosa Parks on the bus, inequitable mobility, segregation, and discrimination have been inherited barriers faced by communities of color, low-income individuals, and women, to name a few. From one generation to the next, such experiences have triggered both setbacks and turning points for social equity, including multiple Supreme Court rulings and the Civil Rights Act.

Yet, transit inequity and related community-level issues remain embedded in the fabric of city life. Gentrification is a key problem as metropolitan areas evolve. This is a residual effect of neighborhood segregation patterns and policies. Promising strategies and tools, including community organizing and engagement, were highlighted as steps to address some of these persisting inequities. The 2021 Bipartisan Infrastructure Law also includes the largest public transit investment in history, along with incentives to overcome inequities. Moving forward, it is vital to acknowledge that transportation technology and development are opportunities to further connect physical and social mobility. Today's public servants must take advantage of innovations to ensure that unjust policies of the past do not get passed on to the next generation once again.

Discussion Questions

1. What is your experience with public transit? Have you ever encountered or observed inequities on a bus, light rail, or commuter train?
2. Transit inequity has led to many turning points, such as passage of federal laws and court rulings. Find a recent news article that illustrates an example of transit inequity in your community or within your home state. Can you identify a strategy that transit administrators could adopt to reduce such disparities?
3. Oshkosh, Wisconsin is one example of a small city that adopted a zero-fare bus program for K–12 students. Major metropolitan areas, such as Los Angeles County, have adopted similar programs on bus and rail for K–12 and community college students. Beyond a ride to school, what are some additional benefits to students and their families of such programs?
4. Shared mobility shifts how people get from one place to another. Via is a microtransit company that partners with cities, transit authorities, school districts, universities, and more. Visit https://ridewithvia.com/resources/case-studies/ and review one of their case studies. What are the advantages and disadvantages of this public-private partnership?

Additional Resources

1. Congressional Black Caucus Foundation. "New Routes to Equity: The Future of Transportation in the Black Community." https://www.cbcfinc.org/publication/new-routes-to-equity-the-future-of-transportation-in-the-black-community/
2. Daniel Knowles, *Carmageddon: How Cars Make Life Worse and What to Do About It* (New York: Abrams Press, 2023).
3. Karner, Alex, Jonathan London, Dana Rowangould, and Kevin Manaugh. "From Transportation Equity to Transportation Justice: Within, Through, and Beyond the State." *Journal of Planning Literature* 35, no. 4 (2020): 440–459.

4. Williams, Rashad Akeem. "From Racial to Reparative Planning: Confronting the White Side of Planning." *Journal of Planning Education and Research*, August 5, 2020, https://doi.org/10.1177/0739456X20946416

Notes

1. Virginia Miller, "Record 10.8 Billion Trips Taken on U.S. Public Transportation in 2014," *American Public Transportation Association,* March 9, 2015, www.apta.com/mediacenter/pressreleases/2015/pages/150309_ridership.aspx
2. David Zipper, "How to Save America's Public Transit Systems from a Doom Spiral," *Vox*, March 27, 2023, www.vox.com/future-perfect/23653855/covid-transit-fares-buses-subways-crisis
3. Hannah Getahun, "American Car Culture Is Changing Thanks to Younger Generations. But Gen Z and Millennials See Vehicle Ownership Much Differently," *Business Insider*, May 13, 2023, www.businessinsider.com/gen-z-changing-american-car-culture-2023-5
4. David Rosenbloom, "Taking Social Equity Seriously in MPA Education," *Journal of Public Affairs Education* 11, no. 3 (2005): 247–252.
5. August Meier and Elliott Rudwick, "Negro Boycotts of Segregated Streetcars in Virginia, 1904-1907," *The Virginia Magazine of History and Biography* 81 (1973): 479–487.
6. Paul Barrett, "Chicago's Public Transportation Policy, 1900–1940s," *Illinois Periodicals Online* (2001), http://www.lib.niu.edu/2001/iht810125.html
7. Raymond A. Mohl, "Reviewed Works: *Ghosts along the Freeway* by Christine Craton, Tim Schwab; *Crossroads: A Story of West Oakland* by Marjorie P. Dublin, Bill Jersey, Pierre Valette," *The Public Historian* 19, no. 4 (1997): 112–114.
8. Jay Young, "Infrastructure: Mass Transit in 19th- and 20th-Century Urban America," *Oxford Research Encyclopedias* (March 2015), http://oxfordre.com/americanhistory/view/10.1093/acrefore/9780199329175.001.0001/acrefore-9780199329175-e-28
9. Henry Hampton and Steve Fayer, *Voices of Freedom: An Oral History of the Civil Rights Movement from the 1950s through the 1980s* (New York: Random House Publishing Group, 1990).
10. Ibid.
11. John F. Kain, "Housing Segregation, Negro Employment, and Metropolitan Decentralization," *Quarterly Journal of Economics* 82, no. 2 (1968): 175–197.
12. Laurent Gobillon, Harris Selod, and Yves Zenou, "The Mechanisms of Spatial Mismatch," *Urban Studies* 44, no. 12 (2007): 2401–2427.
13. David M. Cutler, Edward L. Glaeser, and Jacob L. Vigdor," Is the Melting Pot Still Hot? Explaining the Resurgence of Immigrant Segregation," *Review of Economics and Statistics* 90, no. 3 (2008): 478–497.
14. Ian Carlton, "Histories of Transit-Oriented Development: Perspectives on the Development of the TOD Concept," *University of California-Berkeley Institute of Urban and Regional Development* (2007), http://iurd.berkeley.edu/wp/2009-02.pdf
15. Daniel C. Vock, "Public Transit Ridership Reaches Highest Level Since 1956," *Governing,* March 10, 2014, www.governing.com/news/headlines/Public-Transit-Ridership-Reaches-Highest-Level-Since-1956.html
16. Casey Dawkins and Rolf Moeckel, "Transit-Induced Gentrification: Who Will Stay, and Who Will Go?" *Housing Policy Debate* 26, nos. 4–5 (2016): 801–818.
17. Gerard C. Wellman, "The Social Justice (of) Movement: How Public Transportation Administrators Define Social Justice," *Public Administration Quarterly* 39, no. 1 (2015): 123.
18. Camilla Stivers, "'So Poor and So Black': Hurricane Katrina, Public Administration, and the Issue of Race," *Public Administration Review* 67 (2007): 48–56.
19. Susan Gooden, Dale Jones, Kasey J. Martin, and Marcus Boyd, "Social Equity in Local Emergency Management Planning," *State and Local Government Review* 41, no. 1 (2009): 1–12.
20. Nilay Yavuz and Eric W. Welch, "Addressing Fear of Crime in Public Space: Gender Differences in Reaction to Safety Measures in Train Transit," *Urban Studies* 47, no. 12 (2010): 2491–2515.
21. Sarah Goodyear, "More Women Ride Mass Transit than Men. Shouldn't Transit Agencies Be Catering to Them?" January 30, 2015, https://www.citylab.com/transportation/2015/01/more-women-ride-mass-transit-than-men-shouldnt-transit-agencies-be-catering-to-them/385012/
22. See https://www.metrotransit.org/everydayequity
23. Stephanie Farmer, "Uneven Public Transportation Development in Neoliberalizing Chicago, USA," *Environment and Planning A: Economy and Space* 43, no. 5 (2011): 1154–1172.
24. Mohamad G. Alkadry, Brandi Blessett, and Valerie L. Pat-

terson, "Public Administration, Diversity, and the Ethic of Getting Things Done," *Administration & Society* 49, no. 8 (2017): 1191–1218.

25. East Central Wisconsin Regional Planning Commission, "2021 State of the System Report: Oshkosh Metropolitan Planning Organization. East Central Wisconsin Regional Planning Commission," April 29, 2022. https://www.ecwrpc.org/wp-content/uploads/2022/04/2021-State-of-the-Sytem-Oshkosh-MPO.pdf
26. City of Oshkosh, "Resolution 10-353 Oppose Census Bureau Rules which Impact Federal Transit Aid and Reduce Oshkosh Transit's Federal Transit Funding," November 5, 2010, https://www.ci.oshkosh.wi.us/WebLink/DocView.aspx?id=598632&dbid=0&repo=Laserfiche
27. Peter Mosher "Transportation Finance," Wisconsin Legislative Fiscal Bureau, Information Paper #39, January 2023, https://docs.legis.wisconsin.gov/misc/lfb/informational_papers/january_2023/0039_transportation_finance_informational_paper_39.pdf
28. Shawn Johnson, "A Decade After Act 10, I's a Different World for Wisconsin Unions," Wisconsin Public Radio, February 11, 2021. https://www.wpr.org/decade-after-act-10-its-different-world-wisconsin-unions
29. Midwest Environmental Advocates, "Milwaukee Zoo Interchange," accessed July 25, 2023. https://midwestadvocates.org/issues-actions/actions/milwaukee-zoo-interchange
30. Chuck Quirmbach, "DOT Will Pay $13M in Milwaukee Zoo Interchange Lawsuit Settlement," Wisconsin Public Radio, May 20, 2014, https://www.wpr.org/dot-will-pay-13m-milwaukee-zoo-interchange-lawsuit-settlement
31. ESTHER, "Congressman Petri, Congressman Ribble Say YES to Transit!" accessed July 25, 2023, https://esther-foxvalley.org/content/congressman-petri-congressman-ribble-say-yes-transit-click-here-video
32. Federal Transit Administration, MAP-21," accessed July 25, 2023, https://www.transit.dot.gov/regulations-and-guidance/legislation/map-21/map-21
33. WISEdash, Enrollment," WISEdash Public Portal, accessed July 25, 2023, https://wisedash.dpi.wi.gov/Dashboard/dashboard/18110
34. Wisconsin Department of Public Instruction, "School Nutrition Program Statistics," accessed July 25, 2023, https://dpi.wi.gov/school-nutrition/program-statistics/archive#epr
35. U.S. Census Bureau, "S1702, Poverty Status in the Past 12 Months of Families," U.S. Census Bureau, accessed July 25, 2023, https://data.census.gov/table?q=poverty+oshkosh+ wisconsin+2016&tid=ACSST1Y2016.S1702
36. Wisconsin Department of Public Instruction, "Unusually Hazardous Transportation, " accessed July 25, 2023, https://dpi.wi.gov/sfs/support/school-operations/pupil-transportation/public-uht
37. Wisconsin State Legislature, "Section 121.54(1), Wis. Stats," accessed July 25, 2023, https://docs.legis.wisconsin.gov/document/statutes/121.54(1)
38. ESTHER, "How Will I Get to School? Public Transportation and 6-12 Students," "June 7, 2017.
39. Bremen Keasey, "Oshkosh School Board Approves Plan to Save $9.2 Million by Refinancing 2020 Referendum Debt, " *Oshkosh Northwestern*, March 31, 2022, https://www.thenorthwestern.com/story/news/education/2022/03/31/oshkosh-school-board-save-9-million-after-refinancing-referendum-debt/9446625002/
40. Oshkosh Media, "Oshkosh Common Council - 2/11/20," *YouTube*, February 11, 2020, https://youtu.be/nno-SRK706Q?t=4062
41. Samantha June Larson, ElizabethBouche, JullianaBanayag, AdrianHanrahan, AshleeRahmlow, Sarahjean-Schluechtermann, PriscillaIdoko, Maya Van Thiel, "An Evaluation of the GO Transit City Bus Program for K-12 Students in Oshkosh. "Winnebago County, May 2023, https://www. co.winnebago.wi.us/sites/default/files/uploaded-files/Student%20Transit%20Report_Finalwith-Appendices.pdf
42. UCLA Institute of Transportation Studies, "For the Press: Transportation and COVID-19," accessed July 25, 2023, www.its.ucla.edu/news/for-the-press/transportation-coronavirus-covid19/
43. Yi Qi, Jinli Liu, Tao Tao, and Qun Zhao, "Impacts of COVID-19 on Public Transit Ridership." *International Journal of Transportation Science and Technology* 12, no. 4 (2021): 34–45.
44. Susan Shaheen, Adam Cohen, Nelson Chan, and Apaar Bansal, "Sharing Strategies: Carsharing, Shared Micromobility (Bikesharing and Scooter Sharing), Transportation Network Companies, Microtransit, and Other Innovative Mobility Modes." In *Transportation, Land Use, and Environmental Planning,* ed. Elizabeth Deakin (Amsterdam: Elsevier, 2020), 237–262.
45. Laura Bliss, "Uber Was Supposed to Be Our Public Transit," *Citylab,* April 29, 2019, https://www.citylab.com/transportation/2019/04/innisfil-transit-ride-hailing-bus-public-transportation-uber/588154/
46. Via Transportation "Tools," accessed July 25, 2023, https://ridewithvia.com/resources/tools/
47. U.S. Department of Transportation, "Fact Sheet: Equity in the Bipartisan Infrastructure Law," July 5, 2022, https://www.transportation.gov/bipartisan-infrastructure-law/fact-sheet-equity-bipartisan-infrastructure-law

12 WORKING TOWARD ENVIRONMENTAL JUSTICE FOR ALL

Celeste Murphy-Greene

From the Editors

The environment affects countless dimensions needed for a healthy life, from the air we breathe, the water we drink, the resources we use, to the hazards we experience. Environmental justice movements seek to address all of these issues, from where pollution occurs, to influencing environmental policy, to administering environmental protection programs. Promising solutions include better legal protections of rights, establishing advisory boards, adopting environmental justice and climate change programs like those in Chicago, IL and Richmond, VA, and the seven-step Collaborative Problem Solving Model.

In recent years, Environmental Justice (EJ) has shifted from a peripheral environmental issue to part of mainstream public policy. The social unrest of the summer of 2020 caused by the murder of African American George Floyd heightened people's awareness of the social, environmental, and economic inequality existing in the United States. As protests called attention to racial inequality, environmental justice grabbed headlines and policymakers took note. As EJ scholar Robert Bullard stated, "What was once a footnote is now a headline."[1]

This chapter provides an overview of environmental justice. First, a definition of EJ will be provided along with a history of the environmental justice movement, including the major events, policies, and milestones. Next, an examination of current issues, including recent federal, state, and local policies will be provided. Additionally, the chapter delves into climate and energy justice. Case studies are presented to illustrate how climate change impacts communities globally. The cases demonstrate efforts underway to mitigate those impacts. Finally, the chapter focuses on the future of environmental justice and challenges yet to be addressed.

Overview of Environmental Justice

It is important to first understand the difference between equality, equity, and justice. Equality is when the same or equal benefits, assistance, or rights are provided to everyone. The Equal Protection Clause of the

Fourteenth Amendment of the U.S. Constitution states, "No state shall make or enforce any law which shall abridge the privileges or immunities of citizens of the United States; nor shall any State deprive any person of life, liberty, or due process without due process of law; nor deny any person within its jurisdiction equal protection of the laws."[2] Thus the U.S. Constitution guarantees equal protection to all citizens.

Equity differs from equality as it takes into consideration the varying needs of individuals and allocates resources according to those needs. Justice is achieved when systematic barriers causing inequity are removed. When the justice principle is applied to the environment, the U.S. Environmental Protection Agency defines environmental justice as "the fair treatment and meaningful involvement of all people regardless of race, color, national origin, or income with respect to the development, implementation, and enforcement of environmental laws, regulations, and policies." In this regard, "fair treatment means that no group of people, including racial, ethnic or socioeconomic group should bear a disproportionate share of the negative environmental consequences resulting from industrial, municipal, and commercial operations or the execution of federal, state, local and tribal programs and policies."[3]

The three main focus areas of EJ are 1) The distribution of the effect of environmental pollution, 2) the environmental policymaking process, and 3) the administration of environmental protection programs. Therefore, EJ focuses on the fairness of environmental policies and procedures and uses a participatory approach to the development, implementation, and enforcement of environmental protection programs. EJ also involves recognizing and addressing the historic causes of inequities and working with administrative agencies and diverse populations to address these inequities.

Social Vulnerability and Environmental Justice

When exploring the issue of EJ, it is important to understand the factors that lead to the creation of an environmental justice community. Understanding what such a community looks like requires delving into the issue of social vulnerability. This is a term that refers to "the resilience of communities (the ability to survive and thrive) when confronted by external stresses on human health, such as natural or human-caused disasters, or disease outbreaks. Reducing social vulnerability can decrease both human suffering and economic loss."[4] Conducting an environmental justice analysis helps determine a community's social vulnerability. Figure 12.1 displays four categories of factors to consider in the analysis: 1) Demographic, 2) Geographic, 3) Economic, and 4) Human Health and Risk. Each of these includes indicators that help determine vulnerability. Negative predictors for each indicator include 1) low income, 2) low education level, 3) lack of access to health care, 4) lack of knowledge and understanding of laws and legal rights, 5) lack of use of the dominant language, and 6) lack of property ownership.

The combination of negative predictors for these factors leads to a vulnerable community at risk of exposure to environmental hazards and lack of protection under the law. Pollution takes many forms,

Figure 12.1 Environmental Justice Analysis

Factors	Indicators
Demographic	Age of population, population density, property ownership, education level, race/ethnicity, understanding of laws and legal rights
Geographic	Climate, geomorphic features, hydrologic features
Economic	Income level, infrastructure conditions
Human Health and Risk	Health care access, emissions and toxic pollutant exposures, pesticide locations and concentrations, health data

including air pollution from factories, cars, and pesticides that are sprayed. Groundwater and waterways are impacted by agricultural runoff and hazardous waste sites.

Different perspectives are used to identify vulnerable populations. Two of these are location and occupation. The *location perspective* is used to analyze the demographic, health, and economic data of an area. This method is commonly used when conducting an EJ assessment. Another perspective is the *occupational perspective,*[5] which views data of an entire occupational group, such as migrant workers, and analyzes laws, social, economic, and health factors impacting them. For example, migrant workers are a vulnerable occupational subgroup at risk for exposure to environmental hazards, such as pesticides.[6]

In order to address environmental inequities in the United States, the EJ movement evolved. The discussion turns now to the history of the EJ movement from inception to current events.

History of the Environmental Justice Movement

The EJ movement began in 1971 when the Council on Environmental Quality issued a report acknowledging the impacts of racial discrimination on the urban poor and their environment.[7] (see Figure 12.2). This report is the first national recognition of racial disparities regarding the disproportionate impact of pollution on minority communities. However, in 1982 the event that ignited the movement took place in Warren County, North Carolina when a group of community members protested the planned siting of a hazardous waste landfill. To avoid properly disposing of hazardous

Figure 12.2 Chronological History of the Environmental Justice Movement

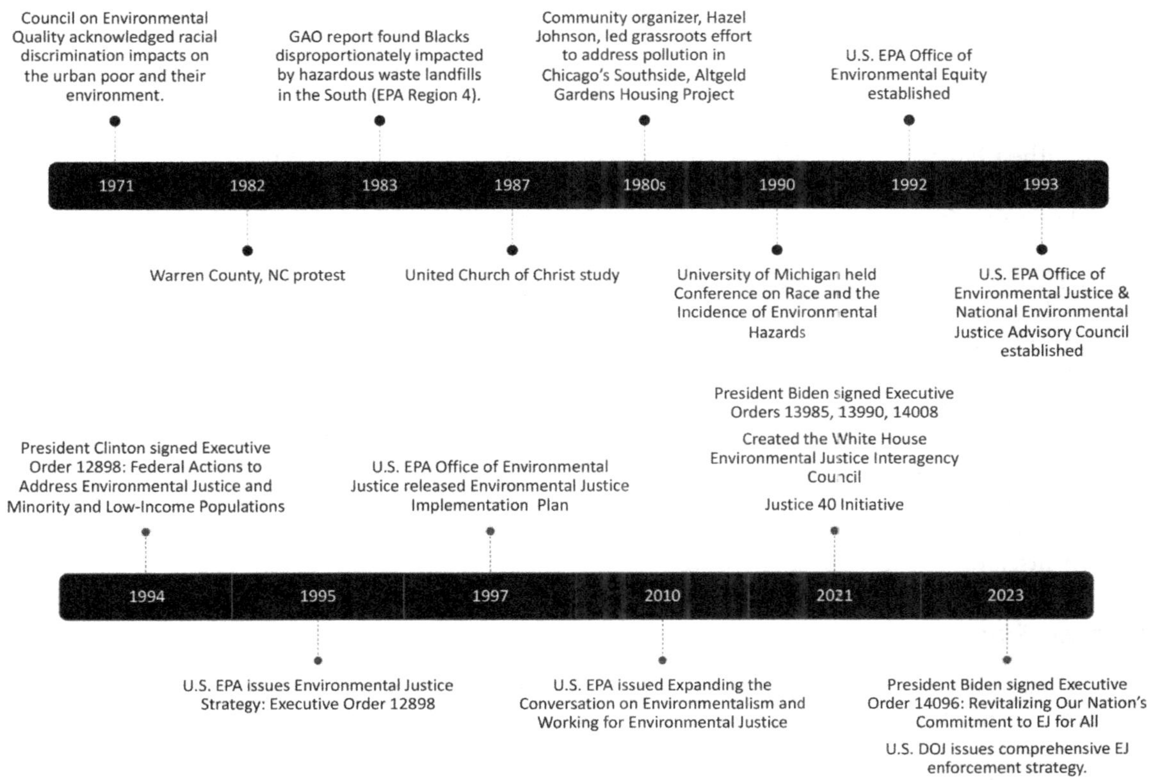

waste, as required by the Toxic Substances Control Act (TOSCA), Ward Transformer Company, based in Raleigh, North Carolina, illegally dumped polychlorinated biphenyls (PCBs) along 200 miles of road shoulder across 13 counties.[8] The state prosecuted and convicted the three men responsible for the illegal dumping.

Afton, a town in Warren County, had been chosen as the disposal site for the hazardous waste. Of the 93 sites considered, Afton had the highest Black population and Warren County was among the poorest in the state. As the disposal site was constructed between 1978 and 1982, community members met regularly and connected with civil rights leaders from groups like the Southern Christian Leadership Conference (SCLC) and the United Church of Christ Commission on Racial Justice. Despite two legal attempts to stop construction of the hazardous waste landfill, including a suit by the National Association for the Advancement of Colored People (NAACP), local residents resorted to daily protests to block trucks carrying contaminated soil to the facility.

The protests in Warren County set off a chain of events at the national level. In 1983 the U.S. Government Accountability Office reported that Blacks were disproportionately impacted by hazardous landfills in EPA's Region 4, which is the American southeast. In 1987 the United Church of Christ issued a report citing race as the most significant variable associated with the location of commercial hazardous waste facilities.[9]

Also, in the 1980s, community activist and Chicago resident, Hazel Johnson, an African American woman, worked to organize community members on Chicago's South Side and alert local, state, and national policymakers to the health issues plaguing her community. Ms. Johnson, a resident of the Altgeld Housing Project, labeled it a "toxic doughnut," due to the many landfills and polluting facilities located around her neighborhood. After her husband died of cancer, Ms. Johnson founded the grassroots organization "People for Community Recovery" and mobilized her community to address such issues as asbestos in the walls of homes to cyanide in the drinking water. Ms. Johnson's community organizing efforts earned her the 1992 President's Environment and Conservation Challenge Award. Hazel Johnson died in 2011 and is considered the "Mother of Environmental Justice."[10]

The 1990s were a time of great advancement for the EJ movement. Dr. Robert Bullard, the "Grandfather of the Environmental Justice Movement," wrote extensively on the topic and in 1990 published the first textbook on EJ, *Dumping in Dixie.* Also, in 1990 the University of Michigan convened the Conference on Race and the Incidence of Environmental Hazards, where academics and policymakers addressed environmental inequities in minority communities.

In response to growing evidence of environmental health inequities throughout the United States, in 1992, the U.S. EPA created the Environmental Equity Workgroup. This workgroup was tasked with examining what was then referred to as environmental equity. Realizing the importance of the issue, the U.S. EPA established the Office of Environmental Equity later that same year. In 1993 the name was changed to the Office of Environmental Justice and the National Environmental Justice Advisory Council (NEJAC) was established. The goal of NEJAC is to provide independent advice to the U.S. EPA on environmental justice. It has 25 members appointed from stakeholder groups representing non-governmental organizations (NGOs), community members, academics, businesses, tribal governments, and state and local governments.

Federal Environmental Justice Policies

A major step in the EJ movement was in 1994 when President Clinton signed Executive Order 12898: Federal Actions to Address Environmental Justice in Minority and Low-Income Populations.[11] The Executive Order (EO) was the first federal-level policy to address EJ. It required all federal agencies and departments to develop and execute a plan to address EJ and it established the Interagency Working

Group (IWG). The IWG, chaired by the EPA administrator, comprises the heads of 11 cabinet-level federal departments and agencies and meets monthly to collaborate on projects addressing EJ.

After EO 12898 was signed, the challenge for the U.S. EPA and all federal agencies and departments was how to implement this new policy. In order to guide implementation, in 1995, the U.S. EPA issued the Environmental Justice Strategy: Executive Order 12898, which set forth goals and objectives for achieving EJ. In 1997, the U.S. EPA released the Environmental Justice Implementation Plan. This provided a framework for achieving the EJ goals set by the agency.

One of the main policies the U.S. EPA is responsible for implementing is the National Environmental Policy Act (NEPA). NEPA requires all agencies conducting projects that may significantly impact the environment to complete an Environmental Impact Statement (EIS) or Environmental Assessment (EA), depending on the project's scope. An EIS is required for more comprehensive projects. For the agency to fully integrate EJ principles into its work, goals had to be incorporated into the preparation of each EIS and EA. Thus, incorporating EJ into each EIS and EA is consistent with a key part of the Environmental Justice Implementation Plan.

Presidential Priorities and Environmental Justice

Each presidential administration brings its own policy priorities. Since the signing of Executive Order 12898 in 1994, one of the challenges with implementation has been maintaining support and funding. For example, during the George W. Bush Administration, the Northwest Regional Office of Environmental Justice was closed and in 2004 the Office of Inspector General criticized the U.S. EPA for not implementing EO 12898. A year later, the General Accountability Office also criticized the EPA for not implementing EO 12898.

Taking office in 2009, the Obama Administration renewed and reenergized executive-level commitment to EJ. President Obama appointed Lisa Jackson, the first African American woman to lead the U.S. EPA and she set EJ as a top priority for the U.S. EPA. In 2010 the EPA issued reports that expanded the conversation on EJ. For example, Plan EJ 2014, which marked the 20th anniversary of EO 12898, created a roadmap for the EPA to achieve EJ priorities.

During the Trump administration, the U.S. EPA Office of Environmental Justice experienced a major overhaul. Several longtime staff members resigned due to the anti-government rhetoric espoused by the president. Despite this challenge, the EPA's EJ work moved forward, launching an interactive environmental tool called EJScreen. This tool allows anyone to log into www.epa.gov/ejscreen and find information related to a location's proximity to a Superfund site, hazardous waste, lead paint, and other pollutants.

After taking office in January 2021, the Biden administration set EJ as a top priority. Within the first 100 days in office, the president established the White House Environmental Justice Advisory Council (WHEJAC) and signed three executive orders pertaining to social equity and environmental justice. The WHEJAC includes community members, academics, and state and local officials who advise the president on EJ issues. These are the orders issued:

1) EO 13985: Advancing Racial Equity and Support for Underserved Communities Through the Federal Government

2) EO 13990: Protecting Public Health and the Environment and Restoring Science to Tackle the Climate Crisis

3) EO 14008: Tackling Climate Change at Home and Abroad

4) Additionally, on April 21, 2023, Biden issued EO 14096: Revitalizing Our Nation's Commitment to Environmental Justice for All.

EO 13985: *Advancing Racial Equity and Support for Underserved Communities Through the Federal Government* requires all federal agencies to conduct an equity assessment. This assessment is intended to identify potential barriers that confront underserved communities and individuals. One example of an area where barriers may exist is in procurement and contracting opportunities. EO 13985 works to remove those barriers within federal agencies.

EO 13990: *Protecting Public Health and the Environment and Restoring Science to Tackle the Climate Crisis* directs all federal agencies to take action to confront the climate crisis and places EJ as a top priority. The order states:

> Our Nation has an abiding commitment to empower our workers and communities; promote and protect our public health and the environment; and conserve our national treasures and monuments, places that secure our national memory. . . . In carrying out this charge, the Federal Government must be guided by the best science and be protected by processes that ensure the integrity of Federal decision-making. It is, therefore, the policy of my Administration to listen to the science; to improve public health and protect our environment; to ensure access to clean air and water; to limit exposure to dangerous chemicals and pesticides; to hold polluters accountable, including those who disproportionately harm communities of color and low-income communities; to reduce greenhouse gas emissions; to bolster resilience to the impacts of climate change; to restore and expand our national treasures and monuments; and to prioritize both environmental justice and the creation of the well-paying union jobs necessary to deliver on these goals. To that end, this order directs all executive departments and agencies (agencies) to immediately review and, as appropriate and consistent with applicable law, take action to address the promulgation of Federal regulations and other actions during the last 4 years that conflict with these important national objectives, and to immediately commence work to confront the climate crisis.[12]

EO 13990 directs all agencies to review the promulgation of federal regulations and policies from the previous presidential administration and rescind policies inconsistent with the above stated goals. This EO also established an Interagency Working Group focusing on the Social Cost of Greenhouse Gases.

EO 14008: *Tackling Climate Change at Home and Abroad.*[13] EO 14008 prompts several initiatives. First, it establishes the White House Environmental Justice Interagency Council (WHEJIC). The WHEJIC is made up of the heads of federal agencies and departments that are charged with coordinating with the WHEJAC in developing performance metrics to ensure accountability. The WHEJIC is also charged with publishing an annual performance scorecard. EO 14008 also includes the Justice40 Initiative, which requires 40% of the overall benefits from federal investments in climate change and clean energy to be allocated to disadvantaged communities. Additionally, Justice40 establishes an Office of Environmental Justice at the U.S. Department of Justice to coordinate EJ issues at the Department.

Continuing the momentum gained on advancing EJ, on April 21, 2023, President Biden signed Executive Order 14096: *Revitalizing Our Nation's Commitment to Environmental Justice for All.* EO 14096 revitalizes and strengthens the policies set forth in EO 12898, signed by President Clinton in 1994. As stated in EO 14096:

> To fulfill our Nation's promises of justice, liberty, and equality, every person must have clean air to breathe; clean water to drink; safe and healthy foods to eat; and an environment that is healthy, sustainable, climate-resilient, and free from harmful pollution and chemical exposure. . . . We must advance environmental justice for all by implementing and enforcing the Nation's environmental and civil rights laws, preventing pollution, addressing climate change and its effects, and working to clean up legacy pollution that is harming human health and the environment. Advancing environmental justice will require investing in and supporting culturally vibrant, sustainable, and resilient communities in

> which every person has safe, clean, and affordable options for housing, energy, and transportation. . . . Achieving this vision will also require improving equitable access to parks, tree cover, playgrounds, sports fields, rivers, ponds, beaches, lakes, and all of the benefits provided by nature, including America's public lands and waters. . . . Communities with environmental justice concerns face entrenched disparities that are often the legacy of racial discrimination and segregation, redlining, exclusionary zoning, and other discriminatory land use decisions or patterns. These decisions and patterns may include the placement of polluting industries, hazardous waste sites, and landfills in locations that cause cumulative impacts to the public health of communities and the routing of highways and other transportation corridors in ways that divide neighborhoods. . . . Nearly three decades after the issuance of Executive Order 12898 of February 11, 1994 (Federal Actions to Address Environmental Justice in Minority Populations and Low-Income Populations), the Federal Government must build upon and strengthen its commitment to deliver environmental justice to all communities across America. Our Nation needs an ambitious approach to environmental justice that is informed by scientific research, high-quality data, and meaningful Federal engagement with communities with environmental justice concerns and that uses the tools available to the Federal Government, including enforcement of civil rights and environmental laws. Our Nation must also take further steps to dismantle racial discrimination and institutional bias that disproportionately affect the health, environment, safety, and resiliency of communities with environmental justice concerns. . . .[14]

To achieve its goals, EO 14096 directs all federal agencies to submit an Environmental Justice Strategic Plan (EJSP) to the Chair of the Council on Environmental Quality. EO 14096 also requires all federal agencies to create performance metrics and other measures of accountability to track the agency's performance in achieving environmental justice goals.

Federal Civil Rights Law and Constitutional Rights

Along with the executive orders there are additional policy tools used to implement EJ efforts. The first is Title VI of the Civil Rights Act of 1964,[15] which prohibits discrimination on the basis of race, color, and national origin in programs and activities receiving federal financial assistance. Up until 2001, to prove discrimination in environmental cases, one needed to demonstrate the disparate impact of environmental pollution on certain groups. However, in 2001, the Supreme Court weakened Title VI in the case *Alexander v. Sandoval*. In this case, the Supreme Court ruled that the *intent* rather than *disparate impact* was needed to prove discrimination. This made EJ cases more challenging to prove in court.

As described earlier, the second policy tool used to implement EJ is the Fourteenth Amendment of the U.S. Constitution.[16] According to it, all citizens of the United States are provided equal protection under the law. The assumption is that these same protections apply to environmental protection and environmental justice communities.

States and Environmental Justice

In addition to policy advancements at the federal level, states have also been taking action. States with EJ policies include California, New York, Oregon, Rhode Island, Arkansas, Kentucky, Minnesota, North Carolina, and New Mexico. California passed a law requiring environmental regulators to monitor the impact of pollution on minority and vulnerable populations. State-formed EJ advisory boards in California, North Carolina, and Virginia allow stakeholders, such as community members, universities, and non-profit organizations, to have their voices represented. Another way states integrate EJ into their policies and practices is through interactive Geographic Information Systems mapping and grant programs. For instance, the State of North Carolina has an excellent interactive community online mapping tool. (The link to this tool is in the Resources section at the end of the chapter.) Each year more progress is being made to address EJ at the state level.

Local Level Environmental Justice Actions

In addition to state-level initiatives, localities are also implementing EJ policies and practices. Chicago, Illinois, and Richmond, Virginia provide examples.

Chicago's Citywide Approach to Environmental Justice

On May 10, 2023, Chicago Mayor Lori E. Lightfoot issued an Executive Order to advance EJ for all Chicagoans (Executive Order No. 2023-3). This order does the following:

- Ensures completion of the citywide Cumulative Impact Assessment (CIA) that provides data on how environmental burdens and other stressors vary across Chicago
- Formally establishes the structure and role of a community advisory body and interagency working group, both charged with carrying forward EJ actions
- Requires the City to develop and implement robust community engagement standards, and to create a coordinator role within the Office of Climate and Environmental Equity
- Advances City reforms to zoning, transportation planning, permitting, and enforcement policies to address cumulative impacts.[17]

The executive order was a major step forward in helping the city work toward achieving EJ for all residents. It determines how environmental burdens impact all residents; increases community engagement; and increases interagency communication.

Richmond, Virginia's Equity-Focused Solutions to Climate Change

Cities across the United States are currently dealing with the impacts of climate change. These impacts come in the form of extreme heat and recurrent flooding. The impacts of climate change do not impact all residents equally. Often, those who are most vulnerable socially, economically, and environmentally are also likely to suffer the greatest impacts. Because climate change disproportionately impacts the most vulnerable populations in society—poor, elderly, and minorities—this phenomenon has become a social justice issue. The intersection of climate change and social justice is referred to as climate justice.

The City of Richmond is working to address climate justice with its justice-focused climate action plan, RVAgreen2050. This is a resilience plan that uses an equity-focused and justice-focused approach to identify vulnerable communities at risk of the impacts of climate change. Richmond's plan is a two-pronged approach focusing on mitigation and adaptation in order to create a more resilient community. The equity-centered plan seeks to reduce greenhouse gas emissions by 45% by 2030 and achieve zero emissions by 2050. To adapt to these changes, the plan involves partnerships with local universities, nonprofits, and government agencies.

One of the key components in Richmond's adaptation plan is to address the impacts of the historic practice known as redlining. Redlining is a form of geographical discrimination used in financial lending to constrain persons of color from purchasing homes or securing a mortgage in predominantly white residential areas. The practice of redlining was used in the United States beginning in the 1930s and its effects are still felt. It is a discriminatory practice that makes it difficult, if not impossible, to live in more desirable areas of Richmond where there are more shade trees, which make neighborhoods cooler on hot summer days.

Redlining, combined with social and environmental inequity, produces cascading threats. As urban areas experience rising temperatures due to climate change, the result is Urban Heat Islands (UHIs). The main cause of UHIs is lack of green space and the predominance of impermeable surfaces such as concrete and asphalt that radiate heat from the sun. According to the U.S. EPA, the average surface temperature in urban areas can range from 18 to 27 degrees F hotter during the day and from 9 to 18 degrees F warmer at night than in rural areas.[18] Increased heat exposure for prolonged periods results in numerous health-related problems, such as chronic obstructive pulmonary disease, asthma, cardiovascular disease, heat stroke, and heat exhaustion. The effects of UHIs impact minorities disproportionately because many lack air conditioning and access to health care. The University of Richmond's Mapping Inequality Project provides maps of redlined communities and the Virginia Museum of Science provides expertise in helping identify Richmond's UHIs. A Heat Vulnerability Index (HVI) includes these factors: poverty, age, disability, working outdoors, vehicle access, housing status, housing cost burden, lack of central air conditioning, and health conditions (COPD, heart disease, high blood pressure, asthma, diabetes, kidney disease, obesity).

In 2017, the City of Richmond partnered with the Science Museum of Virginia, the University of Richmond, and the local non-profit Groundwork RVA to increase awareness and understanding of the city's urban heat burden. Together they developed strategies to address the UHI burden. Groundwork RVA is a local chapter of Groundwork USA. With the support of the U.S. EPA, the National Park Service, the City of Richmond, and Groundwork USA, Groundwork RVA involves youth in leadership programs to increase greenspace and green infrastructure to enhance neighborhood climate resilience. Green infrastructure is defined as:

> A strategically planned and managed network of wilderness, parks, greenways, conservation easements, and working lands with conservation value that supports native species, maintains ecological processes, sustains air and water resources, and contributes to the health and quality of life for America's communities and people.[19]

Integrating green infrastructure reduces impermeable surfaces that radiate heat and reduces UHIs and flooding caused by climate change. Green infrastructure provides multiple benefits, including providing cooling to urban areas, reducing runoff and flooding from increased precipitation, increasing biodiversity to support pollinators and native species, and enhancing the aesthetic beauty of communities. To increase the amount of green infrastructure in Richmond, Groundwork RVA's Green Team engages at-risk recent high school graduates to help create sustainable landscapes and community greening projects. The Green Team helps youth build work experience and contributes to the health and sustainability of their community.

In addition to the efforts of Groundwork RVA, the City of Richmond encourages residents to help reduce urban heat by incorporating the following activities:

- Plant and care for native trees and native vegetation in neighborhoods
- Install a vegetated or green roof
- Create green space on vacant lots or help maintain an existing green space
- Install permeable surfaces on roadways, sidewalks, parking lots, and alleys.

The City of Richmond is an excellent example of how municipalities can address environmental and climate justice by partnering with local universities, non-profit organizations, and community groups to build more resilient communities. Such partnerships provide pathways forward and the EPA provides guidance as explained next.

The Power of Partnerships in Addressing Environmental Justice: The Collaborative Problem-Solving Model

As communities across the nation confront EJ issues, the U.S. EPA offers a strategic approach built on partnerships. The Collaborative Problem-Solving Model is a seven-step process:

1. Issue Identification, Communicating Vision and Strategic Goal Setting
2. Community Capacity Building and Leadership Development
3. Consensus Building and Dispute Resolution
4. Multi-Stakeholder Partnerships and Leveraging Resources
5. Constructive Engagement by Relevant Stakeholders
6. Sound Management and Implementation
7. Evaluation, Lessons Learned, and Replication of Best Practices

One application of the Collaborative Problem-Solving Model is in Spartanburg, South Carolina, where in 1996 a resident, Harold Mitchell, put these tools into action. Mr. Mitchell founded Regenesis, a nonprofit he established to address the environmental, economic, and health issues facing his community. The two communities of Arkwright and Forest Park, located outside of Spartanburg, were areas where, due to old zoning laws, residential housing was located within yards of polluting industrial sites and hazardous waste landfills. The poverty rate in these largely African American communities was 25% and the unemployment rate was 10%. For years residents suffered from ill health and lack of jobs, poor access to health care, few grocery stores, and few recreational facilities.

Using the Collaborative Problem-Solving Model, Mr. Mitchell was able to leverage $300 million to successfully transform a once highly polluted and economically depressed area into a healthy and thriving community.[20] Some of the major EJ achievements of Regenesis (visit at https://regenesis.com/en/) include:

- Environmental cleanup of two Superfund sites and six Brownfield sites
- Reducing crime and illegal activities
- Improved housing for the community
- Improved health care services
- Improved transportation access
- Better emergency preparedness
- Eliminating food desert
- Several job training initiatives.

By collaborating with local universities, community members, and government officials at the federal, state, and local levels, the Arkwright and Forest Park communities were transformed into thriving communities. This project is an international model for EJ and revitalization. In 2000 Regenesis was selected by the Federal Interagency Working Group on Environmental Justice as one of 15 national demonstration projects.

Environmental Justice Around the Globe

As more attention and resources are focused on EJ efforts, issues of climate and energy justice and resiliency develop more traction. However, climate change is a multi-dimensional and multi-national issue. This chapter discussed climate justice as it pertains to Urban Heat Islands. On an international level, climate change impacts less developed, poorer countries at a more significant rate than developed countries. The top 10 countries at greatest risk are: 1) Puerto Rico, 2) Myanmar, 3) Haiti, 4) Philippines, 5) Mozambique, 6) The Bahamas, 7) Bangladesh, 8) Pakistan, 9) Thailand, and 10) Nepal.[21] As extreme weather events impact communities across the globe, climate change is a global public health threat. According to the United Nations Security Council, in 2019 weather-related hazards displaced 24.9 million people in 140 countries.[22]

Energy justice accompanies environmental and climate justice movements. Energy justice focuses on enabling communities to access safe, affordable energy. It expands on the environmental and climate justice movements by elevating the shift away from a fossil-fuel-based energy system and by correcting undue burdens unjustly imposed on marginalized communities. Energy justice is often used interchangeably with the term *energy equity*. Frontline communities dealing with the firsthand impacts of natural resources extraction bear the most immediate effects, but the ripple effect touches everyone. Working with communities to create renewable, clean energy and to encourage energy independence using techniques such as microgrids helps eliminate pollution and promotes sustainability and resiliency.

Resilient communities are those able to rebound from economic, environmental, and social disruption. These disruptions can take the form of economic downturns, a major weather event such as a tornado, hurricane, flood, typhoon, or a mass shooting. Building resilience requires an inclusive approach that includes all community members. The future of EJ will build on addressing environmental injustices that plague communities around the globe. All nations must work collaboratively to meet the goals of the Paris Agreement, a binding international treaty on climate change, and to take action to address the growing threat of climate change.

Summary of Key Points

Achieving EJ requires a whole community approach, ensuring that the voices of the poor, minority, elderly, tribal nations, and other underrepresented groups, are heard in the decision-making process. Fortunately, EJ advancements at the federal, state, and local levels over the last 40 years demonstrate commitment to this effort. But while much progress has been made, much remains to be done. States and local governments must act to address the EJ issues that plague communities. Holding polluters accountable and using such tools as the Collaborative Problem-Solving Model will help frontline communities address legacy pollution issues.

The path to achieving EJ involves building resilient communities using transparency, inclusiveness, and an equity-focused approach.[23] Justice-focused resilience strategies are currently being implemented in communities such as Richmond, Spartanburg, and elsewhere, yet there remains much to be done. Acknowledging past discriminatory practices, such as redlining, and addressing the lasting economic, environmental, and health impacts of those practices is key. While much progress has been made since the EJ movement began, more work remains if we are to achieve environmental justice for all. Using a participatory approach based on trust-building and community engagement will help communities address environmental injustices.

Discussion Questions

1. How do you identify an environmental justice community? What are the factors included in an environmental justice analysis?
2. Discuss the key components of the Collaborative Problem-Solving Model.
3. What are some strategies used to address Urban Heat Islands?
4. What strategies described in this chapter would work in your community?
5. Are there environmental hazards near you? Access www.epa.gov/ejscreen to learn.

Additional Resources

1. U.S. EPA Environmental Justice Screening Tool: https://www.epa.gov/ejscreen
2. U.S. EPA Environmental Justice Collaborative Problem-Solving Model: https://www.epa.gov/environmentaljustice/epas-environmental-justice-collaborative-problem-solving-model-0
3. Green Infrastructure Center: http://www.gicinc.org/
4. National Wildlife Federation Native Plant Finder: https://www.nwf.org/nativeplantfinder
5. State of North Carolina EJ Community Mapping Tool link: https://www.deq.nc.gov/outreach-education/environmental-justice/deq-north-carolina-community-mapping-system

Notes

1. Robert Bullard, "Introduction: Environmental Justice—Once a Footnote, Now a Headline," *Harvard Law Review* 45, no. 2 (2021): 243–248.
2. Constitution of the United States. Constitution Annotated. Retrieved on May 11, 2023 from https://constitution.congress.gov/browse/essay/amdt14-S1-3/ALDE_00013743/
3. U.S. Environmental Protection Agency, "Learn About Environmental Justice," Environmental Protection Agency, accessed July 25, 2023, https://www.epa.gov/environmentaljustice/learn-about-environmental-justice
4. Agency for Toxic Substances and Disease Registry, "At a Glance: CDC Social Vulnerability Index," Centers for Disease Control, accessed March 12, 2021, www.stsdr.cdc.gov/placeandhealth/svi/at-a-glance_svi.html
5. Celeste Murphy Greene, "The Occupational, Safety, and Health of Florida Farm Worker: Environmental Justice in the Fields," *Journal of Health and Human Services Administration* 25, no. 3 (2002): 281–314.
6. Celeste Murphy-Greene and Leslie A. Leip, "Assessing the Effectiveness of Executive Order 12898: Environmental Justice for All?" *Public Administration Review* 62, no. 6 (2002):650–658.
7. A. Bryant and P. Mohai, "Race, Poverty, and the Environment," *EPA Journal* 18, no. 1 (1992): 8.
8. Jennifer Kagan, "Social Equity and Environmental Justice." In *Achieving Social Equity: From Problems to Solutions,* ed. Mary Guy and Sean McCandless, Irvine, CA: Melvin and Leigh, Publishers, 2020): 142–157.
9. United Church of Christ, "Toxic Wastes and Race in the United States," (New York: The Commission for Racial Justice, 1987), xiii–xvi.
10. Adam Mahoney, "Here's Why Congress Is Recognizing Hazel M. Johnson, the 'Mother of Environmental

Justice,'" *Grist*, May 17, 2021, https://grist.org/equity/hazel-johnson-environmental-justice-month-chicago/

11. U.S. Environmental Protection Agency, "Summary of Executive Order 12898: Federal Actions to Address Environmental Justice in Minority and Low-Income Populations," Environmental Protection Agency, accessed July 25, 2023, www.epa.gov/laws-regulations/summary-executive-order-12898-federal-actions-address-environmental-justice
12. Federal Register, "Executive Order 13990: Protecting Public Health and the Environment and Restoring Science to Tackle the Climate Crisis," *Federal Register* 86, no. 4 (Washington, DC: National Archives, January 25, 2021), https://www.govinfo.gov/content/pkg/FR-2021-01-25/pdf/2021-01765.pdf
13. Federal Register, "Executive Order 14008: Tackling Climate Change at Home and Abroad," accessed July 25, 2023, https://www.federalregister.gov/documents/2021/02/01/2021-02177/tackling-the-climate-crisis-at-home-and-abroad
14. Federal Register, "Executive Order 14096: Revitalizing Our Nation's Commitment to Environmental Justice for All" accessed July 25, 2023, https://www.federalregister.gov/documents/2023/04/26/2023-08955/revitalizing-our-nations-commitment-to-environmental-justice-for-all
15. U.S. Department of Justice, "Title VI of the Civil Rights Act," United States Department of Justice, accessed July 25, 2023, www.justice.gov/crt/fcs/TitleVI-overview
16. United States Constitution, amend. 14, sec. 1, accessed July 25, 2023, https://constitution.congress.gov/browse/essay/amdt14-S1-3/ALDE_00013743/
17. City of Chicago, "Mayor Lightfoot Announces Executive Order to Advance Environmental Justice for All Chicagoans," City of Chicago, May 10, 2023, https://www.chicago.gov/city/en/depts/cdph/provdrs/environmental_health/news/2023/May/mayor-lightfoot-executive-order-environmental-justice.html
18. U.S. Environmental Protection Agency, "Reducing Urban Heat Islands: Urban Heat Island Basics," (Washington, DC: U.S. Environmental Protection Agency, 2008), accessed July 25, 2023, https://www.epa.gov/heat-islands/heat-island-compendium
19. Mark Benedict and Edward McMahon, *Green Infrastructure: Linking Landscapes and Communities* (Washington, DC: Island Press, 2006).
20. United States Environmental Protection Agency, "EPA's Environmental Justice Collaborative Problem Solving Model," (Washington, DC.: US. Environmental Protection Agency, 2008), accessed July 25, 2023, https://www.epa.gov/environmentaljustice/epas-environmental-justice-collaborative-problem-solving-model
21. David Eckstein, Vera Kunzel, and Laura Schafer, "Global Climate Risk Index 2021," (Bonn: Germanwatch e.V., 2021), accessed July 25, 2023, https://www.germanwatch.org/sites/default/files/Global%20Climate%20Risk%20Index%2020212.pdf
22. United Nations, "The Paris Agreement," United Nations, accessed July 25, 2023, www.un.org/en/climatechange/paris-agreement
23. Celeste Murphy Greene, *Environmental Justice and Resiliency in an Age of Uncertainty* (New York: Routledge, 2022).

13 MEETING THE CHALLENGE OF LIBERATION WORK: PRACTICAL APPLICATIONS FOR DEIA OFFICERS

Kimberly Desmond

From the Editors

While achieving social equity involves law, politics, management, agencies, and promising solutions, it is ultimately people at the frontlines who make social equity happen. An example of this important on-the-ground work is provided by DEIA officer Kimberly Desmond, who is Chief Race and Equity Officer of San Diego, California. In this chapter, she shares personal and professional experiences and explains not only the skills and education required to do the work but also the complex roles, duties, expectations, and networking that are required. She presents a model she developed—the Liberation Model—and explains how it can be used to drive change and promote equity for all.

Diversity, equity, inclusion, and accessibility (DEIA) officers are vital to integrating equity work into local government. The work dismantles systemic inequities, especially racism, and pivots around the key components of visualizing, normalizing, organizing, and operationalizing racial equity to create a culture of systemic and organizational change. Race Forward is a prime example of a national organization that functions as a catalyst to advance DEIA work in local communities. Founded in 1981, its purpose is to bring an innovative approach to complex systemic issues so that people can take effective action toward racial equity. There are close to 400 governmental jurisdictions currently addressing systemic racism with the goal of achieving equity in their communities.[1]

While DEIA offices are growing in number across the country, readers may wonder what the work entails. For instance, what are the duties of a DEIA officer? What education and training are required to work in this position? What skills and talents do DEIA officers need? These are not easy questions, and there are no easy answers. I will answer these questions by sharing my lived experience as an African

American woman. Born and raised in America, my past is the galvanizing force that propelled me into a career doing humanitarian work to dismantle systemic and institutional racism. I present approaches and strategies that I use to move government forward in a drive to integrate equity into policies, practices, and budget decisions. Table 13.1 offers reflection questions to guide readers toward self-exploration, for this is what prompts behavior change that, in turn, leads to systemic change. I also present what I call my Liberation Model, which I use to sustain racial justice work within city government.

Toward My DEIA Work in the Public Sector

I was born in the 1980s to my mother who was raised in Paris, Texas, and my father who grew up in Chicago, Illinois. My parents met in Denver, Colorado, which served as the backdrop for my cultural experiences.

Systemic racism impacts my life personally. While I do not want this chapter to be all about my most painful traumatic experiences with racism, I believe it is important to position the impact created by the deprivation that resulted from restricted freedom and structural inequities. Specifically, I want to bring attention to how designed racism produces inequitable health and education outcomes, creates a set of conditions that informed my family's reality of the deaths of my brother and father, and created the unjust interactions with the mass incarceration system that consumed the life of so many of my relatives.

My personal experience with racism, family history, education, training, and preparatory work was the catalyst for my career and purpose within local government. I pursued degrees in the fields of education, sociology, and community counseling because I sought an explanation for my personal trauma. I sought an explanation for the death of many family members and friends, and I sought an explanation for why human life is packaged into consumable recycled commodities.

Ultimately, I was seeking my own humanity and a path to forgive my mother and father because I blamed them for every painful experience. Then I began to understand the role that racism played in designing and perpetuating impoverished neighborhoods. As a child, I often wondered why poverty was the norm on my block and why low-wage positions carved a path toward low-income housing instead of homeownership. And how low reading and math scores prevented college readiness. I also wondered about high mortality rates for African American/Black women, unsafe living conditions infested with rodents, and mold-stained walls. I was curious about why so many people in my life visited the inside of prison walls. I was curious about how rich people lived without worrying about food and housing, and how they loved their children without the consistent stress associated with inhumane living conditions. I also wondered if they knew about the people trapped in poor conditions or if they felt obligated to help.

I was curious about how love, pain, and trauma coexist. And I could see how beautiful values grow in the midst of poverty. The truth about my experience is that my grandmother picked cotton in the southern part of Texas in a job that was exploitative, she lived through segregated schools, restaurants, recreation center pools, and housing, and had limited access to many areas of the city. She lived through Jim Crow laws that governed "separate-but-equal" accommodations and that codified discrimination and systemic racism. The restrictions on her prevented my mom from having the capacity to build generational wealth. I was raised to be conscious of both implicit and explicit racism because the collateral damage was a part of everyday life. The associated trauma was a gravitational force that damaged my family's collective humanity and restricted freedom and access to basic needs. The truth about my experience is that my family is also communal, spiritual, and committed to love in ways that taught me how to be resourceful and persistent. I refuse to let the totality of my experience with racism steal the abundance of ancestral gifts that prepared me for a career to liberate humanity.

I continually learn about the powerful gravitational force that racial discrimination has on all races and ethnic groups and I have come to realize that addressing racism is a radical hypothesis. Why? Because the dehumanization of African American/Black people is enshrined in the Constitution of this country. As we critique the impact of systemic racism, we begin to understand that meritocracy cannot exist as a norm because the sum of our available choices is connected to the social, political, and economic structures that prevent opportunity.

I entered DEIA work because the liberation of my personal humanity demanded an intervention from oppression. This intervention included relief from the exploitation tethered to the apparati of racism. I entered this field to understand how systems produce racial disparities within public safety and how structures perpetuate structural exclusion from education, transportation, employment, essential health care, and environmental justice. Additionally, I wanted to remove barriers to healthy food, safe drinking water, and housing. I entered this field to better understand myself, critically examine how my family is hindered by racism, and to ultimately change the systems that prevent liberation. I entered this field to look at society and have honest conversations about racial disparities, to turn protest into progress, to eliminate systemic racism, and to treat equity work as an opportunity. Becoming a Chief Race and Equity Officer is more than a job; it is a divine purpose that is connected to the social justice movement fought by my ancestors.

Moving Toward Liberation

In my role, I consider what social, economic, political, and environmental conditions must exist to actualize liberation, and this leads to the imperative to connect with emancipation. If emancipation is a process that we follow to be set free from oppression, involuntary servitude, and control, then liberation is the expression of freedom that exists without restriction and without restraint from racism, oppression, and injustice.

Liberation goes beyond tolerance. It encompasses unrestricted opportunities to self-actualize and thrive without personal humanity being stolen by racist ideology. I envision liberation through the lens of emancipation of enslaved African American/Black communities and countless massacres and forced relocations of Indigenous peoples through acts of genocide. The process of emancipation sets the conditions for Chief Race and Equity Officers to build equitable systems that are positioned to eliminate racial disparities and systemic racism.

As a model, liberation encompasses love, freedom, equity, and social justice as interconnected principles that are only possible when viewed through the lens of emancipation. To be free from racism, authority, exploitation, colonization, and oppression, is to create the conditions for liberation. This freedom occurs when social, economic, political, and environmental circumstances are not constrained by systemic racism. The conditions for liberation allow individuals to thrive without restriction, exploitation, or control. Liberation is what a society would resemble without racial disparities or economic exploitation.

While equity and justice can occur as singular or multiple outcomes, liberation, on the other hand, is a persistent condition that, when it exists, makes it possible for people to self-actualize individually and collectively. Self-actualization means moving through life without the constraints posed by poverty and racism, both of which set social, economic, political, and environmental constraints. In other words, liberation is the persistent expression of freedom and social justice as a result of emancipation from exploitation.

Often, people attempt to compliment me by stating, “You made it out, and you’re smart. Therefore, there is no excuse that will prevent success” within a country full of opportunity. In response, I say, “To survive racism in this country includes navigating the inheritance of generational poverty and trauma, receiving the unwanted gifts of a constant state of dehumanization, experiencing unimaginable grief, and living in environments that structure neglect." To survive racism is to constantly navigate racial microaggressions and to leap over mountains of accumulated inequity, mountains that prevent the convergence of economic opportunity, dignity, and liberation.

As I reflect on my personal career path, positionality, and experience as a Black woman in America, I find peace in the belief that my position as a DEIA officer is directly connected to modern day freedom fighters and civil rights activists. This is true in spite of the fact that there is a misconception and stigma attached to government employees due to their positionality within an institution that has structurally neglected Black or African American, American Indian or Alaska Native, Asian, and Native Hawaiian or Other Pacific Islander communities. DEIA officers are judged by unrealistic standards that measure our ability to eliminate systemic racism in a system that has never eradicated racial disparities. In fact, our ancestors were murdered when they challenged a system not built to ensure freedom and liberation for all.

When individuals attempt to place the burden and responsibility on me to eliminate racism, I remind them of the meticulous intricacies that created a centuries-long tapestry of colonialism, dehumanization, economic exploitation, enslavement, and genocide. We replicate hierarchies of power when we expect one person or position to solve the complexities that uphold systemic racism. It is up to all of us to be reflective, especially of our own identities, histories, and positionalities. We must "do the work" to understand ourselves and our lives. As a DEIA officer, I have found that asking and answering several key questions helps. Take the time to reflect on your answers to the questions in Table 13.1.

Table 13.1. Reflection Questions

#	Question	Personal response
1	Have you ever experienced dehumanization or any type of inequity personally?	
2	How do you define the difference between interpersonal, systemic, and institutional racism?	
3	What is the difference between a moral obligation and an economic obligation to intervene when someone who is different from you is experiencing inequity? Specifically, should you intervene when the humanity of another person is compromised or stolen?	

Doing the Work: Four Guiding Principles of the Liberation Model

At this point, I want to shift from my personal experience to innovative models for dismantling systemic racism in local government. DEIA work requires adopting foundational principles that guide social justice and anti-racism efforts. To operationalize equity work, I have found several key principles that support strategies and inform the development of equity plans. These plans fit well within a Liberation Model I developed for this work.

Throughout the history of the Civil Rights Movement, words like *freedom*, *justice*, and *liberation* were used to build social justice movements and label a direction toward justice. To build on the path set forth by many revolutionary change makers, my own work is based on the four principles shown in Table 13.2. They pave a road toward equity-driven strategies and are the foundation for culture change work.

Table 13.2. The Four Principles

Principle #1. Love	bell hooks[a] defines Love as, "the will to extend oneself for the purpose of nurturing one's own or another's spiritual growth."
Principle #2. Freedom	Centers opportunity, freedom of choice, and unrestricted access to an overall quality of life without the constraints of oppression.
Principle #3. Equity	Occurs when we eliminate institutional racism and systemic disparities, providing everyone with equitable access to opportunity and resources to thrive, no matter where they live or how they identify.
Principle #4. Social Justice	"[A] communal effort dedicated to creating and sustaining a fair and equal society in which each person and all groups are valued and affirmed. It encompasses efforts to end systemic violence and racism and all systems that devalue the dignity and humanity of any person. It recognizes that the legacy of past injustices remains all around us, so therefore promotes efforts to empower individual and communal action in support of restorative justice and the full implementation of human and civil rights."[b]

Notes: a. bell hooks, All about Love: New Visions (New York: William Morrow, 2000).
b. John Lewis Institute for Social Justice, https://www.ccsu.edu/johnlewisinstitute

So what do these four principles look like in practice? I use my own experience to provide context. During my career, I have had the opportunity to partner with many thoughtful city employees, elected officials, community members, and academic partners to develop two local government offices, both of which were developed to dismantle systemic racism and to design more equitable structures within local government. The workforce for the City and County of Denver is approximately 13,000 city employees, serving over 800,000 community members. The workforce for the City of San Diego is approximately 11,000 city employees, serving over 1.4 million community members; it is the 8th largest city in the country.

In my roles as Chief Race and Equity Officer for the City of San Diego and as Interim/Director of the Mayor's Office of Social Equity and Innovation in the City and County of Denver, it became clear that liberation would be the force needed to truly address systemic racism. There is no linear or individual strategy that can be deployed to dismantle systemic racism. The political, social, and economic systems are interconnected and impact everyone, regardless of where they live, or how they identify. This is why problems are complex, multi-dimensional, and long-standing. In my role as Chief Race and Equity Officer, I deploy varied culture change strategies with each aimed at building reliable, equitable data collection practices that identify opportunities for change.

I find a Liberation Model helpful because it treats systemic and structural change as a core component to eliminating disparities and racism. The Love, Freedom, Equity, and Social Justice principles in Table 13.2 lead directly into the Liberation Model and are foundational to intentional change. The purpose of the model is to activate strategies and action steps that dismantle systemic racism and inequity.

To activate the "Love" principle is to launch a culture change strategy that promotes ongoing learning and development. It builds an understanding of how systemic racism operates. For city employees to eliminate racism within government systems, there must be a work culture where individuals understand their own implicit biases, call out economic exploitation where it exists, and understand how colonialism infects judgment. To activate the "Freedom" principle is to identify opportunities to create, revise, and/or redesign policies and practices as they relate to the provision of neighborhood services. The purpose of this is to ensure that distinctly different neighborhoods are treated equitably. To activate the "Equity" principle is to address disparities and produce measurable outcomes. To activate the "Social Justice" principle is to recognize that the legacies of past injustices and systemic racism remain and impact our collective humanity, regardless of our race/ethnicity.

Applying the Liberation Framework: Linking Principles and Strategies

There is a moral and economic imperative associated with dismantling the tools that perpetuate the apparati of racism. Focusing on social justice means there is a collective obligation for everyone to dedicate time, resources, experiences, and expertise. Equally important is a liberatory frame of reference that centers on opportunity, freedom of choice, and quality of life free from oppression. The Liberation Model combines the four principles to ensure that systemic change eliminates all inequities, regardless of neighborhood or life circumstances. The principles of love, freedom, equity, and social justice can be applied through strategies that employ learning and development, policies and practices, data collection, and monitoring of outcomes.

Strategy 1: Learning and Development (Love)

The Learning and Development strategy is "Love" activated as an intentional process to outline behaviors and attributes for employees to display in agencies that value inclusion. According to bell hooks,[2] "to truly love we must learn to mix various ingredients—care, affection, recognition, respect, commitment, and trust, as well as honest and open communication." Activating "Love" is a culture change strategy. It cultivates a workplace environment where employees acknowledge and appreciate different cultural experiences and backgrounds among colleagues and community members. For example, when listening to complaints about problematic policies, city employees display the action of love through trusting community members when they contextualize their individual experiences with historic inequity when elected officials make a commitment to provide information and transparency about a policy change, and when city employees treat community members with respect as they express frustration at the impact of policy or budget decisions.

Engaging with an employee workforce of over 11,000 individuals in 30 departments is not a straightforward process. There are multiple communication channels and decision nodes, and conflicting political priorities of elected officials must be balanced. The larger a jurisdiction is, the more complicated it is for everyone to achieve a common understanding. Therefore, it is imperative to outline uniform terminology, build common knowledge about inequity and racism, and identify common data collection standards that can be used to determine whether outcomes are equitable.

When conducting training, we teach employees how to de-bias decisions by using an equity lens. This lens consists of a set of questions that probe the benefit, burden, or unintended consequences of each decision made by city departments. The learning and development strategy creates opportunities to learn about how past policies and statutes legalized racial segregation (Jim Crow laws) and how discriminatory practices excluded access to insurance, loans, and mortgages (redlining, for example). Each example illuminates the codification of racial segregation, which led to the current disparities in housing, education, health, and economic status. The point is that disparities experienced today have a causal root in past policies.

A learning and development strategy creates opportunities for city employees to shift the narrative and incorporate diverse perspectives and cultural experiences. It also provides a means to de-bias ideologies that perpetuate damaging stereotypes. At its core, strategies that change the narrative are an intentional approach to cultivating inclusive places for those who are underrepresented and for those who are impacted by systemic racism, enabling them to engage in dialogue about what they experience. While media often feed preexisting racial stereotypes, narrative projects counteract and disrupt implicit biases among city employees.

Strategy 2: Policies and Practices (Freedom)

The Policies and Practices strategy is "Freedom" activated. It is a process to name and address policy opportunities that can be created or revised to build equity in structures and systems. The role of local government is to provide a range of vital services for people within each neighborhood. These include emergency management/plans, transportation, housing, planning, waste collection, stormwater services as well as water quality management/flood prevention, parks/recreation access, public safety, and licensing and business support, to list only a few.

In the past, systemic racism was designed into institutions and social structures. Now we have the opportunity to learn from the past and unravel what is unjust. This is made possible by redesigning policies and programs so they serve our collective humanity. When policies steal someone's humanity, preventing access and opportunity, we should revise them. Policies should be designed to prevent harm, not prevent the opportunity to access freedom. Ameliorative examples include having standards that remove lead from water, building streets that are not vulnerable to sinkholes, repairing dams/levees, and replacing water pumps to prevent catastrophic flooding.

As examples show, policies and practices at the local level are varied. Still, each presents a pathway toward freedom and opportunity. The following list names six I have found to be important.

1. Ordinances. These are local laws put in place by a municipality to regulate safety, public health, and land zoning. These laws are enforceable.
2. City council policies. These are standard practices and procedures implemented by the City Council. They provide guidance to city departments.
3. Administrative regulations. These provide direct administrative guidance. They outline the scope, purpose, key functions, communication expectations, and responsibilities that guide operational expectations for city departments.
4. Mayoral executive orders. These are directives and sets of commands. The mayor uses these orders to provide instruction and to direct immediate specific action for each city department.
5. Resolutions. These reflect a collective political interest and are issued by the city council. They are used to express the council's formal opinions and intentions. Resolutions go into effect on the date of final passage and are used to guide department decisions.
6. Proclamations. These are official declarations issued by a local government authority and are used to make an announcement or acknowledgment. Proclamations are not policies but they set a tone for what is valued.

Legislating policies and issuing orders, resolutions, and proclamations will not guarantee liberation or equitable outcomes. Nor do they dismantle systemic racism or repair the totality of cultural deprivation. This is where the work of the Chief Race and Equity Officer enters the picture. The officer's job is to understand how to remove policies that codify systemic racism and how to create policies that create opportunity and access.

Strategy 3: Data Collection (Equity)

As a Chief Race and Equity Officer, one of the roles that we can play in partnership with department leaders is to provide a model that captures strategies, action steps, and outputs. Data collected can then be used to inform city budget investments and to monitor progress. In this part of the Liberation Model, data are essential because they make it possible to track strategies and goals and they provide measures of success for departments.

The data collection strategy activates "Equity" as an outcome. Table 13.3 demonstrates the contrast between an equality standard and an equity assessment. Equality occurs when each individual, family, neighborhood, or community is given the same resources and opportunities without recognition that each person has different circumstances. In the City of San Diego, equity occurs when we eliminate institutional racism and systemic disparities, providing everyone with equitable access to opportunity and resources to thrive, no matter where they live or how they identify. While the equality standard is well-meaning, the equity assessment provides information about real disparities. The contrast between equity and equality is important because it sets the context for how to address disparities. The table also demonstrates how achieving equity relies on data collection.

Table 13.3. Equality versus Equity Assessment

Department Name	Equality Standard	Equity: Identified Disparity
Parks and Recreation	Each recreation center (40 total) should provide recreation center programming with the following options: robotics classes, basketball teams, and arts/culture activities.	A recreation center assessment determined that only 20 recreation centers provide robotics classes, basketball teams, and arts/culture activities.
Public Utilities	Each neighborhood should have access to safe drinking water.	The US Environmental Protection Agency (EPA) mandated an inventory of every single service line delivering drinking water. A citywide assessment determined the presence of 10 service lines with lead contaminants.
Transportation	Each neighborhood (40) should have complete sidewalks with accessible curb ramps.	A sidewalk assessment determined that 15 neighborhoods in low-income areas do not have complete sidewalks with accessible curb ramps.

Positioning equity as an outcome creates the conditions for using metrics to track progress and close gaps. Specifically, equity is achieved when disparities disappear. Chief Race and Equity Officers are uniquely positioned to partner with departments to assist them in identifying disparities by first creating standards for citywide programs and services. Citywide standards make it possible for each department to operationalize its outputs and set a baseline for its accomplishments. Having the baseline makes it possible to identify which neighborhoods or demographic groups are not meeting the equity goal. Once a disparity is identified, a window of opportunity opens for policy solutions, budget reallocations, or program design changes.

Strategy 4: Social Justice

Data collection helps lead to the fourth strategy, social justice. Data aggregated at the neighborhood level are far more useful than when aggregated citywide. This is because citywide data obscure the unique conditions and needs of individual neighborhoods. Census tract information provided by the U.S. Census is available free of charge. Even more useful are individualized studies of neighborhoods.

The pursuit of social justice refers to ongoing commitments to dismantle ideological, internalized racism—racism that is seen as so normal, so taken for granted, that it is not identified as such. Indeed, the Liberation Model displayed in Table 13.4 is based on my experience as a Chief Race and Equity officer. I designed it to help governments drive systemic and structural change in local government. The Model involves linkages between processes, outcomes, the four principles, and the four strategies. As a reminder, each principle (Love, Freedom, Equity, and Social Justice) is guided by a focus on either a process or outcome. Additionally, each principle is cross-walked over a specific strategy or action steps to operationalize equity as a measurable outcome.

Table 13.4. The Liberation Model: A Framework to Drive Structural and Systemic Change

	Process		Outcome	
Principles	**Love**	**Freedom**	**Equity**	**Social Justice**
Strategy	**Strategy #1**	**Strategy #2**	**Strategy #3**	**Strategy #4**
	Learning and Development	Policies and Practices	Data Collection	Social Justice
Action Steps	**Action Step #1** Create training content that normalizes conversations about racial equity, types of racism, and historical policies that codify racism. **Action Step #2** To address biases and stereotypes, launch a story-telling project to shift the narrative about different cultural experiences.	**Action Step #1** Select a specific policy or practice to change a systemic disparity. **Action Step #2** Adopt an equity lens and ask questions. **Action Step #3** Launch an Equity Plan process to create strategies in each department.	**Action Step #1** Set an "Equal" standard or baseline goal. **Action Step #2** Identify disparities to determine which demographic is not meeting the "Equal" standard. **Action Step #3** Launch a study to collect data that is not otherwise available.	**Action Step #1** Personal ongoing commitment to dismantle ideological, internalized, systemic racism.

The Liberation Model is both a tool and a process for guiding change. It captures specific practices, policies, and programs that can enhance the services provided by departments. Once a department identifies a specific program, practice, or policy, data metrics are integrated into the strategy to aid in evidence-based decision-making.

In my role as a Chief Equity Officer, I have helped change policies and practices, designed learning and development content, conducted randomized control trials in partnership with academic partners, and created processes for creating citywide Equity Plans. The principles (Love, Freedom, Equity, and Social Justice) guided each strategy and allowed me to shift the culture of large-scale organizations. Government agencies are huge and no single employee creates wide-scale change alone, so I am thankful for all my colleagues, community partners, and elected officials who contribute to the movement. Table 13.5 provides examples from two departments: 1) Parks and Recreation and 2) Engineering and Capital Projects.

Duties and Responsibilities

The work described in Table 13.5 does not just happen. It requires that people do their best to foster fairness for all. The Chief Race and Equity Officer is the catalyst for making this happen. The essential duties attached to this role align with integrating equity into every level of local government. The position partners with departments to review, revise, and/or create policies, programs, practices, and budgets in order to eliminate systemic racism and inequity.

Priority actions for DEIA officers include:

- Collaborating with internal performance and data analytics departments to conduct a citywide assessment to identify disparities/gaps in a city's services and programs
- Developing and launching an assessment to determine how city employees are conducting equity and inclusion work
- Creating a citywide racial equity action plan and compiling goals, strategies, and measures of success for each department
- Launching liberation teams that operate at the department level to connect day-to-day work to the action steps identified in department equity plans
- Adopting a Liberation Model; and
- Partnering with Race Forward to launch a theoretical orientation that positions local government to dismantle systemic racism. This pivots around visualizing, normalizing, organizing, and operationalizing racial equity in order to implement change.

Across this work, there are five important implications for priorities and programming. First, DEIA officers are required to facilitate learning and development. In the City of San Diego, the Department of Race and Equity facilitates training on racial equity and inclusion with a curriculum that contextualizes historic oppression, systemic racism, and implicit/explicit biases. This training provides City departments with tools for building equitable outcomes.

Second, officers need to conduct liberation-centered coaching (LCC). In collaboration with the Performance and Analytics Department in the City of San Diego, the Department of Race and Equity provides liberation-centered coaching to direct an inquiry-driven approach that leads to strategy development and action. LCC offers support to City departments as they execute tailored tactical

Table 13.5. Applying the Liberation Model

Department Name: Parks and Recreation				
	Process		Outcome	
Principles	**Love**	**Freedom**	**Equity**	**Social Justice**
Strategy	**Strategy #1** Learning and Development	**Strategy #2** Policies and Practices	**Strategy #3** Data Collection	**Strategy #4** Social Justice
Action Steps	**Action Step #1** Create content for training that normalizes conversations about racial equity, racism, and policies that codify racism to provide context around different cultural perspectives from those who utilize recreation centers.	**Action Step #1** Create administrative regulations that outline standards for each recreation center.	**Action Step #1** Set an "Equal" standard to determine the baseline goal for each recreation center (40 total) to determine a programming schedule. **Action Step #2** Identify the disparity that exists between recreation centers to determine which locations do not provide robotics classes, basketball teams, and arts/culture activities.	**Action Step #1** Personal ongoing commitment from everyone to review a decision-making matrix to address inequity at specific recreation centers during monthly funding allocation meetings.

Department Name: Engineering and Capital Projects				
	Process		Outcome	
Principles	**Love**	**Freedom**	**Equity**	**Social Justice**
Strategy	**Strategy #1** Learning and Development	**Strategy #2** Policies and Practices	**Strategy #3** Data Collection	**Strategy #4** Social Justice
Action Steps	**Action Step #1** Create content for training that normalizes conversations about racial equity, types of racism, and historic policies that codify racism to provide context to how historic capital disinvestment created structurally excluded communities.	**Action Step #1** Revise Policy 800-14 to integrate an equity factor score into the prioritization matrix to inform all capital investments in parks, libraries, stormwater, transportation, and public safety. **Action Step #2** Consider revision to *Council Policy 200-01. In 1979, the City Council adopted Policy 200-01, which defines the different types of streets. The policy outlines who is financially responsible for maintaining and constructing various types of streets. This policy does not mention unimproved streets or alleys, as Resolution No. 107424 previously placed the financial responsibility for them on the abutting property owner.	**Action Step #1** Set an "Equal" standard to determine the baseline goal for all city streets and alleys. **Action Step #2** Identify the disparity that exists across neighborhoods to identify unimproved streets and unimproved alleys. Note: The Transportation Department launched a study to capture potholes, cracks, and surface issues on the road to determine neighborhood impact and future investment.	**Action Step #1** Personal ongoing commitment from everyone to review the prioritization matrix to outline a budget allocation plan during weekly meetings.

Note: *Policy example from City of San Diego.

equity plans. The primary objective is to coach departments as they design equity into their services and resources and as they identify disparities that impact distinct neighborhoods, demographics, and intersectionalities, including race, ethnicity, gender, people with disabilities, LGBTGIA, and so forth.

In LCC sessions with departments, inquiry-based questions are used to probe and identify how historic decisions designed inequity into neighborhoods and programs, which resulted in disparate impacts on communities of color. The historic decisions include water quality, environmental justice issues (air quality, hotter temperatures due to no tree canopies, hazardous material), and unequal public safety interactions with police departments. Table 13.6 displays questions used in LCC to guide the creation of tactical equity plans.

Table 13.6. Inquiry-Based Questions and Action Steps for Liberation-Centered Coaching

Question	Inquiry-Based Questions	Action Steps
1.	What is the equal outcome that is created by the current or future policy?	Departments are asked to set an equal standard for all programs and resources delivered to each neighborhood.
2.	What disparities do the identified policy or practice seek to address? • Consider the geographic location of the neighborhood. • Consider the impact on city employees.	Departments are asked to consider how policies impact people and neighborhoods differently based on how they are positioned in society.
3.	Is there a specific neighborhood or demographic impacted by the identified policy or practice?	Departments are asked to identify a specific neighborhood impacted by their decisions. For example, some neighborhoods have low homeownership rates, lack healthy food options, and/or have inferior infrastructure (streets, sidewalks, alleys, hospitals, and schools).
4.	What data are available to help your department understand the historical impact? Note: Consider housing, education, and income data disaggregated by categories of diversity.	Departments are asked to review past policies and practices and to consider revisions to produce more equitable outcomes.
5.	What is the unintentional impact of current and/or future policy?	Departments are asked to review the impact of a policy or practice for specific demographics.

Third, DEIA officers should practice inclusive community engagement. In the City of San Diego, the Department of Race and Equity partners with each City department to cultivate an intentional approach to inclusive engagement. The result is that spaces are created for community members to contribute their lived experiences and offer ideas for how to transform local government policies, programs, practices, and budget priorities.

Fourth, DEIA officers should help create equitable outcomes. The Department of Race and Equity utilizes data to measure the progress of clearly defined goals and strategies. A measurable process includes using data to track how city budgets address the creation of new sidewalks, new traffic signs that prevent fatalities, more affordable housing, new libraries, and improvements in parks. With parks, for example, the equipment is broken/missing or neglected in some neighborhoods. And in some areas, there is a high potential for flooding if there is a failure in critical stormwater systems (drain structure, water channels, water pipes). Data can be used to measure the status, maintenance, and replacement of vital infrastructure assets (streets, sidewalks, sewers, dams, water pumps, fire protection systems).

Fifth, DEIA officers should integrate a budget equity framework in their work with departments. The Budget Equity Framework uses an equity lens to evaluate budgets and submit budget adjustment requests. It prompts the identification of disparities, which leads to the inclusion of equity highlights in the department's Executive Budget Review and City Council Budget Review Committee presentations. In the City of San Diego, for example, a Budget Equity Impact Statement is included in Volume II of the Proposed and Adopted Budget documents to provide a summary describing how each department budget directly benefits a specific neighborhood or program. The equity impact statement also identifies operational impacts and potential unintended consequences and/or burdens connected to a specific budget request. Each department uses an equity lens to analyze how policies, programs, practices, and budget decisions will achieve equitable outcomes. As part of this, there are three big questions that drive analysis: 1) How does this budget allocation directly benefit specific neighborhoods and city employees; 2) What are the operational impacts to policy, programs, or practices; and 3) What are the potential unintended consequences and/or burdens to specific neighborhoods and city employees?

This discussion has explained strategies for engaging in DEIA work. Now I explain the personal and experiential requirements to become a DEIA officer and what it takes to maintain work/life harmony while doing the job.

Cognitive and Emotive Requirements for DEIA Officers

DEIA work requires both cognitive and emotive skills. In terms of education, many DEIA officer positions require at least a Bachelor's degree from an accredited college or university in fields such as psychology, sociology, counseling, education, and/or political science. Further, many positions require between five to eight years of experience in a learning and development environment that includes curriculum design and facilitation. It is also ideal to have a background in systems work, which means work that addresses complex problems through collaborating with multiple levels of leadership. Further, given the importance of engagement, a strong applicant will have five to 10 years of experience partnering with multiple systems within and across government, nonprofits, and businesses.

Community engagement experience is also a must. Candidates for DEIA positions must have experience using community engagement models and practices that create inclusive interactions between community members and city employees. When applying for a DEIA post in local government, strong candidates should also have three to five years of experience partnering with city departments to revise or create policies and practices. This includes being familiar with how to translate the technical language of federal, state, and local regulations into language understandable to the public.

While the requirements above are expressed in terms of years of prior experience, other skills needed are less directly expressed. Ideally, DEIA officers should be politically astute. A high level of sophistication is needed in order to work with elected officials and balance multiple political priorities within high-pressure environments. Further, officers must understand systemic and institutional racism, which refers to a deep understanding of the attitudes and practices that constitute the scaffolding of systemic racism.

Just as important as the cognitive skills are the emotive skills. DEIA work requires officers to have a high level of emotional intelligence and strong interpersonal skills. The work is intense and often pockmarked with resistance. Self-awareness—the ability to recognize and understand one's own emotive state—is necessary as one faces the realities of systemic racism and resistance to change. Self-regulation of one's emotions is another critical skill. This refers to officers' ability to regulate and manage their own emotions, especially when confronted with hostility and anti-blackness. Emotive self-regulation means appearing calm when one may not feel calm, adapting well to unexpected events, managing conflict constructively, and diffusing tense or difficult situations. Interpersonal skills are also needed because officers must be able to put information to work in daily interactions and communications to develop rapport with leaders/colleagues and to deploy active listening skills. Other-awareness and empathy are also important so that officers understand how their words are perceived by others and so that they pick up on the power dynamics that influence social interactions.

Self-care is essential if DEIA officers are to stay on the job and be effective. Self-care practices include setting boundaries around one's work demands and finding harmony between work and personal life. Resolving historic disparities does not happen quickly, nor does it happen without setbacks and resistance. I like to spend time away from work in nature, walking on the beach, reading, watching survival shows, and spending quality time with family. Rest and restoration are key to doing liberation work lest compassion fatigue and burnout get in the way of the critical thinking and executive functioning that are necessary.

I use the following three pillars to guide my self-care practices. First, I engage in restoration, which refers to actively resting and disconnecting from my ongoing tasks. I use time off to renew my energy without distractions from work. Second, I engage in rejuvenation. As a humanitarian, changing systems that were created to break people can be emotionally draining. To rejuvenate, I celebrate small and large successes. I also allow myself to fail and to lean toward forgiveness when things do not work out as planned. Rejuvenation also includes creating time to think in order to cultivate innovative ideas. There are no singular solutions to eliminate racism. Finally, I engage in revolution. As a core component of my personal learning journey, I create opportunities to engage in learning from historic judicial dissents and decrees, and I review best practices from other cities, both success points and failures. I believe that history is a great teacher; therefore, I am a constant student.

As an African American female, I maintain self-care by understanding the limits to my responsibility as an individual within a position that is created to eliminate racism. We have lost countless leaders who were murdered for pushing a policy agenda to bolster freedom and address racial disparities. Therefore, I understand it is not my burden to carry the work alone within a system not designed to produce liberation. There are no simplistic policies or strategies that can be deployed to eliminate systemic racism.

Summary of Key Points

The work that I do in local government is the work of my ancestors. It is a generational commitment to continually fighting injustice and racism until we are all free and liberated from systems that were intentionally created to confine our minds, bodies, and spirit. The pursuit of freedom in this country is not something that we have fully actualized, which is why the work of a Chief Race and Equity Officer is needed in local government. In this role, we are modern freedom fighters and civil rights leaders, redesigning organizational culture, changing policies, partnering with community members, and working with elected officials to continuously redesign policy making.

The principles of love, freedom, equity, and social justice lead directly into the Liberation Model and serve as the foundation for intentional cultural change. Through learning and development, adopting an equity lens to examine policies and practices, collecting data to make evidence-based judgments, and by insisting upon social justice, cities can carve a path toward a better future for all residents.

In closing, I hope you find that the Liberation Model I shared in this chapter is a useful tool to pursue systemic and structural change as a core component to eliminating disparities and systemic racism. I want this chapter to cultivate innovation and enthuse visionary leaders to continue the work of our ancestors. There is no singular or simplistic approach to eliminating systemic racism, so don't be afraid to fail, learn, innovate, and share with each other. We are all needed in the social justice movement.

Journey well!

Discussion Questions

1. Apply an equity lens to a program or practice in your community. Think about who it benefits, who it burdens, and what its unintended consequences might be. Does it benefit some people more than others? Given the way it operates, what are the potential unintended consequences and/or burdens to specific groups or neighborhoods?
2. Think about the four principles of love, freedom, equity, and social justice. Are these compelling for you? How might you apply them to an equity issue important to you?
3. Imagine you are a DEIA officer for a city near you and your task is to convince a department head to critically assess operations that have run the same way for over a decade. The department head argues that this new-fangled notion of "social equity" is a passing fad and not something that merits upsetting the way operations have worked for years. What is the first step you take? The second step? The third step?

Additional Resources

1. Government Alliance for Race and Equity (GARE) at https://www.racialequityalliance.org/
2. Nicole Humphrey, Shannon Portillo, Domonic A. Bearfield, Alesha Doan, "The Oblivious Organization: Understanding Racial Stereotypes in the Public Sector," *Journal of Social Equity and Public Administration*, 1, no. 2 (2023): 51–64.
3. Isabel Wilkerson, *Caste: The Origins of Our Discontents* (New York: Random House, 2020).

Notes

1. More information is at https://www. https://www.racialequityalliance.org/home . Race Forward# is home to the Government Alliance on Race and Equity (GARE), which is a national network of local governments working to achieve racial equity and advance opportunities for everyone.
2. bell hooks, *All about Love: New Visions* (New York: William Morrow, 2018).

14 IN PURSUIT OF SOCIAL EQUITY: ISSUES OF PROCESS, ACCESS, QUALITY, AND OUTCOMES

Mary E. Guy and Sean A. McCandless

From the Editors

This concluding chapter accentuates themes from previous chapters and explains that achieving social equity is a journey, not a destination. Equity audits are explained as a method to identify inequity in access, processes, quality, and outcomes. An interview with Zina Merritt, Chief Diversity Management Officer for the U.S. Government Accountability Office, provides optimistic insights into the future of social equity initiatives. The chapter closes with a reminder that it is both an honor and an obligation to be responsible, personally and collectively, for ensuring that "We the People" truly means "We."

There is an urgency to social equity, so how do we put our arms around it? We can give it a name, build it into strategic and operational plans, and audit programs to assess their degree of equity. We can focus on procedural fairness, access to services, quality of services, and outcomes. We can pass laws and implement monitoring systems, such as Title IX, the Civil Rights Act, and the Equal Employment Opportunity Commission. We can differentiate it into procedural equity and substantive equity, two sides of the fairness coin. But before any of these are effective, we must "see" it.

These chapters are prisms that heighten awareness of racism, colorism, sexism, homophobia, transphobia, ethnocentrism, ageism, ableism, and other "isms." Each chapter presents a unique dimension to social equity. Had there been space and more weeks in a semester, many more chapters would have been added. They would focus on the urban-rural divide, on the young versus old chasm, on the intersections that combine to further complicate lives, and on social equity issues in an increasingly globalized world. You name it: Fairness is a variable that belongs in every decision calculus.

For those who are advantaged by inequity, it is tempting to overlook it. But ignoring it delivers advantage to some while disadvantaging others. Public service professionals do not have a choice. It is incumbent on each of us to see it and to be ever sensitive to how our work perpetuates inequity or resolves it, from repairing potholes on all streets and not just on wealthy avenues, to ensuring accessible transportation and safe housing, to creating rules for programs so they are fairly delivered. The challenge is to have the knowledge and sensitivity to identify inputs, processes, and outcomes in such a way that equity issues are illuminated. This is how knowledge drives action and makes progress.

The Public Service Imperative

Achieving social equity and then maintaining it requires constant vigilance. Like a stretched rubber band, advantage returns to its original shape in the absence of forces that maintain balance. Just as the social equity emphasis of the 1970s retracted into the "efficiency" and "business" imperatives of the 1990s, the attention to social equity after George Floyd's murder is already meeting with pushback.

It is up to public service professionals to keep social equity issues on the radar. Such professionals wear two hats: one reflects their personal identity and one reflects their professional obligation to see the equity implications in their programs. Does one policy interact with another to compound advantage or disadvantage? What is the balance that can be achieved? Whether approaching the subject proactively or retroactively, there is a price to be paid when power imbalances are not taken into account. For example, in the latter 20th century, tight-knit urban communities of people of color were shattered by the construction of thoroughfares connecting downtown business communities to suburbs. Policies that advantaged the well-heeled disadvantaged the poor. Neighborhoods were razed to make room for urban redevelopment projects. History is rhyming as gentrification threatens historic urban neighborhoods. It falls on the shoulders of transportation planners, city managers, community development officers, public health professionals, and neighborhood activists to turn the prism, to look at who is advantaged and who is disadvantaged by public policies. A good way to keep social equity foremost in administrators' minds is by periodically conducting equity audits, which are explained next.

Equity Audits

Equity audits are an evidence-based means for evaluating policies, procedures, and programs to ensure they are equitable. By using four lenses—procedural fairness, access, quality, and outcomes—the audit reveals where inequities lurk and pave the way for corrective action. Equity audits range from back-of-the-envelope analyses to comprehensive interviews and examinations of documents. They are an opportunity to look anew at the status quo, to identify inequities, and to point a way forward. To conduct an audit, evaluate the policy and/or program in five steps as listed here:

1. ***Procedural Fairness*** – This refers to the processes used in policy development, program design, and services rendered. It involves due process, transparency, equal rights, and representativeness. Procedural inequities occur when members of a particular group are targeted in a way that disadvantages them, such as with traffic stops, or when discriminatory hiring and promotion practices disadvantage members of one group while advantaging another. Representativeness ensures that those affected by policies and programs have a voice in their planning and operations.

2. ***Access*** – As a form of distributional equity, access refers to the opportunity to participate in processes and programs. For example, inequity exists when residents on one side of the city have poorly maintained streets and parks and residents on the other side have well-maintained streets and parks. Another example is when members of a group cannot obtain information or participate in decision-making that affects them.
3. ***Quality*** – As a form of process equity, quality refers to the degree to which services meet minimally acceptable levels. It ranges from safe water and air to street maintenance and well-equipped schools.
4. ***Outcomes*** – These are the effects that policies and programs produce. Do all groups benefit similarly from the program? Are any groups disadvantaged?
5. ***Summary and Recommendations*** – After taking stock of findings that result from the assessment of procedural fairness, access, quality, and outcomes, close the audit with a summary of findings that enumerate where inequities exist and how they can be corrected.

Efficiency, Effectiveness, Economy, and Equity

Ever since Leonard White wrote the first public administration textbook, the field has had a long-standing obsession with being businesslike, meaning efficient and economical (and ideally effective). The point of these chapters is that equity is an equally important criterion. While a representative bureaucracy, vibrant citizen engagement, due process, and transparent rules are means for enabling equity, merely having systems in place is not enough. Achieving social equity begins by appreciating how outcomes are experienced by different communities and by identifying who and/or what is responsible for adverse impacts. Adverse impacts can be identified by answering these questions: For whom is this program good? Who does it disadvantage? These questions should be asked and answered for each program and each new set of regulations. And those who speak up when public opinion is solicited skew the answer so administrators must work smarter to solicit input from the quiet quadrants of the community. Those in pockets of privilege will insist that their voices are heard while those with disadvantaged identities will remain in the shadow. Status affects not only who speaks up but also who gets heard. In the absence of watchdogs who are mindful of this, the letter of the law for citizen participation is followed but the spirit is lost.

Appreciating differences in outcomes and identifying the cause is just the beginning in the process of achieving social equity. In a capitalist economy, public service is the conscience that corrects imbalances. This balancing act is a "comes with" in the American economic system. Although it works poorly in theory, the nation's 250-year history shows it can be made to work in practice. To have the advantages that capitalism brings, it is up to the public service environment to fill the chinks left by the inequality that capitalism requires.

Advocacy for bureaucratic neutrality usually comes from positions of privilege and power, and it is precisely this privilege that has sculpted notions about what is "normal." Now comes the work to probe these notions and show them for what they are. Public service professionals are on the frontlines of these issues—issues that require unwavering defense of social equity. While it is not unusual for someone to back out of discussions because they want to "stay neutral," in fact, neutrality is never neutral. It is embedded in the status quo, such that keeping things the way they are advantages the current power structure. To see inequity requires challenging the status quo, not accepting it.

Social Equity as a Moving Target

True equity is a moving target. Equitable structures put in place in 2010 may require modification now because they may have become inequitable. What is fair today may become unfair tomorrow as economic conditions change or as exceptions become the rule. Each person's identity forms a lens through which fairness and justice are interpreted; intersections complicate and reshape the lens. Deeply held beliefs and attitudes shape interactions, expectations, notions of entitlements, and expectations about what opportunities will lie ahead.

Among these deeply held beliefs is the idea that the United States is a nation that subscribes to the rule of law, but law alone cannot make equity happen. For example, the Equal Pay Act was passed in 1963, but equal pay did not happen. The Lilly Ledbetter Act was passed 45 years later to try again, but the burden remains not on employers who make the salary decisions but on those disadvantaged by unequal pay to file suit, one victim at a time. The aggrieved person must engage with the legal system and insist that the employer follow the law.

Many chapters mentioned constitutional provisions that seemingly make treating one human differently from another a violation of law. Yet many court cases are cited in this book, some of which legitimate social inequity. In other words, law is an instrument that contributes to social equity but law alone cannot achieve it. Laws are nothing more than institutionalized norms and norms change as years pass. In fact, passage of a law does not happen until a majority of the population is already "there" in terms of behaving in accordance with it. However, having a law on the books is not enough. For example, sticky floors, trap doors, glass ceilings, and glass walls are terms used to describe the barriers that make women's escalation up the career ladder so difficult,[1] despite a spate of legislation that prohibits employment discrimination. These metaphors are equally apt for describing the plight of other disadvantaged groups: racial minorities, immigrants, LGBTQs, and those with intersecting disadvantages. The metaphors capture how being "outside the norm" limits promotion opportunities and diminishes the likelihood that their voices will be heard.

First, the "sticky floors" metaphor is used when explaining why someone whose experience is primarily at the lower rungs in an organizational hierarchy is not qualified to move up the career ladder. Of course, lower positions are the ones that women and people of color are more likely to be hired into so this perpetuates the predominance of white men in higher positions. Second, "trap doors" are those events that highlight someone's mistake, short-circuiting their movement into the mainstream or escalation up the career ladder. The person with a prison record encounters this when trying to reenter the workforce. On the job, a white male who performs poorly in a managerial position will probably be retained and "given another chance" or promoted to another position. But if the incumbent is of a demographic group that has never held that position before, perhaps a black female, the failure will be exaggerated and will be used to explain why black women "just don't work out" for the job. (Note: no one suggests that white men "just don't work out.")

Third, in the employment setting, glass walls are a metaphor for staff positions and similar posts that are close to power but do not have power. The "other," whether women or people of color or LGBTQ, are often in these positions and are used as examples of diversity even though they do not have decision-making authority or supervisory authority. When promotion time comes, they are passed over precisely because they lack experience as decision-makers and supervisors. Finally, glass ceilings are the best known of these metaphors, characterizing how the "other" reaches a given level but never gains upward promotion largely because no one of that demographic has ever been promoted higher.

What Could Have Been Still Can Be

The course of history is shaped by a confluence of forces. This is as true of academic disciplines as it is of the practice environment. Public administration and city management provide examples. About a century ago, when the International City/County Management Association (ICMA) was in its early days and when the American Society for Public Administration (ASPA) was in its formative years, the work of city government *could* have been conceptualized as more like caring for a large extended family rather than like management of a business. It was not. Had children's welfare, jobs, and housing been prioritized over corporate growth, the allocation of resources would have occurred differently. Instead, cities were thought of more as businesses, and this is how theories have developed since. To Jane Addams,[2] this was outmoded thinking even back then. To the awakening interest in social equity, cities-as-businesses remain out of sync with people's needs. The primacy of business over people's lives disregarded those factors that are elemental to social equity: affordable, safe housing; safe environments for children; clean streets, clean water, fresh fruits and vegetables; adequate clothing, and transportation. As Camilla Stivers has persuasively argued, in the early days of public administration, so many opportunities to focus on social equity were left behind in the rush to perform like a business.[3]

Just as Jane Addams recognized as she worked to improve the plight of the poor in Chicago, cities concentrate the best and the worst of American society. Today we know that one's zip code is a powerful indicator of life expectancy, education, health, and income. Factors combine, such as lack of transportation to get to jobs and to markets that sell nutritious foods, affordable housing so that residents are not living on the street, access to affordable health care, and meaningful political representation. It is not too late to return to Addams' progressive focus on people's lives.

What Would Social Equity Look Like?

A fully equitable community has yet to be achieved. For communities and agencies that seek to be attentive to the equity implications of their inputs, processes, and outcomes, the United Nations' Sustainable Development Goals provide a model.[4] The goals address global challenges of poverty, inequality, climate, environmental degradation, prosperity, and peace and justice. They provide a blueprint to achieve a better and more sustainable future for all.

What if the federal Office of Information and Regulatory Affairs reviewed each proposed regulation for its social equity impact? What if states reviewed construction proposals for not only their environmental impact but also their social equity impact? The questions would be "Whose voices were heard in the planning for this project?" "Is there a class that will be disproportionately disadvantaged?" What might unintended consequences be? In other words, mindful attention to social equity can be built into projects from the beginning. And continuous mindfulness is essential.

Imagine what it would be like if there were no health disparities between Whites and persons of color. Consider what retirement would be like if persons of color had the same level of retirement savings as Whites. If women had the same level of savings as men? Think about school systems where all facilities are in good repair and school officials' demographic characteristics are representative of the students they serve. A third of the states now offer a gender-neutral birth certificate option.[5] What would it take for other states to follow suit?

"We the People": Social Equity and Administrative Responsibility

While it is tempting to enter the "Oppression Olympics" and pit one disadvantaged group against another, public administration gains little by comparing the plight of one intersectionalized category against another. There is a better way to think about social equity. With the goal of forging communities rather than dividing them, a framework for embracing groups and identities offers more promise. Pockets of hope provide starting points. One suggestion is put forward by Eric Klinenberg,[6] a sociologist who argues that rather than divide people, communities will do better by creating public spaces—libraries in neighborhoods, parks, public pools—that provide a civic space and bring people from all walks of life together. This is an integrative approach as compared to a divisive approach. It acknowledges differences while focusing on common ground—the humanness—that everyone brings.

This integrative approach means that achieving social equity requires reexamining everything we take for granted. Recall from chapter 1 that the historical underpinnings of social equity included a parade through philosophies, ideas of what government should do, and a confluence of different approaches to politics, management, and law. Woven throughout the discussion is the power of discourses, which are debates and conversations about what "fairness for all" means. Across the centuries, debates over fairness focus on questions that are as serious as it gets: Who matters to government? Whose ideas, beliefs, and desires prevail? Who is accountable and to whom? Who deserves what? While we can conceive of societies and their governments as arising from social contracts, we have to face a reality: Social contracts may or may not be fair, depending on whose voices are heard when conditions of the contract are determined. Achieving social equity means we have to ask these tough questions and meaningfully expand and protect *who* is involved in any discourse on the meaning of fairness. If we do not, then there cannot be "fairness for all."

The social equity imperative links to ethical principles. Administrators have the ethical duty to serve the public interest and to promote democratic participation. These broad ethical imperatives are why the chapters in this book point to this common ground and provide a lesson for every public service professional, regardless of policy domain, position, or jurisdiction. Everyone serving the public has a responsibility to advance social equity. In too many cases, services and programs have been instruments for perpetuating inequity, but that is precisely the reason why services and programs provide a starting point to redress those very inequities. These responsibilities begin with protecting constitutional rights. As a reminder, social equity has roots in negative freedoms or freedoms *from* government interference. These are evident in the Bill of Rights and are also mirrored in state constitutions.[7] They include freedom of religion, speech, and assembly; freedom from unreasonable searches and seizures; mandates for due process; and more. Further, through the Fourteenth Amendment to the U.S. Constitution, all *persons* (not just citizens) are entitled to due process and equal protection of the law. Over two centuries of legal battles, such rights have increasingly extended to more and more groups, from protections for all persons based on race and sex to recognition of rights based on sexual orientation and immigrant status. Despite progress, there is more work to be done.

Positive freedoms are those that allow people to take charge of their own lives. They are important because they ensure that people can improve their quality of life through the right to quality education, health care, transportation, leisure activities, and safe air and water. While debates about which positive freedoms should be mandated, all public service professionals are called upon to act in ways that serve the four normative pillars of the field—efficiency, effectiveness, economy, and social equity. As they are the ones who "run the constitution," public administrators are stewards of both negative and positive freedoms.

Accountability

Those who work in public service have an ethical obligation to ask how accountability for social equity is to be achieved. This massive question is an outgrowth of how the meaning of "We the People" has expanded since 1787, coupled with the realization that inequities continue to persist despite initiatives designed to mitigate them. The question of how to achieve accountability for social equity acknowledges reality, and alerts administrators to the responsibility to undo inequities that their programs perpetuate. It also requires that those serving the public take seriously their mandate to make social equity coequal to efficiency, effectiveness, and economy.

Being accountable means being responsible for understanding how the four dimensions of social equity—access, processes, quality, and outcomes—intersect with and influence one another.[8] If someone is not informed about, or lacks access to, public services, then they will not benefit from them. If someone is not accorded procedural fairness, then it is likely that service quality is also subpar. And if the processes and quality of a service are inequitable, then outcomes will be negative. Each equity issue includes these four dimensions and inequity in one dimension leads to and compounds inequities in the others. Throughout this book, the authors have pointed to these realities and to how one's own identity, place in society, and the inequities one faces due to prejudice directed at those identities, are likely to predict the privileges and costs one experiences in daily life.

Public Integrity

Understanding social equity's place in the broad scheme of public service is among the highest of ethical obligations. This responsibility is both personal and collective. At the personal level, it means administrators are responsible for their own integrity as well as striving to advance social equity in their own actions. At the collective level, it means being aware of how being accountable for social equity also comes in tandem with maintaining organizational integrity.

The eight provisions of the Code of Ethics of the American Society for Public Administration highlight these personal and collective responsibilities:

1. Advance the public interest.
2. Uphold the Constitution and the law.
3. Promote democratic participation.
4. Strengthen social equity.
5. Fully inform and advise.
6. Demonstrate personal integrity.
7. Promote ethical organizations.
8. Advance professional excellence.[9]

To advance the public interest means upholding the Constitution and the law. In turn, this requires awareness of the ways administrators must be fair. Further, achieving social equity means promoting democratic participation and making sure everyone has a place at the table while also speaking truth to power about inequities and the causes and effects of those inequities. These actions rely on personal integrity. Advancing the public interest is far from a linear process: values flow to and from one another, yet all roads lead back to social equity.

Parsing these complexities, accountability for social equity at the personal level means individual responsibility for multiple things. For one, to serve the public interest, administrators must understand their own prejudices and mitigate the effects of their prejudices. Doing so requires questioning one's own privilege and asking difficult questions such as, "In what ways are my identities influencing my attitudes and behaviors?" And it means asking and answering even more uncomfortable questions: "In what ways am I racist? Sexist? Homo- or trans-phobic?"

Asking and answering the questions then leads to the harder work of taking personal responsibility to counter one's own biases. Administrators have a duty to interact fairly with all constituencies and to take personal responsibility for their own actions. And it entails calling out situations where access, processes, quality, and/or outcomes advantage some while disadvantaging others.

The ethical provisions mentioned in these chapters remind us that social equity is the duty not just of individual administrators but of the whole machine of public service. As a whole, administrators have the duty of ensuring that equity is taken seriously across all of public service, understand how inequities in the workplace affect agency performance, grasp historical inequities and administrative culpability, and advocate with policy leaders to take issues of fairness more seriously. Everyone benefits when services are accessible to all, are procedurally fair, are of equal quality, and promote positive outcomes.

Zina Merritt, Chief Diversity Management Officer for the U.S. Government Accountability Office, is optimistic that the current emphasis on social equity will remain.[10] She has worked in federal civil service for 35 years and notes that the social equity flame burns brighter than it ever has. Hopeful that commitment to equity will remain at the forefront, she explains that when she welcomes new employees, she tells them "it's no longer just about race, ethnicity, and gender; it is about the whole game—the talent, the uniqueness that you bring, your skills, knowledge, abilities, and more." Being proactive, she describes how accessibility has a forward focus: "Push your organizations and agencies to make them more accessible, from physical to technological, and any services that are provided. By doing that, it benefits somebody like me who may not have a disability today, but I might have one tomorrow." In other words, making things more equitable helps everyone, if not today, then in the future. And regardless of one's job, she gives this advice: "Shift the emphasis to the diversity of your people and everything that they bring."

Final Words

Achieving social equity is a continuous task, not one that will reach a destination and be done. It takes grit and perseverance to ask and answer uncomfortable questions about who benefits and who loses. And solutions will not be perfect. But silence about inequities is destructive, for it entrenches unfairness. The challenge to each and every public servant is to stay in the game, asking the hard questions, embracing diverse points of view, implementing the best ideas, monitoring results, and making continuous adjustments to accommodate changes. Resilience is required.

Regardless of the years of experience, we never cease being students of public administration. We always are learning how to do a better job of planning, organizing, staffing, directing, coordinating, reporting, budgeting, and achieving social equity. Competence includes implementing techniques like those discussed in these chapters, and studying what other communities do—both good and bad—in order to replicate successful ventures and to correct what is not working. In the words of Mary Parker Follett, it means learning what it takes to create true communities—communities in which the interests of others are also our own.[11]

When the goal is fairness for everyone, the discussion is always worth having. Achieving social equity may seem like a Sisyphean task, but to paraphrase Martin Luther King, Jr., we may not get there, but if we do not stay on the road, we, for sure, will not get there.[12]

Summary of Key Points

The main points in this chapter are few and straightforward: social equity is everybody's business. The obligation to be continuously mindful of it falls on the shoulders of public service professionals, whether working in health care or literacy, transportation or housing, law enforcement or education, city management, or environmental protection.

Society's eyes and ears are the best tools that public administrators have for identifying problems collaboratively and resolving them. Evidence is clear on the effect that meaningful participation has. More opportunities for participation broaden the number of perspectives that will be represented. While all input may not be equally useful, it is an essential element in policy formulation, rulemaking, program implementation, and determining desired outcomes.[13]

Social equity is neither a new idea nor a pie-in-the-sky dream, and that which is judged equitable by today's standards may not be seen the same tomorrow. It will always be a work in progress. As Zina Merritt says, it is a journey, not a destination.

Social equity reflects a willingness to respect the points of view of everyone in a community, and to integrate people's preferences in decisions that affect them. It improves quality of life for individuals and strengthens social bonds, human capital, civic engagement, and the willingness to defend common interests. In short, social equity is a win-win. It strengthens individuals and it strengthens communities.

Discussion Questions

1. Think about the policy domain that most interests you. What are the social equity considerations that are most salient?
2. It is a rare decision that can maximize all four imperatives of public administration—economy, effectiveness, efficiency, and equity. How should an administrator decide which of these are most important in any given problem? Which imperative should be traded off in favor of another? Can you think of an example affecting your local community?
3. Are you ready to ask the hard questions about systems, processes, and practices that have a disparate impact on communities in your work? Your neighborhood? What do you still need to know and learn?

Exercise

Visit this site: https://www.mncompass.org/disparities/resource-directory. It details services and activities designed to advance social equity in the state of Minnesota. Assume you are a consultant for your home state. List 10 services/activities that you could contribute to a site such as this.

Additional Resources

1. The City of Seattle has been at the forefront of social equity initiatives. Visit the city's civil rights webpage to learn about its activities: https://www.seattle.gov/civil-rights
2. Eric Klinenberg, *Palaces for the People: How Social Infrastructure Can Help Fight Inequality, Polarization, and the Decline of Civic Life* (New York: Crown, 2018).
3. Rothstein, Richard, *The Color of Law: A Forgotten History of How Our Government Segregated America* (New York: W.W. Norton & Co, 2017).

Notes

1. Mary E. Guy, "Organizational Architecture, Gender, and Women's Careers," *Review of Public Personnel Administration* 14, no. 2 (1994), 77–90.
2. Patricia M. Shields, ed., *Jane Addams: Progressive Pioneer of Peace, Philosophy, Sociology, Social Work and Public Administration* (Cham, Switzerland: Springer 2017).
3. Camilla Stivers, *Bureau Men, Settlement Women: Constructing Public Administration in the Progressive Era* (Lawrence, KS: University Press of Kansas, 2000).
4. For more information about the UN Sustainable Development Goals, see https://www.un.org/sustainabledevelopment/sustainable-development-goals/
5. Tim Fitzsimons, "In Gender-Neutral Push, a 4th State Embraces Nonbinary Birth Certificates," *Governing* (January 31, 2019), https://www.governing.com/topics/health-human-services/In-Gender-Neutral-Push-New-Jersey-Latest-State-to-Embrace-Nonbinary-Birth-Certificates.html
6. Eric Klinenberg, 2018. *Palaces for the People: How Social Infrastructure Can Help Fight Inequality, Polarization, and the Decline of Civic Life* (New York: Crown, 2019).
7. Ian Carter, "Positive and Negative Liberty," *Stanford Encyclopedia of Philosophy* (Summer 2018 edition), Edward N. Zalta (ed.), https://plato.stanford.edu/archives/sum2018/entries/liberty-positive-negative/
8. Norman J. Johnson and James H. Svara, "Social Equity in American Society and Public Administration," in *Justice for All: Promoting Social Equity in Public Administration,* ed. Norman J. Johnson and James H. Svara (New York: Routledge, 2015), 3–25.
9. American Society for Public Administration, "Code of Ethics, *American Society for* Public Administration, accessed August 2, 2019, https://www.aspanet.org/ASPA/About-ASPA/Code-of-Ethics/ASPA/Code-of-Ethics/Code-of-Ethics.aspx?hkey=fefba3e2-a9dc-4fc8-a686-3446513a4533
10. Zina Merritt, personal interview, March 24, 2023.
11. Mary Parker Follett, *The New State: Group Organization, the Solution to Popular Government* (Mansfield Centre, CT: Martino Publishing, [1918]2016).
12. Martin Luther King, Jr. *I Have Been to the Mountaintop*. Speech delivered in Memphis, Tennessee, April 3, 1968. Accessed January 21, 2024, at https://www.huffpost.com/entry/martin-luther-king-mountain-top-speech_n_4632452
13. Eric Joseph van Holm, "Unequal Cities, Unequal Participation: The Effect of Income Inequality on Civic Engagement," *American Review of Public Administration* 49, no. 2 (2019), 135–144.

Index

About the Editors and Contributors

Mary E. Guy (she/her) holds a University of Colorado Distinguished Professorship at the University of Colorado Denver. Her research focuses on social equity, the difference that gender makes, workforce diversity, and the citizen-state encounter. She served as inaugural editor-in-chief of the *Journal of Social Equity and Public Administration* and is an elected Fellow of the National Academy of Public Administration and past President of the American Society for Public Administration.

Sean A. McCandless (he/him) is an associate professor in the Public and Nonprofit Management program of the University of Texas at Dallas. His research centers on social equity, human resources, organizational dynamics, and societal discourses and is featured in global academic outlets. He presently serves as the co-chair (with S. Nicole Diggs, North Carolina State University) of the Diversity and Social Equity Committee of the Network of Schools of Public Policy, Affairs, and Administration (NASPAA).

Rashmi Chordiya (she/her) is an assistant professor of public administration at Seattle University's Institute of Public Service. Her work bridges academic scholarship and social justice visions to support liberatory justice in public service and administrative contexts. She approaches diversity and social justice work from an embodied lens that is trauma-informed and healing-centered, compassionately centering the margins. Her forthcoming book is *Beyond Diversity, Equity and Inclusion: Dreaming Liberatory Justice in Public and Nonprofit Organizations.*

Kimberly Desmond (she/her) is the Chief Race and Equity Officer for the City of San Diego, and formerly the Interim Equity Officer/ Director for the Mayor's Office of Social Equity and Innovation in the City and County of Denver. Her work focuses on operationalizing racial equity in local government through creating systems that improve policy, service delivery, and equitable distribution of resources. She ensures that equity is prioritized and integrated into programs, practices, and budget decisions.

Ty Price Dooley is Associate Professor and Interim Dean in the College of Public Affairs and Education at the University of Illinois Springfield, where he served as the Inaugural Director of the School of Public Management and Policy from 2021 to 2023. His research interests include social justice, program evaluation, housing policy, policing, and community development. In addition to scholarly presentations and publications, his work includes funded projects for state and local entities totaling over $1.5 million.

Lynnsey Erickson (she/her) is Deputy Mayor of Oshkosh, Wisconsin, and has served on the Oshkosh Common Council since April 2020. She also works in local public health with a focus on systems change and addressing social and structural determinants that drive inequities. She holds a master's degree in Public Administration from the University of Wisconsin Oshkosh and a bachelor's degree in Gender and Women's Studies and Psychology from the University of Wisconsin Madison.

Michelle D. Evans (she/her) is an associate professor at the University of Tennessee at Chattanooga. Her research focuses on equity, intersectionality, pedagogy, volunteer motivation, and whistleblowing, and has appeared in *Teaching Public Administration, Review of Public Personnel Administration, Human Resource Management Review, Administrative Theory & Praxis,* and *Public Integrity*. She co-edited *Intersectionality and Crisis Management: A Path to Social Equity* with Hillary J. Knepper and Tiffany Henley. Previously she worked for more than 20 years for Special Olympics.

Cornel Grey is an assistant professor in the Department of Gender, Sexuality, and Women's Studies at Western University. Dr. Grey's research focuses primarily on the health of Black queer communities. His current projects include a qualitative study on the role of skin-to-skin contact in the lives of Black queer men and an archival study that looks at queer models of care during the 1980s and 1990s HIV/AIDS crisis.

Megan E. Hatch is an associate professor of Urban Policy and City Management in the Maxine Goodman Levin School of Urban Affairs at Cleveland State University. She studies the variation in policies within the US federalist system and the effects those disparities have on social equity, individuals, and institutions. Within this theme, she examines three policy areas: rental housing, state preemption of local laws, and the CDBG program.

Hillary J. Knepper (she/her) is the Associate Provost for Student Success and a full professor in the Department of Public Administration at Pace University. Previously she was an administrator in nonprofit and public organizations and brings this strong practitioner perspective to her research on equity with emphasis on marginalized and vulnerable populations. Her recent work can be found in *Administrative Theory & Praxis, Public Administration Review, Journal of Public Affairs Education*, and *Public Integrity*.

Samantha June Larson (she/her) is an associate professor of Public Administration and Research Director of the Whitburn Center for Governance and Policy Research at the University of Wisconsin Oshkosh. Her research focuses on how public service can advance social equity, belonging, resilience, and healing. She has authored multiple publications and served in public and nonprofit organizations with rural, environmental, and educational missions for over 15 years.

Simone Martin-Howard's multidisciplinary research focuses on health, crime, and the criminal justice system; public and nonprofit service delivery in vulnerable communities around the world; and health and social equity. Dr. Martin-Howard's work has appeared in *Public Administration Review*; the *Journal of Public and Nonprofit Affairs*; *Crime & Delinquency*; the *Journal of Urban Health*; the *Journal of Health and Human Services Administration*; *Women & Criminal Justice*; and the *Journal of Public Management and Social Policy*.

Pamela Medina is an associate professor of Public Administration and Nonprofit Management at California State University San Bernardino. Her research interests include social equity, public participation, and technology use in the public sector. Her most recent work has been published in *Journal of Public Affairs Education*, *Administrative Theory & Praxis*, and *Nonprofit Management & Leadership*.

Kim Moloney is an assistant professor at Hamad Bin Khalifa University in Doha, Qatar. She has three research interests: (1) intersection of public administration with international organizations and transnational administration, (2) intersection of public administration with the opportunity and challenges of small states, and more recently, (3) interaction of public administration with social cohesion and social equity. Her latest book, *Who Matters at the World Bank*, was published by Oxford University Press in 2022.

Celeste Murphy-Greene is Chair and Associate Professor of the Political Science, History, and International Studies Department at Hampton University. Additionally, Dr. Murphy-Greene serves as the Executive Director of the Center for Environmental Justice and Resilience. Dr. Murphy-Greene has been researching, writing, and teaching about environmental justice for over 25 years. Her most recent publication is the edited book *Environmental Justice and Resiliency in an Age of Uncertainty*. Dr. Murphy-Greene earned her PhD at Florida Atlantic University.

John C. Ronquillo (he/him/él) is the inaugural director of the Institute for Public Leadership and associate professor at the University of Maryland School of Public Policy. His research has been published in *Public Administration Review*, the *American Review of Public Administration*, *Decision Support Systems, Public Integrity, Voluntas: International Journal of Voluntary and Nonprofit Organizations*, the *Transylvanian Review of Administrative Sciences*, and in numerous edited volumes.

Meghna Sabharwal is a professor in the public and nonprofit management program at the University of Texas at Dallas. Her research is focused on public human resources management, specifically diversity, equity, and inclusion. She has published three books and over 70 peer-reviewed journal articles and chapters and is the winner of five best paper awards. She is the Associate Editor of the *Review of Public Personnel Administration* and *Public Integrity*.

Kareem K. M. Willis (he/they) is a scholar and activist deeply rooted in the LGBTQ+ community. Their commitment as a social justice scholar-practitioner involves advocating for disempowered individuals and communities, striving to provide access to resources, and carving out inclusive spaces that empower them to embrace their potential. Their research delves into social equity and justice, unraveling underlying issues within public administration, nonprofit management, and philanthropy. Dr. Willis earned a PhD from Rutgers University-Newark.